BARRON'S

ESSENTIAL WORDS FOR THE IELTS®

THIRD EDITION

Lin Lougheed
Ed.D., Teachers College
Columbia University

Publishing Globally

NEW AGE INTERNATIONAL (P) LIMITED, PUBLISHERS
New Delhi • Bangalore • Chennai • Cochin • Guwahati
Hyderabad • Kolkata • Lucknow • Mumbai
Visit us at www.newagepublishers.com

ACKNOWLEDGMENTS

The author would like to thank all the teachers and students around the world who have helped form the content of this book. The author is especially grateful to Daniel Norman for his contribution on the history of the circus and to Kristen Girardi, the editor, for her generous and careful attention to every single detail in the book.

AUDIO AND AUDIOSCRIPTS

The MP3 files and audioscripts for all listening segments can be found online at *http://barronsbooks.com/tp/ielts/audio/*

BARRON'S Essential Words for the IELTS with MP3 CD, 3rd Edition by Dr. Lin Lougheed

Third Indian Sub-Continent Edition: 2019 by **New Age International (P) Ltd., Publishers**

This special low-priced edition is for sale in **India, Bangladesh, Bhutan, Maldives, Nepal** and **Sri Lanka** only.

Originally Published in the *United States of America.*

BRANCHES

- **Bangalore** 37/10, 8th Cross (Near Hanuman Temple), Azad Nagar, Chamarajpet, Bangalore- 560 018 **Tel.:** (080) 26756823, **Telefax:** 26756820, **E-mail: bangalore@newagepublishers.com**
- **Chennai** 26, Damodaran Street, T. Nagar, Chennai-600 017, **Tel.:** (044) 24353401 **Telefax:** 24351463, **E-mail: chennai@newagepublishers.com**
- **Cochin** CC-39/1016, Carrier Station Road, Ernakulam South, Cochin-682 016 **Tel.:** (0484) 2377303, **Telefax:** 4051304, **E-mail: cochin@newagepublishers.com**
- **Guwahati** Hemsen Complex, Mohd. Shah Road, Paltan Bazar, Near Starline Hotel, Guwahati-781 008 **Tel.:** (0361) 2513881, **Telefax:** 2543669, **E-mail: guwahati@newagepublishers.com**
- **Hyderabad** 105, 1st Floor, Madhiray Kaveri Tower, 3-2-19, Azam Jahi Road, Near Kumar Theater, Nimboliadda, Kachiguda, Hyderabad-500 027, **Tel.:** (040) 24652456 **Telefax:** 24652457, **E-mail: hyderabad@newagepublishers.com**
- **Kolkata** RDB Chambers (Formerly Lotus Cinema) 106A, 1st Floor, S N Banerjee Road Kolkata-700 014, **Tel.:** (033) 22273773, **Telefax:** 22275247 **E-mail: kolkata@newagepublishers.com**
- **Lucknow** 16-A, Jopling Road, Lucknow-226 001, **Tel.:** (0522) 2209578, 4045297 **Telefax:** 2204098, **E-mail: lucknow@newagepublishers.com**
- **Mumbai** 142C, Victor House, Ground Floor, N.M. Joshi Marg, Lower Parel, Mumbai-400 013 **Tel.:** (022) 24927869, **Telefax:** 24915415, **E-mail: mumbai@newagepublishers.com**
- **New Delhi** 22, Golden House, Daryaganj, New Delhi-110 002, **Tel.:** (011) 23262368, 23262370, **Telefax:** 43551305, **E-mail: sales@newagepublishers.com**

ISBN: 978-93-87788-35-0
C-21-10-12845

Printed in India at D. D. Offset, Noida.

PUBLISHING GLOBALLY
NEW AGE INTERNATIONAL (P) LIMITED, PUBLISHERS
7/30 A, Daryaganj, New Delhi-110002
Visit us at **www.newagepublishers.com**
(CIN: U74899DL1966PTC004618)

CONTENTS

Introduction

Barron's Essential Words for the IELTS will help familiarize you with the vocabulary you will find in the reading and listening sections of the IELTS exam (International English Language Testing System). As the number of words you understand when you are reading and listening increases, your speaking and writing vocabulary will improve as well.

VOCABULARY AND THE IELTS

Vocabulary is not tested directly on the IELTS. There are no questions on the IELTS that ask specifically for the meaning of a word. However, comprehension *is* tested. Can you understand what you read? Can you understand what you hear? The more words you know, the more you will understand. The more words you know, the more fluently you will be able to speak and write.

Essential Words for the IELTS will teach you 600 words that you might find on the exam in reading and listening and that you might use in writing and speaking. You will also learn how to use various clues for understanding the meaning of new words.

- **Context clues.** The context provides clues about the meaning of a word. The topic of the passage or paragraph can help you understand a new word, and there may also be an explicit definition, synonym, or paraphrase in the text. You will practice using the context to understand new vocabulary.
- **Synonyms and paraphrases.** One idea can be expressed in different ways. You will reinforce the vocabulary you are learning by identifying words and phrases with similar meanings.
- **Compound words, prefixes, and suffixes.** These can help you analyze a word to determine the meaning. You will learn to recognize common prefixes and suffixes and understand how words are joined together to form new words.
- **Word families.** These are the different parts of speech—noun, verb, adjective, and adverb—that share a similar meaning. The book presents word family charts to help you learn the most common forms.
- **Dictionary.** If none of the above have helped you understand the meaning of a word, you can use a dictionary designed for learners of English. You can use an online dictionary to help you learn the correct pronunciation of new words.

In *Essential Words for the IELTS*, you will practice one very effective vocabulary strategy that will improve your comprehension. This effective strategy is to use a word four ways: **Read** the word, **write** the word,

listen to the word, and **speak** the word. Every activity in each chapter will help you develop this strategy.

Keep a notebook of new words you are learning. Each vocabulary list in this book consists of twenty words selected from the accompanying reading passage. You will probably find additional words in each reading passage that are new to you. You can keep your own lists of these words and other words you come across. You can apply the same skills and strategies to learning these words as you do to the vocabulary word lists in the book.

When you learn a new word, you should practice the same strategy. If you hear a new word, write the new word in a sentence. Read the sentence to yourself. Say the sentence aloud. Every chance you get, review the words you are learning. Say them, write them, read them, and listen to them.

IELTS STUDY CONTRACT

You must make a commitment to study English. Sign a contract with yourself. You should never break a contract—especially a contract with yourself.

- Print your name below on line 1.
- Write the time you will spend each week studying English on lines 4–8. Think about how much time you have to study every day and every week, and make your schedule realistic.
- Sign your name and date the contract on the last line.
- At the end of each week, add up your hours. Did you meet the requirements of your contract?

MY IELTS STUDY CONTRACT

I, ____________________, promise to study for the IELTS. I will begin my study with *Barron's Essential Words for the IELTS*, and I will also study English on my own.

I understand that to improve my English I need to spend time on English.

I promise to study English ______ hours a week. I promise to learn ______ new words every day.

I will spend ______ hours a week listening to English.
I will spend ______ hours a week writing English.
I will spend ______ hours a week speaking English.
I will spend ______ hours a week reading English.

This is a contract with myself. I promise to fulfill the terms of this contract.

____
Signed

____
Date

SELF-STUDY ACTIVITIES

Here are some ways you can improve your English vocabulary on your own. Check the ones you plan to try. Add some of your own ideas.

Internet-Based Self-Study Activities:

LISTENING

___ Podcasts on the Internet
___ News websites: CNN, BBC, NBC, ABC, CBS
___ Movies in English
___ YouTube
___ Ted.com
___ ______________________________
___ ______________________________

SPEAKING

___ Use Skype to talk to English speakers (*http://www.skype.com*)
___ ______________________________
___ ______________________________

WRITING

___ Write e-mails to website contacts
___ Write a blog
___ Leave comments on blogs
___ Post messages in a chat room
___ Use Facebook and MySpace
___ ______________________________
___ ______________________________

READING

___ Read news and magazine articles online
___ Do web research on topics that interest you
___ Follow blogs that interest you
___ ______________________________
___ ______________________________

Other Self-Study Activities

LISTENING

___ Listen to CNN and BBC on the radio
___ Watch movies and TV in English
___ Listen to music in English
___ ______________________________
___ ______________________________

SPEAKING

___ Describe what you see and do out loud
___ Practice speaking with a conversation buddy
___ Sing or recite song lyrics
___ ______________________________
___ ______________________________

WRITING

___ Write a daily journal
___ Write a letter to an English speaker
___ Make lists of the things you see every day
___ Write descriptions of your family and friends
___ ______________________________
___ ______________________________

READING

___ Read newspapers and magazines in English
___ Read books in English
___ Read song lyrics
___ ______________________________
___ ______________________________

Suggestions for Self-Study Activities

Whether you read an article in a newspaper or on a website, you can use that article in a variety of ways to improve your vocabulary while you practice reading, writing, speaking, and listening in English.

- Read about it.
- Paraphrase and write about it.
- Give a talk or presentation about it.
- Record or make a video of your presentation.
- Listen to or watch what you recorded. Write down your presentation.
- Correct your mistakes.
- Do the same again.

PLAN A TRIP

- Go to *www.cntraveler.com*
- Choose a city, choose a hotel, go to that hotel's website and choose a room, and then choose some sites to visit (*reading*).
- Write a report about the city. Tell why you want to go there. Describe the hotel and the room you will reserve. Tell what sites you plan to visit and when. Where will you eat? How will you get around? Now write a letter to someone recommending this place (*writing*).

- Pretend you have to give a lecture on your planned trip (*speaking*). Make a video of yourself talking about this place. Then watch the video and write down what you said (*listening*). Correct any mistakes you made and record the presentation again. Then choose another city and do this again.

SHOP FOR AN ELECTRONIC PRODUCT

- Go to *www.cnet.com*
- Choose an electronic product and read about it (*reading*).
- Write a report about the product. Tell why you want to buy one. Describe its features. Now write a letter to someone recommending this product (*writing*).
- Pretend you have to give a talk about this product (*speaking*). Make a video of yourself talking about this product. Then watch the video and write down what you said (*listening*). Correct any mistakes you made and record the presentation again. Then choose another product and do this again.

DISCUSS A BOOK OR A CD

- Go to *www.amazon.com*
- Choose a book or CD or any product. Read the product description and reviews (*reading*).
- Write a report about the product. Tell why you want to buy one or why it is interesting to you. Describe its features. Now write a letter to someone and recommend this product (*writing*).
- Pretend you have to give a talk about this product (*speaking*). Make a video of yourself talking about this product. Then watch the video and write down what you said (*listening*). Correct any mistakes you made and record the presentation again. Then choose another product and do this again.

DISCUSS ANY SUBJECT

- Go to *http://simple.wikipedia.org/wiki/Main_Page* This website is written in simple English.
- Pick any subject and read the entry (*reading*).
- Write a short essay about the topic (*writing*).
- Give a presentation about it (*speaking*). Record the presentation. Then watch the video and write down what you said (*listening*). Correct any mistakes you made and record the presentation again. Choose another topic and do this again.

FOLLOW THE NEWS

- Go to *http://news.google.com*
  Google News has a variety of links.

- Pick one event and read the articles about it (*reading*).
- Listen to an English-language news report on the radio or watch a news program on TV about the same event (*listening*). Take notes as you listen.
- Write a summary of what you read and heard. Then write a short essay about the event (*writing*).
- Pretend you are a news reporter. Use the information from your notes to report the news (*speaking*). Record the presentation. Then watch the video and write down what you said (*listening*). Correct any mistakes you made and record the presentation again. Then choose another event and do this again.

EXPRESS AN OPINION

- Read a letter to the editor in the newspaper (*reading*). You can read sample letters to the editor at *www.publishaletter.com.*
- Write a letter in response in which you say whether or not you agree with the opinion expressed in the first letter. Explain why (*writing*).
- Pretend you have to give a talk explaining your opinion (*speaking*). Record yourself giving the talk. Then watch the video and write down what you said (*listening*). Correct any mistakes you made and record the presentation again. Then read another letter to the editor and do this again.

REVIEW A BOOK OR MOVIE

- Read a book (*reading*). Think about your opinion of the book. What did you like about it? What didn't you like about it? Who would you recommend it to and why?
- Pretend you are a book reviewer for a newspaper. Write a review of the book with your opinion and recommendations (*writing*). You can find examples of book reviews at *www.powells.com/review.*
- Give an oral presentation about the book. Explain what the book is about and what your opinion is (*speaking*). Record yourself giving the presentation. Then watch the video and write down what you said (*listening*). Correct any mistakes you made and record the presentation again. Then read another book and do this again.
- You can do this same activity after watching a movie (*listening*). You can find links to movie reviews to use as models at *www.mrqe.com.*

SUMMARIZE A TV SHOW

- Watch a TV show in English (*listening*). Take notes as you listen.
- After watching, write a summary of the show (*writing*).
- Use your notes to give an oral summary of the show. Explain the characters, setting, and plot (*speaking*). Record yourself speaking. Then watch the video and write down what you said (*listening*).

Correct any mistakes you made and record the presentation again. Then watch another TV show and do this again.

LISTEN TO A LECTURE

Listen to an academic speech or other type of lecture on the Internet. Go to any of the following or similar sites and look for lectures on topics that are of interest to you:

http://lecturefox.com

http://freevideolectures.com

http://podcasts.ox.ac.uk

http://www.ted.com/talks

Listen to a lecture and take notes as you listen. Listen again to check and add to your notes (*listening*). Use your notes to write a summary of the lecture (*writing*).

Pretend you have to give a lecture on the same subject. Use your notes to give your lecture (*speaking*). Record yourself as you lecture. Then watch the video and write down what you said (*listening*). Correct any mistakes you made and record the lecture again. Then listen to another lecture and do this again.

HOW TO USE THIS BOOK

The book is divided into ten units, each one focusing on a different theme. There are three topics per unit, and each introduces twenty new vocabulary words in the context of the unit theme. You will practice these vocabulary words by doing exercises that look just like the questions on the IELTS. You can use this book in conjunction with *Barron's IELTS* and *Barron's IELTS Practice Exams* to reinforce the skills practiced in those books and improve your performance on the practice tests.

You can study the units in any order you like. Many of the words introduced in earlier units are repeated in later units. For this reason, you may find it helpful to study the units in order, but it isn't necessary.

NOTE

The book includes many footnotes to show you the British English equivalents of American English words. You will also hear a variety of accents on the audio so that you can become more comfortable with the variations in English. Both British English and American English spelling are acceptable on the exam.

Each unit follows the same format:

Words and Definitions
Each lesson begins with a list of twenty vocabulary words and a separate list of twenty definitions, followed by a reading passage. You will look for the vocabulary words as you read the passage and use the context to help you match each word with its correct definition.

Reading Comprehension
The reading passage is followed by IELTS-style reading comprehension questions. There are a variety of question types throughout the book so you will have an opportunity to practice most of the types of reading comprehension questions that appear on the IELTS.

Word Families
Next you will find word family charts—noun, verb, adjective, and adverb forms of five or six words selected from the unit vocabulary list. You will practice these words in an exercise that asks you to select the correct form of a word to complete each sentence.

Paraphrases
In this section, you will choose paraphrases for sentences from the reading passage. This is an opportunity to strengthen new vocabulary and develop your reading comprehension skills.

Dictionary Skill/Word Skill
This section uses one or two words from the vocabulary list to help you practice using a dictionary or analyzing a word to determine its meaning.

Listening
You will listen to a talk or conversation and answer IELTS-style listening comprehension questions. The different types of talks and conversations and the different question types found in the four listening sections of the IELTS are distributed throughout the book.

Writing
You will write in response to an IELTS-style writing task. This is also an opportunity for you to use some of the vocabulary words in your response. IELTS Task 1– and Task 2–type writing tasks are evenly distributed throughout the book.

Speaking
You will practice speaking in response to two or three IELTS-style speaking questions. This is also an opportunity for you to use some of the vocabulary words in your response.

Unit 1: The Natural World

ENVIRONMENTAL IMPACTS OF LOGGING

Words

Write the letter of each definition with the word it defines. If you don't know the definition, use the context of the reading passage to help you. Look for the words in bold as you read the passage.

PARAGRAPH 1

Words	Definitions
1 .... logging	**A** n., the natural world
2 .... array	**B** n., damage to air, water, etc.
3 .... environment	**C** n., the cutting down of trees for commercial use
4 .... habitat	**D** n., a large number; a collection
5 .... pollution	**E** n., the natural area where a plant or animal lives
6 .... extend	**F** v., to disappear
7 .... fell	**G** n., the goodness in food
8 .... nutrients	**H** adj. living in the water
9 .... terrestrial	**I** adj., living on the land
10 .... aquatic	**J** v., to cut down
11 .... vanish	**K** v., to reach past; get bigger

PARAGRAPH 2

Words	Definitions
12 .... myriad	**L** adj., whole; complete
13 .... intact	**M** adj., many; numerous
14 .... intercept	**N** n., loss of soil from the action of water or wind
15 .... stabilize[1]	**O** v., to keep from changing; maintain
16 .... erosion	**P** v., to catch; to interrupt the progress of something

[1]BrE: stabilise

PARAGRAPHS 3–5

Words	Definitions
17 .... vegetation	**Q** n., plants
18 .... inhibit	**R** n., the removal of all trees from a large area
19 .... defense[1]	**S** v., to prevent; slow down
20 .... deforestation	**T** n., protection

Reading

Environmental Impacts of Logging

(1) **A**

From shipping crates to paper bags, the **logging** industry supplies the raw materials for an **array** of products. However, this is not without untold harm to the **environment**. The damage includes **habitat** loss, **pollution**, and climate change, with the effects spanning the globe from the rainforests of Central Africa, Southeast Asia, and South America to the northern forests of Canada and Scandinavia. The effects of logging **extend** beyond just the **felling** of a swath of trees. **Nutrients**, water, and shelter for plants, animals, and microorganisms throughout the ecosystem are also lost; many life forms—both **terrestrial** and **aquatic**—are becoming endangered as forests **vanish**.

(2) **B**

Trees protect the soil beneath them; thus, tree loss can affect its integrity. For example, the rainforest floor, home to **myriad** plant life as well as insects, worms, reptiles, amphibians, and small mammals, relies on a dense canopy of branches and leaves to keep it healthy and **intact**. The canopy prevents surface runoff by **intercepting** heavy rainfall so that water can drip down onto the porous earth. Tree roots also **stabilize** the soil and help prevent **erosion**. In return, a healthy soil encourages root development and microbial activity, which contribute to tree growth and well-being. A major factor in logging-related soil damage comes from road building, with trucks and other heavy equipment compressing the spongy soil, creating furrows where water collects, and disrupting the

[1]BrE: defence

underground water flow. Eventually, the topsoil wears away, leaving behind an infertile layer of rocks and clay.

(3) **C**

Logging can also damage aquatic habitats. **Vegetation** along rivers and stream banks helps maintain a steady water flow by blocking the entry of soil and other residue, while tree shade **inhibits** the growth of algae. Removing trees obliterates these benefits. When eroding soil flows into waterways, the organic matter within it consumes more oxygen, which can lead to oxygen depletion in the water, killing fish and other wildlife.

(4) **D**

Trees provide a natural **defense** against air pollution. They remove carbon dioxide from the atmosphere while they emit oxygen, and their leaves filter pollutants from the air. Cutting down trees keeps pollutants airborne, where they can mix with water vapor[1] and form acid rain. Water quality in nearby streams and rivers also deteriorates as tree loss contributes to increased sedimentation.

(5) **E**

In a healthy forest ecosystem, trees draw moisture from the soil and release it into the atmosphere while they provide shade to lessen evaporation. Thus, **deforestation** affects rainfall patterns, leading to flooding as well as drought and forest fires. Deforestation is responsible for about one-fifth of carbon dioxide emissions worldwide, making it a major contributor to climate change—in particular, global warming. In the Amazon basin alone, deforestation is responsible for millions of tons of carbon being released into the atmosphere annually. Some logging companies burn large tracts of forest just to facilitate access to one area—a practice[2] that discharges even more carbon dioxide.

(6) **F**

Forests, especially the tropical rainforests, are a vital natural resource with extensive biodiversity and irreplaceable wildlife habitats. More responsible logging practices would help ensure that they are protected for future generations.

[1]BrE: vapour
[2]BrE: practice *n.*, practise *v.*

Answer the questions about **Environmental Impacts of Logging**.

Questions 1–4

The reading passage contains six paragraphs, ***A–F****. Which paragraphs discuss the following information?*

Write the correct letter, ***A–F****.*

.... **1** The impact of logging on the weather

.... **2** How trees inhibit soil erosion

.... **3** How deforestation contributes to air pollution

.... **4** The impact of erosion on fish

Questions 5–8

Complete the summary using words from the list below.

aquatic	defense	habitats	myriad
arrays	fells	intercepts	vegetation

The logging industry **5**.......... trees to get the wood that is used to make many products. This practice has **6**.......... effects on the environment. The natural **7**.......... of many terrestrial and aquatic animals are damaged. Trees protect the environment in many ways. They are an effective **8**.......... against both air pollution and soil erosion.

Word Families

A

Complete each sentence with the correct word from the word family chart. Make nouns plural where necessary. Use the correct form of verbs.

noun	noun	verb
defense	defender	defend

1 The shade of trees provides a ....against the drying effects of the sun.

2 Fish cannot .... themselves from the effects of water pollution.

3 A .... of the environment works to protect plants and animals from damage caused by logging.

noun	adjective	adverb
environment	environmental	environmentally

4 It is important to develop more .... friendly logging practices.

5 Logging causes a great deal of .... damage.

6 The .... needs to be protected from the effects of logging.

noun	verb
erosion	erode

7 When soil ...., there are no nutrients left to help plants grow.

8 Soil .... leads to the pollution of streams and rivers.

noun	verb	adjective	adverb
extent	extend	extensive	extensively

9 The Amazon Rainforest .... from Brazil into neighboring countries.

10 The Amazon Rainforest is the most .... rainforest in the world.

11 The .... of environmental damage caused by logging is frightening.

12 Rainforests around the world have been .... logged.

noun	noun	verb
pollution	pollutant	pollute

13 Factories add .... to the air and water.

14 Eroding soil .... water.

15 Deforestation contributes to the effects of both air and water ....

Word Families

B

Choose the correct word family member from the list below to complete each blank.

1 environment	environmental	environmentally
2 pollution	pollutants	pollutes
3 extent	extend	extensive
4 stability	stabilizes	stable
5 erosion	erode	eroded
6 Defenses	Defenders	Defends

Modern industry has caused damage to our natural **1**.......... in many ways. The air and water are filled with **2**.......... . One result of this is acid rain, which has caused **3**.......... damage to vegetation in many areas. When large amounts of vegetation die off, the environment loses **4**.......... . If there are no plants to hold the soil, it starts to **5**.......... . This leads to myriad problems, including water pollution and habitat loss. **6**.......... of wildlife work hard to prevent further damage to natural areas.

Paraphrases

Read the sentence from the reading passage. Then, choose the sentence that has the same meaning.

1 *For example, the rainforest floor, home to myriad plant life, as well as insects, worms, reptiles, amphibians, and small mammals, relies on a dense canopy of branches and leaves to keep it healthy and intact.* (paragraph 2)

A A variety of plants and animals live in the rainforest, both on the ground and in the branches and leaves of the trees.

B The rainforest floor and the many plants and animals that live there depend on the protection of the tree canopy.

C The thick rainforest tree canopy stays healthy as long as the forest floor is healthy.

2 *Vegetation along rivers and stream banks helps maintain a steady water flow by blocking the entry of soil and other residue, while tree shade inhibits the growth of algae.* (paragraph 3)

A Plants around waterways help keep the water moving and stop the spread of algae.

B Trees and other plants grow on river banks because they depend on the water supply to live.

C Plants that grow near moving water provide shade to keep the water cool and fresh.

Word Skill

Prefix *de-*
The prefix *de-* can mean "remove."

Read the sentences. Write a definition for each underlined word.

1 When we deforest an area, many animals lose their habitat.

deforest: ....

2 You can debone a chicken before cooking it.

debone: ....

3 I had to deice the windshield before I could drive.

deice: ....

Listening

Track 1

Listen to the lecture. Choose the correct letter, ***A****,* ***B****, or* ***C****.*

1 Trees provide a habitat for ....
  A birds only.
  B a myriad of animals.
  C aquatic animals.

2 .... are a source of nutrients for birds.
  A Insects
  B Roots
  C Leaves

3 Trees provide aquatic animals with a defense from ....
  A coolness.
  B rain.
  C heat.

4 .... inhibit soil erosion.
  A Branches
  B Roots
  C Trunks

Writing
(Task 2)

Deforestation caused by human activity is happening in many parts of the world, with serious results for the environment. What do you think can be done to solve this problem?

Support your opinion with reasons and examples from your own knowledge and experience.

Write at least 250 words.

Speaking

Talk about the following topics.

What kinds of natural environments do you enjoy spending time in?

What do you think can be done to solve the problems caused by environmental pollution?

BIRD MIGRATION

Words

Write the letter of each definition with the word it defines. If you don't know the definition, use the context of the reading passage to help you. Look for the words in bold as you read the passage.

PARAGRAPH 1

Words	Definitions
1 .... migration	A n., movement from one place to another
2 .... inhabit	B v., to interest greatly
3 .... fascinate	C n., a priority; an urgent need
4 .... observer	D v., to live in
5 .... imperative	E n., a person who watches something
6 .... evolve	F v., to develop and change

PARAGRAPH 2

Words	Definitions
7 .... breed	G v., to reproduce
8 .... optimal	H n., one half of the Earth; one half of a sphere
9 .... hemisphere	I adj., best; most favorable[1]
10 .... species	J n., type; a basic group in biological classification

PARAGRAPHS 4–6

Words	Definitions
11 .... windswept	K v., to provide energy
12 .... endure	L v., to live under difficult conditions
13 .... fuel	M adj., unprotected from the wind
14 .... aspect	N n., a difficult act or achievement
15 .... feat	O n., a part or feature

[1]BrE: favourable

PARAGRAPH 6

Words	Definitions
16 .... nocturnal	**P** adj., active during the day
17 .... obscure	**Q** adj., active at night
18 .... stray	**R** v., to leave the correct route; to become separated from the group
19 .... diurnal	**S** v., to make difficult to see
20 .... navigation	**T** n., finding and following one's route

Reading

Bird Migration

(1) **Migration** is the regular movement of animals between their breeding grounds and the areas that they **inhabit** during the rest of the year. Many types of animals migrate, but bird migration in particular has **fascinated observers** for centuries. Migration is an excellent example of how nature has responded to the biological **imperative** for species to **evolve** and spread out into all possible ecological niches that can provide the conditions necessary for species to breed and raise young.

(2) The most common form of bird migration involves traveling[1] to higher latitudes to **breed** during the warm season and then returning to lower latitudes during the non-breeding period. This form of migration allows birds to breed in areas that provide **optimal** conditions for nesting and feeding their young. Because of the way in which the continents are placed upon Earth, migration of this type takes place primarily into the higher latitudes of the Northern **Hemisphere**. No land birds are known to migrate into the higher latitudes of the Southern Hemisphere; only **species** of seabirds migrate to the Southern Hemisphere to breed.

(3) Although most bird migration takes place between the lower and higher latitudes of the Northern Hemisphere, many species are trans-equatorial, living in the Northern Hemisphere during the breeding season and in the Southern Hemisphere during the rest of the year. A well-known example of trans-equatorial migration is the arctic tern. This tern, which breeds in the arctic regions and winters in antarctic waters, travels 24,000 miles a year during migration.

---

[1] BrE: travelling

(4) Not all migration is long distance. Some species exhibit altitudinal migration. Their breeding areas are in higher elevations, near or at the peaks of mountains, while they spend the non-breeding season in neighboring[1] valleys or other nearby low country. This variety of migration is typical of many grouse species, including the ptarmigan, a form of arctic grouse. Many rock ptarmigan never leave the high arctic tundra, spending their breeding season atop **windswept** arctic peaks and the winter season in nearby valleys, **enduring** some of the coldest conditions on earth.

(5) During migration, most birds fly for a limited period each day, probably about six to eight hours, typically flying distances of several hundred miles. Some birds, however, undertake much longer flights when their routes include crossing large bodies of water or other geographic features such as deserts and mountains. For example, many species regularly cross the Gulf of Mexico, a trip that requires a continuous flight of over 1,000 miles and takes from twenty-four to thirty-six hours or longer. An extreme example of non-stop bird migration is done by the bar-tailed godwit, which makes a continuous flight of over 11,000 miles from Alaska to New Zealand each year. At the start of its trip, about 55 percent[2] of its bodyweight is made up of the fat necessary to **fuel** this amazing journey.

(6) How birds manage to unerringly travel between distant locations is one **aspect** that has fascinated observers for centuries. Modern-day researchers have attempted to understand this **feat**. Most studies have found that migratory birds all have some ability to navigate and an innate drive to travel in a particular direction. **Nocturnal** migrants, those species that travel at night, seem to take their navigational cues from the stars. When the stars are **obscured** by clouds, nocturnal migrants become confused and may return to earth or **stray** off course. **Diurnal** migrants, those migrating during the day, take their cues from the location of the sun. In addition, diurnal migrants have also been shown to use geographic features such as mountain ranges or sea coasts as other cues for **navigation**. Because the stars and the sun move constantly over the course of twenty-four hours, this suggests that migrating birds also have a sense of time.

---

[1]BrE: neighbouring

[2]BrE: per cent

Answer the questions about **Bird Migration**.

Questions 1–4

Do the following statements agree with the information in the reading passage?

Write

TRUE	*if the statement agrees with the information.*
FALSE	*if the statement contradicts the information.*
NOT GIVEN	*if there is no information on this in the passage.*

.... **1** Trans-equatorial birds cross from one hemisphere to the other when they migrate.

.... **2** Many migratory birds breed in the Southern Hemisphere.

.... **3** Migrating birds spend the warm months where conditions for breeding are optimal.

.... **4** Many birds fail in their migration because they do not have enough body fat to fuel the journey.

Questions 5–8

Look at the following descriptions of migratory habits. Match each type of bird with the correct description.

Write the correct letter, ***A*** *or* ***B***.

A Diurnal species of birds
B Nocturnal species of birds

.... **5** They navigate by looking at the sun.

.... **6** They navigate by looking at the stars.

.... **7** They may stop flying when clouds obscure the sky.

.... **8** They navigate by looking at landforms.

Word Families

A

Complete each sentence with the correct word from the word family chart. Make nouns plural where necessary. Use the correct form of verbs.

noun	verb	adjective
evolution	evolve	evolutionary

1 Scientists believe that birds .... from dinosaurs.

2 Our research plans have gone through many .... and are now quite different from our original plans.

3 Through the .... process, birds have developed adaptations that allow them to survive in different environments.

noun	verb	adjective
fascination	fascinate	fascinating

4 The study of birdsong is a .... subject.

5 The study of the lives of birds .... many people.

6 There are several birdwatchers in his family, so his .... with birds is not hard to understand.

noun	noun	verb	adjective
migration	migrant	migrate	migratory

7 Bird .... generally takes place twice a year, in the spring and the autumn.

8 Scientists study the habits of .... birds.

9 Some birds .... thousands of miles to reach their summer breeding grounds.

10 .... stop to rest several times during their journey.

noun	noun	verb	adjective
navigation	navigator	navigate	navigational

11 Migratory birds are born with .... skills; they don't have to learn them.

12 Migratory birds are amazing ....

13 Birds use landforms as well as the sun and stars for ....

14 Birds .... by looking at the sun and stars.

noun	noun	verb	adjective
observation	observer	observe	observant

15 Many people .... birds as a hobby.

16 If birds become aware of the presence of an ...., they quickly fly away.

17 We can learn a great deal about the lives of birds through simple ....

18 You have to be really .... to spot most types of birds.

Word Families

B

Choose the correct word family member from the list below to complete each blank.

1	fascination	fascinate	fascinating
2	observation	observer	observe
3	migration	migrate	migratory
4	evolution	evolved	evolutionary
5	navigation	navigate	navigational

Birds are **1**.......... to many people, and bird watching is a popular hobby. The best time to watch birds is in the early morning, because birds are usually very active at that time of day. The **2**.......... must keep still and quiet in order not to frighten the birds away. If you live in a part of the world where **3**.......... birds spend their breeding season, then you will have the opportunity to see nest-building activity. Over the ages, different species of birds have **4**.......... with different types of nest-building skills. It makes an interesting study to look at the different types of nests built by birds and to watch them as they build their nests. After the breeding season is over and the babies have left the nest, it is time for the birds to head for warmer parts of the world to spend the winter months. Birds **5**.......... to their winter feeding grounds, using the stars or the sun as their guide.

Paraphrases

Read the sentence from the reading passage. Then, choose the sentence that has the same meaning.

1 *Many types of animals migrate, but bird migration, in particular, has fascinated observers for centuries.* (paragraph 1)

A Animal migration is a subject that has been studied for many years.

B People have long observed the fact that many animals, including birds, migrate.

C The migration of birds, more than other animals, has been interesting to people for a long time.

2 *When the stars are obscured by clouds, nocturnal migrants become confused and may return to earth or stray off course.* (paragraph 6)

A When the sky becomes dark, migrating birds know it is time to stop and rest for the night.

B If birds traveling at night can't see the stars, they might stop flying or get lost.

C When clouds move in front of the stars, there is not enough light for migrating birds to see the earth beneath them.

Dictionary Skill

PARTS OF SPEECH

The word *imperative* can be a noun or an adjective.

Read the dictionary definitions below. Then read the sentences and write the letter of the correct definition for each sentence.

im-per-a-tive [im-PER-uh-tiv]
A *adjective.* very important; essential
B *noun.* a priority; an urgent need

.... **1** It is our *imperative* to protect the natural environment.

.... **2** It is *imperative* to keep dogs and cats away from the bird breeding area.

Listening

Track 2

Listen to the talk. Look at the map below labeled A–E. Look at the list of places and write the correct letter, ***A–E****, next to numbers* ***1–5****.*

.... **1** species list

.... **2** restricted area

.... **3** observation platform

.... **4** gift shop

.... **5** donation box

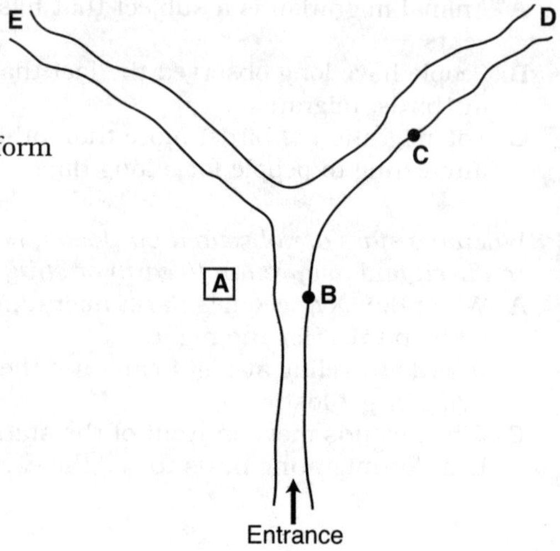

Writing (Task 1)

The chart[1] below shows information about different species of birds observed in Woodchuck County at different times of the year.

Summarize[2] the information by selecting and reporting the main information and making comparisons.

Write at least 150 words.

Species of Birds Observed in Woodchuck County by Season
(partial list)

Species	Winter	Summer
bluebirds		X
cardinals	X	X
crows	X	X
juncos	X	
mockingbirds		X
orioles		X
vireos		X
woodpeckers	X	X

Speaking

Talk about the following topics.

Many people enjoy observing birds because they find them fascinating. Why do you think people are fascinated by birds?

Are you fascinated by birds? Why or why not?

What animals are fascinating to you?

[1]BrE: table
[2]BrE: summarise

PLANT LIFE IN THE TAKLIMAKAN DESERT

Words

Write the letter of each definition with the word it defines. If you don't know the definition, use the context of the reading passage to help you. Look for the words in bold as you read the passage.

PARAGRAPH 1

Words	Definitions
1 .... occupy	**A** adj., small in numbers or amount
2 .... sparse	**B** adj., strong; sudden and destructive
3 .... swing	**C** adj., very severe or difficult
4 .... violent	**D** v., to be in a place; exist in
5 .... extreme	**E** n., a sudden or big change

PARAGRAPH 2

Words	Definitions
6 .... transitional	**F** v., to grow well
7 .... fringe	**G** adj., relating to change from one type to another
8 .... diverse	**H** v., to change to fit a situation or environment
9 .... adapt	**I** n., the edge of something
10 .... thrive	**J** adj., varied; of many kinds

PARAGRAPH 3

Words	Definitions
11 .... resilient	**K** adj., tough; able to endure difficult conditions
12 .... stressor	**L** v., to reduce to the least possible amount
13 .... minimize[1]	**M** n., methods
14 .... moisture	**N** adj., producing a lot of something
15 .... prolific	**O** n., something that causes great difficulties
16 .... mechanisms	**P** n., wetness or water

[1]BrE: minimise

PARAGRAPHS 4–7

Words	Definitions
17 .... evaporation	**Q** v., to decide
18 .... dilute	**R** v., to gradually increase over time
19 .... determine	**S** v., to make weaker by mixing with water
20 .... accumulate	**T** n., the change from liquid to gas; loss of water to the air

Reading

Plant Life in the Taklimakan Desert

(1) The Taklimakan Desert, second in size only to Africa's Sahara Desert, **occupies** some 337,600 square kilometers[1] (130,300 square miles) of northwestern China—an area about the size of Finland. **Sparse** rainfall, daily temperature **swings** of up to 20°C (68°F), and **violent** sandstorms make it one of the most **extreme** environments on Earth.

(2) Eighty-five percent[2] of the Taklimakan Desert consists of shifting sand dunes, some up to 250 meters[3] tall, that are largely free of vegetation. Yet, **transitional** areas between the open desert and oases on the desert **fringe** support **diverse** plant forms that not only have **adapted** to the harsh conditions but actually **thrive** there.

(3) Successful desert plants are **resilient** to scorching summers and frigid winters, drought, and high-salt conditions. The plants' principal defense[4] against these environmental **stressors** consists of drawing in as much water as possible while **minimizing moisture** loss. Three Taklimakan plants—*Populus euphratica, Tamarix ramosissima,* and *Alhagi sparsifolia*—represent some of the most diverse, **prolific** vegetation in the area; although they share many survival strategies, each has developed unique coping **mechanisms** of its own.

(4) The Euphrates poplar, *Populus euphratica*, the only tall tree in the Taklimakan ecosystem, has an extensive root system that allows it to absorb water far from the standing tree. *P. euphratica* controls **evaporation** by opening and closing the stomata, or tiny

[1]BrE: kilometres
[2]BrE: per cent
[3]BrE: metres
[4]BrE: defence

pores, on the leaf surface in response to the amount of moisture being lost through the leaves to the surrounding air. These stomata generally remain open during the day while the plant conducts photosynthesis.

(5) *P. euphratica* can endure high-salt concentrations in the soil. It takes in unlimited amounts of salt through the roots, up the stem, and into leaves, where it **dilutes** the normally toxic salt by increasing the number and volume of its cells.

(6) *Tamarix ramosissima*, a small tree with needlelike leaves commonly known as tamarisk or salt cedar, takes in enormous amounts of water via a far-reaching root system many times the size of the plant above ground. Like *P. euphratica*, tamarisk can naturally **determine** when to close stomata to inhibit evaporation and regulate photosynthesis.

(7) Tamarisk has a high tolerance for salty conditions and even produces its own salt, which it **accumulates** in special glands between the leaves and then releases onto leaf surfaces. Leaves dropping to the ground make the soil more saline, or salty, giving tamarisk a competitive advantage over less salt-tolerant plants.

(8) *Alhagi sparsifolia*, a spiny shrub, thrives in the Taklimakan Desert even though it uses large amounts of water, especially during the summer months. With only a few wispy roots in the upper soil, it is unaffected by occasional flooding. Most of its roots reach down deep, where they take up water from as far as sixteen meters below ground. Unlike *P. euphratica* and *T. ramosissima*, which open and close stomata according to conditions on the leaf surface, *A. sparsifolia* does so according to hydraulic conductance—that is, the ease with which it takes up groundwater.

(9) Although desert plants have adapted for their own survival, they also help protect their ecosystem by stabilizing sand dunes, preventing erosion, presenting a barrier to sandstorms, and conserving biodiversity.

Answer the questions about **Plant Life in the Taklimakan Desert**.

Questions 1–3

Choose the correct letter, ***A, B, C,*** *or* ***D.***

1 Most of the Taklimakan Desert is covered with
- **A** tamarisk.
- **B** spiny plants.
- **C** sand dunes.
- **D** diverse plant life.

2 Plants in the Taklimakan Desert
- **A** grow only in areas above 250 meters high.
- **B** thrive in extreme conditions.
- **C** are not very hardy.
- **D** are mostly tall trees.

3 Environmental stressors in the Taklimakan Desert include
- **A** sparse sunlight.
- **B** lack of salt in the soil.
- **C** extreme temperatures.
- **D** periods of heavy rainfall.

Questions 4–7

Which of the following mechanisms used by plants to survive in the desert environment are mentioned in the passage? Choose ***four*** *answers from the list below.*

A Having strong roots that can hold on during violent sandstorms

B Closing pores to minimize loss of moisture

C Occupying a place in the shade of a larger plant to avoid the scorching desert sun

D Diluting the salt that the plant takes in

E Having large root systems that can reach water far from the plant

F Adding salt to the soil to minimize competition from other plants

G Accumulating water in the leaves of the plant

Word Families

A

Complete each sentence with the correct word from the word family chart. Make nouns plural where necessary. Use the correct form of verbs.

noun	verb	adjective
adaptation	adapt	adaptable

1 One way that plants .... to the dry desert is by developing deep root systems.

2 Plants in the Taklimakan Desert have .... that allow them to live in dry, salty conditions.

3 Most plant species are not .... to a desert environment.

noun	noun	verb	adjective
diversity	diversification	diversify	diverse

4 The .... ways that plants adapt to desert conditions makes a fascinating study.

5 Changes in climate can result in species ....

6 There is a great .... of plant life in the fringe of the Taklimakan Desert.

7 As the climate changes, plant species in an area may .... if conditions improve.

noun	adjective	adverb
extreme	extreme	extremely

8 Temperatures in the Taklimakan Desert reach an .... during hot summer days.

9 The weather in a desert is usually .... dry.

10 Many plants cannot endure the .... heat of the desert.

noun	adjective	adverb
resilience	resilient	resiliently

11 Desert plants are .... to heat and dryness.

12 Desert plants grow .... in the heat.

13 The .... of certain plants allows them to thrive in the desert.

noun	noun	verb	adjective
stress	stressor	stress	stressful

14 Heat and drought both .... plants.

15 A long period of dryness causes a lot of .... to plants.

16 The main .... in a desert is lack of rain.

17 Certain plants thrive in the desert despite the .... conditions.

noun	adjective	adverb
violence	violent	violently

18 The .... of sandstorms keeps many plants from thriving in the desert.

19 .... winds tear up many plants or cover them with sand.

20 The winds blow .... during a sandstorm.

Word Families

B

Choose the correct word family member from the list below to complete each blank.

1 adaptations	adapts	adapted
2 extreme	extremes	extremely
3 stressor	stress	stressful
4 resilience	resilient	resiliently
5 Violence	Violent	Violently
6 diversity	diversify	diverse

Desert plants have a variety of **1**.......... that allow them to endure the desert environment. Because a desert is **2**.......... dry, plants need to be able to take in as much water as possible when it rains and to store the water for a long time. Special root systems and types of leaves enable them to do this. Another source of **3**.......... in a desert is the high temperature, so desert plants need to have **4**........... . **5**.......... storms can occur in a desert, and only plants with strong roots will be able to endure the storms. Considering the difficult conditions in a desert, the **6**.......... of plants that can be found there is truly amazing.

Paraphrases

Read the sentence from the reading passage. Then, choose the sentence that has the same meaning.

1 *Sparse rainfall, daily temperature swings of up to 20°C (68°F), and violent sandstorms make it one of the most extreme environments on Earth.* (paragraph 1)
- **A** The environmental conditions in the Taklimakan Desert are among the most difficult on Earth.
- **B** On any day in the Taklimakan Desert, you might experience little rainfall, high temperatures, or strong sandstorms.
- **C** The Taklimakan Desert has less rain, higher temperatures, and more frequent sandstorms than most other deserts.

2 *Successful desert plants are resilient to scorching summers and frigid winters, drought, and high-salt conditions.* (paragraph 3)
- **A** Many plants suffer because of the extreme desert conditions.
- **B** Plants that live well in the desert are able to endure the harsh environment.
- **C** Few plants live in the desert because of the hot summers, cold winters, dryness, and salt.

Dictionary Skill

DIFFERENT MEANINGS

Many words have more than one meaning.

Read the definitions below. Then read the sentences and write the letter of the correct definition for each sentence.

swing [SWING]
A *noun.* a sudden or big change
B *noun.* back-and-forth movement
C *noun.* a hanging seat that moves back and forth

.... **1** The children played on the *swing* all afternoon.

.... **2** After a rainstorm in the desert, there is a noticeable *swing* back to life.

.... **3** The *swing* of the branches in the breeze made a creaking noise.

Listening

Track 3

Listen to the discussion. Complete the notes below.
*Write **NO MORE THAN ONE WORD** for each answer.*

Taklimakan Desert Plants

Many plants live in the **1** .... areas.

Stressors:

little rain

2 .... temperatures

rapid **3** ....

Adaptations:

ability to close pores

large root systems to **4** .... water

Writing (Task 1)

The charts[1] below show information about three different deserts around the world.

Summarize[2] the information by selecting and reporting the main information and making comparisons.

Write at least 150 words.

Sahara Desert (Africa)

Size	9,000,000 sq km
Average annual rainfall	7.6 cm (north) 12.7 cm (south)
Average temperatures	30°C (summer) 13°C (winter)
Temperature extremes	58°C = highest recorded

Taklimakan Desert (Asia)

Size	337,600 sq km
Average annual rainfall	3.8 cm (west) 1.0 cm (east)
Average temperatures	25°C (summer) –9°C (winter)
Temperature extremes	–26.1°C = lowest recorded

Great Basin Desert (North America)

Size	305,775 sq km
Average annual rainfall	5.1–51 cm
Average temperatures	30°C (summer) –8°C (winter)
Temperature extremes	57°C = highest recorded

[1]BrE: tables
[2]BrE: summarise

Speaking

Talk about the following topics.

Are you interested in visiting extreme environments, such as deserts or high mountains? Why or why not?

Why do you think people like to visit extreme environments?

When you travel, do you adapt easily to new climates?

Unit 2: Leisure Time

PERIPHERAL VISION IN SPORTS

Words

Write the letter of each definition with the word it defines. If you don't know the definition, use the context of the reading passage to help you. Look for the words in bold as you read the passage.

PARAGRAPH 1

Words	Definitions
1 .... focus	**A** adv., without thinking; automatically
2 .... indistinct	**B** v., center attention on one particular object
3 .... blur	**C** adj., at the edge
4 .... unconsciously	**D** n., something not seen clearly
5 .... peripheral	**E** adj., unclear
6 .... tolerate	**F** n., a person who plays sports[1]
7 .... vision	**G** v., to show; model
8 .... athlete	**H** n., area
9 .... demonstrate	**I** v., to accept; allow
10 .... range	**J** n., the ability to see; sight

PARAGRAPH 2

Words	Definitions
11 .... performance	**K** adj., taking attention away from something
12 .... detect	**L** n., a movement
13 .... maneuver[2]	**M** n., how well a person or machine does something
14 .... distracting	**N** v., to expect; be ready for something to happen
15 .... anticipate	**O** v., to notice; become aware of

[1]BrE: sport
[2]BrE: manoeuver

PARAGRAPHS 3–5

Words	Definitions
16 .... scan	**P** v., to cause to be more difficult
17 .... complicate	**Q** v., to look over
18 .... coordinate	**R** adv., in a way that is impossible to see or notice
19 .... boundary	**S** n., an edge; border
20 .... indiscernibly	**T** v., to organize[1]; make work together

Reading

Peripheral Vision in Sports

(1) **Focus** in on something as small as a pin. Notice that as you focus, everything else that fills your whole area of sight is **indistinct**: just a **blur** without any clear detail. We **unconsciously** realize that things fill this **peripheral** area, but we are not aware of what they are, nor do we care. We simply **tolerate** the blur. However, sometimes it is important to pay attention to the blur that surrounds the point where we have focused our **vision**. **Athletes**, for example, must be keenly aware of what is happening all around them. They **demonstrate**, with a very high level of skill, how much we can use our entire **range** of peripheral vision.

(2) An athlete's **performance** depends on training visual abilities, not just muscles. **Detecting** and keeping track of as much motion as possible while performing physical **maneuvers** is quite a feat. Peripheral visual information is processed quickly. The office worker might notice the **distracting** bug moving beside the computer, but the fast moving athlete must detect all kinds of motion from every angle and never lose concentration. Each peripherally viewed movement must be immediately processed as more and more movements keep coming, rapidly. Good footwork and body positioning will help the athlete gain viewing time in this intense environment, improving the opportunity to **anticipate** what will happen next.

(3) The athlete's view, full of movement, requires rapid **scanning** with visual focus changing rapidly among various distances. Tracking fast objects is often **complicated** by the need for the athlete's body to move in response to other aspects of the activity, while head motion must **coordinate** with eye movement to assist in balance. A volleyball player, for example, must pay attention to body positioning in

[1]BrE: organize

relation to the speed and angle of the moving ball as well as to the court **boundaries**, all the while scanning the movement of the other players. Athletes need as much peripheral range as possible.

(4) The environment contributes to athletes' visual sharpness. Contrasting court backgrounds, adequate lighting, non-confusing uniform color combinations, and less off-court motion all help the athlete's peripheral concentration. It seems odd that visiting baseball teams are allowed to dress in gray uniforms when bright colors would help the home team keep a better eye on them.

(5) Everything that catches the athlete's attention causes the eyes to pause almost **indiscernibly** as they gather a quick view of focused detail. As the eyes move in and out of focus, there is a blur between each pause. This is when visual tracking errors can occur. Even the act of blinking, usually at a rate of 25 blinks per minute, or one tenth of a second per blink, interferes with the athlete's vision. Normal, natural blinking means the eyes are closed for two and a half seconds out of every minute, and more than that if the athlete is anxious. This is added to the rapid blurs that occur as the athlete's eyes move in and out of focus on specific objects. These non-visual moments can be somewhat compensated for if the athlete thoroughly tunes into the game. Anticipation, that learned and practiced[1] art, will serve the athlete well, in many ways.

Answer the questions about **Peripheral Vision in Sports**.

Questions 1–7

Do the following statements agree with the information in the reading passage?

Write

TRUE *if the statement agrees with the information.*
FALSE *if the statement contradicts the information.*
NOT GIVEN *if there is no information on this in the passage.*

.... **1** Peripheral vision refers to what we see near the boundaries of our visual range.

.... **2** Focusing our eyes on one object only will cause that object to look indistinct.

[1]BrE: practised

.... 3. In addition to physical abilities, athletes need to be skilled at detecting movements all around them.

.... 4. Office workers tend to find that certain kinds of movements are more distracting than others.

.... 5. A volleyball player does not need to focus on the movements of the other players on the court.

.... 6. Poor lighting and confusing color combinations on uniforms can have a negative effect on an athlete's performance.

.... 7. Athletes blink more often when they are feeling anxious.

Word Families

A

Complete each sentence with the correct word from the word family chart. Make nouns plural where necessary. Use the correct form of verbs.

noun	verb	adjective
complication	complicate	complicated

1 Playing a ball game is not as simple as it may look; there are many ....

2 A game can become very .... when there are many players on the field.

3 The need to pay attention to many things at once .... the game for an athlete.

noun	verb	adjective
coordination	coordinate	coordinated

4 The .... movements of all the team members will help them win the game.

5 An athlete must .... physical skill with sharp vision to play a game well.

6 It is important for an athlete to have good physical ....

noun	verb	adjective
demonstration	demonstrate	demonstrative

7 The athlete gave a .... of the correct way to throw the ball.

8 Professional athletes .... a high level of skills.

9 The way that goal was scored was .... of good teamwork in action.

noun	noun	verb
performance	performer	perform

10 The entire team .... well during the game.

11 The team gave an excellent .... at last night's game.

12 All the .... did a good job.

noun	verb	adjective
tolerance	tolerate	tolerant

13 Good athletes always try to do their best but are still .... of occasional failure.

14 An athlete needs to be able to .... a high level of action around him.

15 An athlete should have .... for hard physical activity.

noun	adjective	adverb
vision	visual	visually

16 In sports, ... abilities can be as important as physical abilities.

17 The coach used drawings to explain the game ....

18 Good .... is important for playing sports well.

Word Families

B

Choose the correct word family member from the list below to complete each blank.

1 performance	performer	perform
2 demonstrations	demonstrate	demonstrative
3 coordination	coordinate	coordinated
4 vision	visual	visually
5 tolerance	tolerate	tolerant
6 Complications	Complicate	Complicated

In order to **1**.......... well, an athlete must have a number of different abilities. Naturally, she should **2**.......... excellent physical skills. In addition to strength, **3**.......... of all parts of the body while moving around the court or field is very important. The athlete also needs to have good **4**.......... abilities. She needs to be able to see what is happening around her so that she can respond to the other players' maneuvers. She has to be **5**.......... of activity around her without losing her ability to focus on her own part in the game. Finally, she needs to be a fast thinker. **6**.......... can occur in any game, and the athlete needs to be able to respond to them quickly.

Paraphrases

Read the sentence from the reading passage. Then, choose the sentence that has the same meaning.

1 *Notice that as you focus, everything else that fills your whole area of sight is indistinct: just a blur without any clear detail.* (paragraph 1)
A When you focus on one thing, the rest of your field of vision is unclear.

B If you look at something for a long time, your eyes begin to hurt.
C Sometimes you can focus clearly on one detail, but sometimes your vision is not clear.

2 *An athlete's performance depends on training visual abilities, not just muscles.* (paragraph 2)
A People who play sports must train frequently.
B People with strong muscles are usually good at sports.
C Good visual skills, as well as strong muscles, are needed to play sports well.

Dictionary Skill

PARTS OF SPEECH

Focus can be either a noun or a verb. *Blur* can also be either a noun or a verb.

Read the dictionary definitions below. Then read the sentences and write the letter of the correct definition for each sentence.

QUESTIONS 1–2

fo-cus [FO-kus]
A *noun.* the center of attention
B *verb.* to center attention on one object; concentrate

.... **1** When playing a game, always *focus* on the ball.

.... **2** Keep your *focus* on the goal.

QUESTIONS 3–4

blur [BLUR]
A *noun.* something not seen clearly
B *verb.* make unclear

.... **3** I couldn't follow the game; it was all a big *blur* to me.

.... **4** Poor lighting can *blur* the players' vision.

Listening

Track 4

Listen to the discussion. Complete the notes below.
Write ***NO MORE THAN ONE WORD*** *for each answer.*

Vision and Basketball

Basketball players have to **1**.......... on the ball. They have to **2**.......... the other players' maneuvers. They **3**........... the whole court to see the actions of the rest of the players. They don't think about this; they do it **4**............ .

Writing

> **Do you believe that professional athletes make good role models for young people?**
>
> **Support your opinion with reasons and examples from your own knowledge or experience.**

Write at least 250 words.

Speaking

Talk about the following topics.

Do you focus better on your studies or work when you are in a quiet environment, or do you prefer to have activity going on around you?

What kinds of things are distracting to you when you study or work?

Do you anticipate any major changes in your work or study situation in the next year?

HISTORY OF THE CIRCUS

Words

Write the letter of each definition with the word it defines. If you don't know the definition, use the context of the reading passage to help you. Look for the words in bold as you read the passage.

PARAGRAPHS 1–2

Words	Definitions
1 .... entertainment	**A** n., a period of 100 years
2 .... century	**B** adj., very old; of the distant past
3 .... ancient	**C** n., place where an event is held
4 .... found	**D** n., a performance or show
5 .... venue	**E** v., to start or establish an institution
6 .... popular	**F** n., something shown to the public; a display
7 .... spectator	**G** n., a person who watches an event
8 .... exhibit	**H** n., repair or rebuilding
9 .... exotic	**I** adj., liked by many people
10 .... renovation	**J** adj., unusual; from a foreign place
11 .... massive	**K** adj., very big

PARAGRAPH 3

Words	Definitions
12 .... remnant	**L** v., to make something smaller
13 .... permanently	**M** n., a small group
14 .... reduce	**N** n., a small leftover piece
15 .... band	**O** n., a person who teaches skills to people or animals
16 .... trainer	**P** adv., for always
17 .... develop	**Q** v., to continue; stay alive
18 .... talent	**R** n., a special ability
19 .... survive	**S** v., to grow and change
20 .... grandeur	**T** n., greatness

Unit 2

Reading

History of the Circus

(1) The circus is one of the oldest forms of **entertainment** in history. Although the modern circus has been around for a few **centuries**, related forms of public entertainment have been in existence for millennia. The animal trainers, clowns, and other circus performers who are familiar to us today can trace their roots to the coliseums, stadiums, and racetracks of the **ancient** world.

(2) The ancient Romans were the first to enjoy the circus. Around the sixth century B.C., the Circus Maximus was **founded** in Rome as a **venue** for public entertainment, mostly chariot races, which were a **popular spectator** sport. Other events held at the Circus Maximus included gladiator fights and **exhibits** of **exotic** animals such as elephants and tigers. These entertainments were less common than chariot races but still very popular. The original Circus Maximus venue was built entirely of wood. By the height of the Roman Empire, it had gone through several **renovations** and had become a **massive** marble stadium that could seat more than 200,000 spectators.

(3) Chariot races continued to be held at the Circus Maximus for almost a century after the last **remnants** of the Roman Empire had vanished. Eventually, the site was **permanently** retired, and public entertainment was **reduced** to small **bands** of traveling[1] performers and animal **trainers**. It was during the Dark Ages that the circus began to **develop** into what we know today. The monarchs of Europe had court jesters, whose duty it was to provide amusement for the court. They combined the **talents** of jugglers, mimes, and clowns. The more common people enjoyed the performances of traveling entertainers, who went from village to village, putting on shows during festivals. These performers made up the medieval circus, which had little in common with the Circus Maximus other than adopting the word *circus* as its name. Leisure time was extremely rare during the Dark Ages, and people had few opportunities to enjoy circus performances. However, the circus **survived** to make a return to its former **grandeur** in the eighteenth century.

(4) England was one of the first nations to embrace the modern circus. During the late 1700s, an Englishman named Philip Astley founded the first modern circus. He was a skilled rider who invented stunt riding on horseback. He performed his stunts in a circus ring, another of his ideas, within an indoor stadium. After his act became popular in London, he was asked by Louis XV to perform in France.

[1]BrE: travelling

He later expanded his act to include clowns, acrobats, and parades of trained animals. The last addition to his act was slapstick humor. He had horseback riders pretend to fall off their horses and then go stumbling after them. Shortly after Astley's death, the circus spread to America.

(5) During the early 1800s, the United States took to the circus quickly after learning of its popularity in Europe. Joshua Brown, an American businessman, introduced the circus tent in 1825. The use of portable tents allowed him to take his act all over the country. His traveling circus was a massive success as a business enterprise and was loved by audiences everywhere. Most circuses today are variations of Brown's circus.

Answer the questions about **History of the Circus**.

Questions 1–4

Do the following describe the ancient circus, the modern circus, or both?

Write the correct letter, ***A***, ***B***, *or* ***C***.

A Ancient circus
B Modern circus
C Both the ancient circus and the modern circus

.... **1** had animal exhibits

.... **2** entertained spectators with races

.... **3** entertainments included falling off horses

.... **4** took place in a massive venue

Questions 5–7

Choose the correct letter, ***A***, ***B***, ***C***, *or* ***D***.

5 The Circus Maximus
A was not a popular place to visit.
B developed during the Dark Ages.
C went through a number of renovations.
D took place in a portable tent.

6 The court jesters of the Dark Ages usually
- **A** were skilled animal trainers.
- **B** had several different talents.
- **C** performed at village festivals.
- **D** entertained the common people.

7 In the eighteenth century, the modern circus was founded by
- **A** a horse rider from England.
- **B** a Roman businessman.
- **C** some performers in France.
- **D** a band of American entertainers.

Word Families

A

Complete each sentence with the correct word from the word family chart. Make nouns plural where necessary. Use the correct form of verbs.

noun	noun	verb
development	developer	develop

1 The circus .... in new ways after it arrived in the United States.

2 Philip Astley is known as the .... of stunt riding.

3 Joshua Brown's introduction of the circus tent was an important contribution to the .... of the circus.

noun	noun	verb	adjective
entertainment	entertainer	entertain	entertaining

4 People often hire clowns to .... children at parties.

5 We spent a very .... afternoon at the circus.

6 The job of a circus .... looks like fun, but it is really very difficult.

7 The circus is still a favorite form of .... today.

noun	adjective	adverb
permanence	permanent	permanently

8 Unlike the traveling bands of performers, court jesters had .... jobs.

9 The .... of the circus as a form of entertainment shows how much people enjoy it.

10 Circuses don't stay in one place .... but travel around from city to city.

noun	verb	adjective	adverb
popularity	popularize	popular	popularly

11 The circus is .... in many parts of the world.

12 The modern circus is .... known as the Big Top.

13 Joshua Brown helped to .... the circus in America.

14 The circus still enjoys great ....

noun	noun	verb
survival	survivor	survive

15 The .... of the circus is due to its ability to change with the times.

16 The circus has .... in many forms throughout the centuries

17 The circus as a form of entertainment is a .... of the hard times of the Dark Ages.

noun	verb	adjective
trainer	train	trained

18 Many circuses use .... elephants in their shows.

19 Some animals are easier to .... than others.

20 A circus animal .... has to be able to work with exotic animals.

Word Families

B

Choose the correct word family member from the list below to complete each blank.

1 development	developer	developed
2 entertainment	entertainer	entertained
3 trainers	trains	trained
4 popularity	popularize	popular
5 survival	survivors	survived
6 permanence	permanent	permanently

The **1**.......... of the modern circus began in England in the eighteenth century. A skilled horseback rider[1] **2**.......... audiences with stunt riding. He later added other kinds of performances to the show, such as clowns and **3**.......... animals. The show became very **4**.........., and the idea spread to other countries. The circus has **5**.......... the test of time and is still enjoyed by people today. It holds a **6**.......... place in our hearts.

---

[1]BrE: horse rider

Paraphrases

Read the sentence from the reading passage. Then, choose the sentence that has the same meaning.

1 *Around the sixth century B.C., the Circus Maximus was founded in Rome as a venue for public entertainment, mostly chariot races, which were a popular spectator sport.* (paragraph 2)

A The Circus Maximus was founded in Rome because that's where the best chariot races were held.

B Originally, the Circus Maximus was a place where people enjoyed watching chariot races.

C Many people raced their chariots at the original Circus Maximus.

2 *However, the circus survived to make a return to its former grandeur in the eighteenth century.* (paragraph 3)

A The circus stayed alive to become great again in the 1700s.

B People started returning to the circus in great numbers in the 1700s.

C In the 1700s, small circuses started becoming bigger.

Dictionary Skill

DIFFERENT MEANINGS

Many words have more than one meaning.

Read the definitions below. Then, read the sentences and write the letter of the correct definition for each sentence.

QUESTIONS 1–2

found [FOWND]

A *verb.* to start or establish an institution

B *verb.* past tense and past participle of the verb *find*

.... **1** After we *found* our seats, we sat down and enjoyed the circus performance.

.... **2** It takes a lot of money, effort, and daring to *found* an entertainment business.

QUESTIONS 3–4

band [BAND]
A *noun.* a small group
B *noun.* a strip of cloth

.... **3** A band of actors walked through the park entertaining visitors with short performances.

.... **4** The performers wore brightly colored bands around their waists.

Listening

Track 5

Listen to the talk. Choose the correct answer, ***A****,* ***B****, or* ***C****.*

1 When was the Springfield Circus founded?
A 25 years ago
B 75 years ago
C 100 years ago

2 What has not changed since the circus was founded?
A The venue
B The ticket price
C The number of performers

3 What kinds of animals begin the show?
A Exotic
B Trained
C Massive

4 What is the most popular part of the show?
A Animals
B Clowns
C Dancers

Writing (Task 2)

In your opinion, why is the circus still a popular form of entertainment in the modern electronic age?

Support your opinion with reasons and examples from your own knowledge or experience.

Write at least 250 words.

Speaking

Talk about the following topics.

What forms of entertainment are popular in your city?

Do you prefer to watch TV and movies or to see live entertainment?

Are you talented in any performing arts? What talents do you have that you would like to develop more?

USES OF LEISURE TIME

Words

Write the letter of each definition with the word it defines. If you don't know the definition, use the context of the reading passage to help you. Look for the words in bold as you read the passage.

PARAGRAPHS 1–2

Words	Definitions
1 .... obesity	**A** adj., very important
2 .... physical	**B** adj., related to thinking
3 .... crucial	**C** n., the condition of being very overweight
4 .... intellectual	**D** adj., related to the body

PARAGRAPH 2

Words	Definitions
5 .... overwhelming	**E** n., a feeling such as anger or love
6 .... suffer	**F** adv., only
7 .... merely	**G** adj., overpowering; very large
8 .... emotion	**H** v., to experience something difficult or painful

PARAGRAPH 3

Words	Definitions
9 .... rejuvenate	**I** adv., intentionally; on purpose
10 .... deliberately	**J** adj., not active
11 .... passive	**K** n., a free time activity
12 .... pastime	**L** v., to refresh; restore

PARAGRAPH 4

Words	Definitions
13 .... reluctant **14** .... depression **15** .... authority **16** .... acknowledge	**M** v., to admit, accept as true **N** n., person with power or special knowledge **O** n., constant sadness **P** adj., not wanting to do something; unwilling

PARAGRAPH 5

Words	Definitions
17 .... obvious **18** .... chunk **19** .... industrious **20** .... engage	**Q** n., a large piece **R** v., to participate in something **S** adj., hardworking **T** adj., easy to see, clear

Reading

Uses of Leisure Time

A

Although it may seem that people are working more, studies show that we have more leisure time than ever before. Yet researchers are reporting higher levels of both stress and **obesity**. These reports appear to be a sign that we are not using our leisure time to our best advantage.

B

Health experts agree that the best way to restore body and mind is to spend time in nature pursuing a comfortable level of **physical** exercise. Spending time in natural surroundings is especially **crucial** now because, for the first time, a majority of the world's population live in cities. Recent studies show that **intellectual** function weakens as a result of the energy expended simply sorting out the **overwhelming** stimuli of city life. Tests demonstrate that people **suffer** decreases in attention span, memory, and problem-solving ability after taking a short walk on a busy city street or **merely** seeing pictures of city life. Tests also show that time spent in the city results in a decreased ability to concentrate and to control **emotions** and impulses. On the other hand, spending time in the country produces the opposite effects.

C

Unfortunately, as society becomes more centered[1] on city life, we have to **rejuvenate** ourselves in nature **deliberately** rather than as a matter of course. Yet research shows that we are not spending our leisure time rejuvenating ourselves. Around the world, the most popular way to spend free time is watching television. This, the most **passive** of **pastimes**, is how Americans spend more than half their leisure time. Globally, the next most popular is using the Internet, also passive, and it ranks as the most favored[2] among the billions in China. The third is shopping, which may be slightly more active but is still as far from nature as possible. Modern shopping malls remove shoppers from everything natural, leaving them to experience the outdoors only between the paved parking lot[3] and the mall doors.

D

Children are most negatively affected by city life. Parents are **reluctant** to let children play freely in the city, fearing for their health and safety, and nature is something many children in the city may never have a chance to experience. Childhood obesity and **depression** are reaching epidemic levels. **Authorities** have begun to **acknowledge** the problem, and innovative programs[4] that give children an opportunity to spend time in nature are being introduced in countries around the world.

E

Vacations[5] are the most **obvious chunk** of leisure time. The countries with the most vacation time are Italy, with an average of forty-two days a year, and France, with thirty-seven. The **industrious** Americans have the least: thirteen days. Yet the country most satisfied with their vacations are not the Italians but the British. The British usually divide up their vacation time, taking it in pieces throughout the year rather than all at once. Of all nationalities, the British spend the most time vacationing outdoors in their national-trust parks, where they **engage** in a comfortable level of physical activity. The British report the greatest satisfaction with their leisure time. Perhaps the rest of the world would do well to follow their lead.

---

[1]BrE: centred
[2]BrE: favoured
[3]BrE: car park
[4]BrE: programmes
[5]BrE: holidays

Answer the questions about **Uses of Leisure Time**.

Questions 1–3

The reading passage contains five paragraphs, ***A–E****. Which paragraphs discuss the following information?*

Write the correct letter, ***A–E****.*

.... **1** The most popular pastimes in different countries around the world

.... **2** Why it is crucial to spend time in nature

.... **3** In which country people spend the largest chunk of vacation time engaged in outdoor activities

Questions 4–6

Choose the correct letter, ***A****,* ***B****,* ***C****, or* ***D****.*

4 We can best rejuvenate ourselves by spending time engaged in
A physical activities.
B passive activities.
C activities with children.
D activities in the city.

5 When children do not spend time in nature, they
A fear for their health and safety.
B suffer from obesity and depression.
C are reluctant to spend time with their parents.
D have more time to develop their intellectual functioning.

6 The overwhelming character of city life affects our
A interest in nature.
B choice of pastimes.
C relationships with children.
D emotions and intellectual function.

Word Families

A

Complete each sentence with the correct word from the word family chart. Make nouns plural where necessary. Use the correct form of verbs.

noun	verb	adjective	adverb
authority	authorize[1]	authoritative	authoritatively

1 The expert wrote .... about exercise and its effects on mental health.

2 The school director has .... the teachers to spend a larger chunk of the school day outdoors with their students.

3 According to an .... source, spending time in nature improves our health.

4 The .... have decided to keep the park open in the evenings so families can spend more time in nature.

noun	verb	adjective	adverb
deliberation	deliberate	deliberate	deliberately

5 The group .... for an hour before they were able to reach a decision.

6 She .... chose the longer route for her walk home in order to have more time outdoors.

7 After ...., he decided to spend some time everyday engaged in outdoor activities.

8 It is obvious that people need to make a .... decision to spend more time in nature.

noun	adjective	adverb
emotion	emotional	emotionally

9 The stress of city life can make .... difficult to control.

[1] BrE: authorise

10 People respond .... to the overwhelming stimuli of the city.

11 Children who don't spend a lot of time playing outdoors can end up with .... problems.

noun	adjective	adverb
industry	industrious	industriously

12 He is always .... even when engaged in leisure time activities.

13 He worked on his project ....

14 His favorite pastime is building model ships and he always goes about this activity with great ....

noun	noun	adjective	adverb
intellect	intellectual	intellectual	intellectually

15 I enjoy reading the works of the great .... of the nineteenth century.

16 Some people look for experiences that engage them ....

17 Some people enjoy spending their leisure time engaged in .... activities.

18 The stress of city life has effects on the ....

noun	adjective	adverb
reluctance	reluctant	reluctantly

19 She .... agreed to spend fewer hours watching TV on the weekend.

20 People can be .... to leave their familiar surroundings to explore unknown places.

21 .... to spend time in nature is a problem for modern children.

Unit 2

Word Families

B

Choose the correct word family member from the list below to complete each blank.

1 emotions	emotional	emotionally
2 industry	industrious	industriously
3 intellect	intellectual	intellectually
4 deliberation	deliberate	deliberately
5 reluctance	reluctant	reluctantly
6 authorities	authorizes	authoritative

It is crucial to acknowledge the importance of leisure-time activities. They are not merely a way to use up free time. They are important for our physical and **1**.......... health. We need to choose activities that rest our minds and bodies so that we can feel rejuvenated when we return to work and can do our jobs more **2**.......... . Some people enjoy **3**.......... pastimes; other people choose different sorts of leisure-time activities. The key is to be **4**.......... about choosing a pastime that is active rather than passive. Many people feel **5**.......... to be physically active after a tiring week at work. However, **6**.......... tell us that this is actually the best way to decrease stress and relax.

Paraphrases

Read the sentence from the reading passage. Then, choose the sentence that has the same meaning.

1 *Spending time in natural surroundings is especially crucial now because, for the first time, a majority of the world's population live in cities.* (paragraph 2)

A Since most of us live in cities now, it is important for us to make time to be in nature.

B Many people live in cities because they are not interested in spending time in nature.
C Spending time in nature is becoming more popular around the world these days.

2 *This, the most passive of pastimes, is how Americans spend more than half their leisure time.* (paragraph 3)
A Americans don't make their own choices about free-time activities.
B Americans prefer to spend half of their free time doing things at home.
C Americans spend most of their free time inactively.

Dictionary Skill

DIFFERENT MEANINGS

Many words have more than one meaning.

Read the definitions below. Then read the sentences and write the letter of the correct definition for each sentence.

QUESTIONS 1–2

en-gage [en-GAYJ]
A *verb.* to participate
B *verb.* to hire

.... **1** The school *engaged* a special teacher to teach classes about nature.

.... **2** Every afternoon, the children *engage* in outdoor activities.

QUESTIONS 3–4

in-dus-try [IN-dus-tree]
A *noun.* hard work
B *noun.* production and sale of goods

.... **3** Many people in this city work in the clothing *industry*.

.... **4** *Industry* will help you move up in your profession, but don't forget to spend some time in leisure activities as well.

Listening

Track 6

Listen to the talk. Complete the notes below.
Write ***NO MORE THAN ONE WORD*** *for each answer.*

Research on Leisure

People engaged in **1**.......... pastimes don't feel rejuvenated.

Popular Pastimes:
2.......... Activities
- Sports
- Playing with children
- Gardening

3.......... Activities
- Reading
- Playing computer games
- Doing puzzles
- Using the Internet

Activities that exercise both our minds and bodies help us avoid **4**.......... and **5**.......... .

Writing (Task 1)

The bar graph below shows basic information about uses of leisure time among different age groups.

Summarize[1] the information by selecting and reporting the main information and making comparisons.

Write at least 150 words.

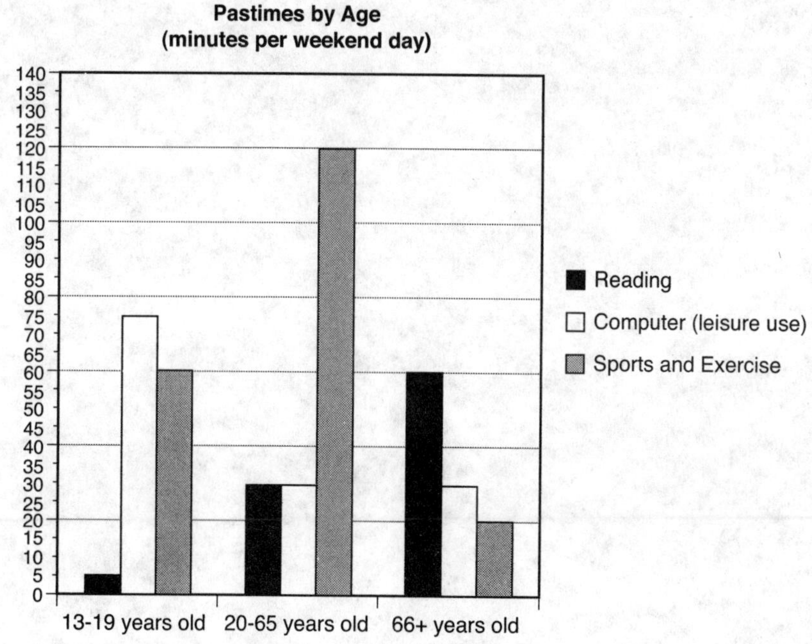

[1]BrE: summarise

Speaking

Talk about the following topics.

What are some of your favorite[1] pastimes? Why do you enjoy them?

Do you prefer physical or intellectual activities for relaxation?

[1]BrE: favourite

Unit 3: Transportation

FIRST HEADLAMPS

Words

Write the letter of each definition with the word it defines. If you don't know the definition, use the context of the reading passage to help you. Look for the words in bold as you read the passage.

PARAGRAPH 1

Words	Definitions
1 .... tricky	**A** v., to throw light on something
2 .... cast	**B** n., a terrible event
3 .... vulnerable	**C** adj., easy to carry
4 .... disaster	**D** adj., difficult
5 .... portable	**E** adj., weak; without defense[1]

PARAGRAPH 2

Words	Definitions
6 .... freight	**F** n., cargo carried by a train, truck, or ship
7 .... innovation	**G** n., an object that produces light
8 .... illuminator	**H** n., a new idea or product
9 .... knot	**I** n., the engine of a train
10 .... locomotive	**J** n., a hard bump in wood

[1]BrE: defence

Unit 3

PARAGRAPH 3

Words	Definitions
11 .... reflector	**K** v., to show or exhibit
12 .... generate	**L** adj., very strong
13 .... display	**M** v., to make or produce
14 .... intense	**N** n., an object that sends light back or makes it stronger

PARAGRAPHS 4–5

Words	Definitions
15 .... drawback	**O** n., a problem; disadvantage
16 .... equip	**P** adj., able to work without waste
17 .... efficient	**Q** v., to provide with something
18 .... mode	**R** adj., strong; able to stand rough treatment
19 .... stringent	**S** n., method
20 .... rugged	**T** adj., strict; firm

Reading

First Headlamps

A

Before electricity, people relied on fire as a source of light. It was a **tricky** business. Flames **cast** limited light, are **vulnerable** to winds and weather, and can lead to **disaster**. Making fire **portable** and dependable was so difficult that lights on moving vehicles were hardly ever considered.

B

The early trains traveled[1] only during the day. The tracks were too dangerous during the dark of night, and passengers wanted to see where they were traveling anyway. In the late 1830s, railroad traffic became heavy enough for **freight** trains to delay passenger trains. To avoid these delays, railroads started running freight trains at night. Horatio Allen's 1831 **innovation**, the "Track **Illuminator**," was suddenly in demand. It was a pile of pine **knots** burning in an iron grate that sat in a box of sand on a platform car. The car was pushed ahead of the **locomotive**. The illuminator did not cast much light, but it warned of the approaching train and was the best technology available.

---

[1]BrE: travelled

C

In 1841, some trains used an oil[2] lamp backed by a curved **reflector**, an improvement, but oil lamps blew out easily in the wind, including the wind **generated** by the movement of the train. At about the same time, Schenectady and Troy Railroad trains **displayed** a whale oil lamp positioned between a reflector and a lens about twelve inches high; it threw light up to 100 feet ahead of the train. Although this was an improvement, the braking distance the trains required was more than the 100 feet of track that were illuminated. In 1849, a calcium lamp was developed that threw light 1,000 feet and lasted four hours; however, the only railroad company to use it was Camden and Amboy. Limelights, which were used to light theater[3] stages on both sides of the Atlantic, were considered too **intense** for trains. Eventually, acetylene, which did not extinguish in the wind, replaced oil in headlamps.

D

In 1851, the first electric headlamp was developed. This headlamp had two major **drawbacks**: It required its own generator, which did not become portable until the 1890s when steam generators became common, and the delicate parts broke easily as a result of the rough rails over which the trains traveled. Russia ran the first train **equipped** with a battery-powered electric headlamp. The French first used steam generators to power electric headlamps on trains. In the United States in 1897, George C. Pyle developed an **efficient** electric headlamp. By 1916, federal law required trains to have electric headlamps.

E

Automobiles, the exciting new **mode** of transportation[4] at that time, needed headlamps, too. The requirements for car headlamps were more **stringent** than those for trains: Because roads were even rougher than rails, cars required more **rugged** parts, and the steam generators had to be smaller than those in trains. Despite these tougher requirements, the Columbia Electric Car was equipped with electric headlamps in 1898.

F

Electric headlamps made travel at all hours and in almost all weather possible, something we take for granted today.

---

[2]BrE: kerosene
[3]BrE: theatre
[4]BrE: transport

Answer the questions about **First Headlamps**.

Questions 1–8

The reading passage contains six paragraphs, ***A–F****. Which paragraphs discuss the following information?*

Write the correct letter, ***A–F****. Some letters may be used more than once.*

.... **1** a lamp that used burning wood

.... **2** lamps rugged enough to use with cars

.... **3** a lamp that generated its own electricity

.... **4** the drawbacks of using flames for light

.... **5** lamps that used reflectors to cast more intense light

.... **6** the year the first train was equipped with electric headlamps

.... **7** a reason why acetylene lamps are more efficient than oil lamps

.... **8** a reason why freight trains traveled at night

Word Families

A

Complete each sentence with the correct word from the word family chart. Make nouns plural where necessary. Use the correct form of verbs.

noun	adjective	adverb
efficiency	efficient	efficiently

1 .... is an important quality for any new product.

2 Candles do not light a room ....

3 .... headlamps made safe travel at night possible.

noun	noun	verb
generator	generation	generate

4 There are a variety of ways to .... electricity.

5 The .... of electricity can cause air pollution.

6 If the power lines are down, you can use a gasoline .... in order to have electricity in your house.

noun	noun	verb
illuminator	illumination	illuminate

7 The .... of an electric lamp is stronger than that of a candle.

8 In the past, people used candles to .... their houses.

9 An .... can provide an area with light.

noun	noun	adjective
innovation	innovator	innovative

10 The electric headlamp was an important .... for the safety of car and train travel.

11 The development of electric headlamps was the work of a number of .... people.

12 Several .... worked on the development of electric headlamps.

noun	verb	adjective	adverb
intensity	intensify	intense	intensely

13 Using a stronger battery will .... light.

14 Some materials burn more .... than others.

15 A locomotive needs a headlamp with high ....

16 The light from candles is not very ....

noun	noun	verb	adjective
reflector	reflection	reflect	reflective

17 A piece of metal can be used to .... light.

18 You can see your .... in a mirror.

19 A .... on a lamp makes the light more intense.

20 If a lamp is coated with .... material, it will cast a stronger light.

Word Families

B

Choose the correct word family member from the list below to complete each blank.

1	efficiency	efficient	efficiently
2	innovators	innovations	innovative
3	illumination	illuminator	illuminated
4	reflector	reflect	reflective
5	intensity	intensify	intensely
6	generation	generators	generate

Traveling at night was tricky before people had developed headlamps that worked **1**.......... . Early **2**.......... for use on locomotives included lamps that **3**.......... by burning pine knots or whale oil. Some of these lamps used metal as a **4**.......... material to **5**.......... the light. Later, electric headlamps were developed. The problem with these lamps involved finding a portable way to **6**.......... the electricity that they used.

Paraphrases

Read the sentence from the reading passage. Then, choose the sentence that has the same meaning.

1 *Flames cast limited light, are vulnerable to winds and weather, and can lead to disaster.* (paragraph 1)
A Fire is not a good source of light during bad weather.
B The lack of light from fire can lead to disaster.
C Firelight is dim, dangerous, and not reliable.

2 *Limelights, which were used to light theater stages on both sides of the Atlantic, were considered too intense for trains.* (paragraph 3)
A Both Europeans and Americans thought limelights were too small for trains.
B The stage lights used in both America and Europe were too strong for trains.
C Theater stages in many countries depended on the strong light of limelights.

Dictionary Skill

DIFFERENT MEANINGS

Many words have more than one meaning.

Read the definitions below. Then read the sentences and write the letter of the correct definition for each sentence.

QUESTIONS 1–2

dis-play [dis-PLAY]
A *noun.* a showing, an exhibit
B *verb.* to show or exhibit

.... **1** The new, more efficient headlamps for use on trains were on *display*.

.... **2** Everyone was excited to see cars that *displayed* the new electric headlamps.

QUESTIONS 3–4

knot [NOT]
A *noun.* a hard bump in wood
B *verb.* tie something in a certain way

.... **3** Burning pine *knots* is a way to create light.

.... **4** If you *knot* your shoelaces well, they won't untie.

Listening

Track 7

*Listen to the lecture. Choose **FOUR** letters, **A–G**.*

Which **FOUR** drawbacks of early train travel does the lecturer mention?

A difficulty traveling at night

B frequent delays

C safety problems

D dirt

E cost of tickets

F uncomfortable rides

G crowded passenger cars

Writing (Task 2)

In your opinion, what has been the most significant transportation innovation of the past 200 years?

Support your opinion with reasons and examples from your own knowledge or experience.

Write at least 250 words.

Speaking

Talk about the following topics.

What modes of transportation are commonly used in your city? Which do you think are the most efficient?

What do you think are some of the advantages of train travel?

What do you think are some drawbacks of train travel?

MAJOR SUBWAYS OF EUROPE

Words

Write the letter of each definition with the word it defines. If you don't know the definition, use the context of the reading passage to help you. Look for the words in bold as you read the passage.

PARAGRAPHS 1–2

Words	Definitions
1 .... intrinsic	**A** n., the main or most important feature
2 .... underground	**B** v., to fill so much as to make movement difficult
3 .... centerpiece[1]	**C** adj., basic
4 .... pedestrian	**D** n., a person traveling[2] on foot
5 .... clog	**E** adj., below the ground

PARAGRAPH 2

Words	Definitions
6 .... disruptive	**F** adj., stopping the usual course of activity
7 .... release	**G** n., the working of something; being used
8 .... vent	**H** v., to let something out
9 .... operation	**I** n., an opening to let air, steam, or smoke out

PARAGRAPH 3

Words	Definitions
10 .... destruction	**J** n., the act of ruining something
11 .... expand	**K** n., something that serves as protection
12 .... shield	**L** v., to make bigger
13 .... surface	**M** n., the outer part or top of something

[1]BrE: centrepiece
[2]BrE: travelling

PARAGRAPHS 4–6

Words	Definitions
14 .... rival	**N** n., the style of a building
15 .... architecture	**O** v., to make an object or place beautiful
16 .... decorate	**P** n., central office for a military commander
17 .... showcase	**Q** v., to compete with
18 .... utilize[1]	**R** n., a setting in which to present something
19 .... headquarters	**S** v., to use
20 .... spring up	**T** v., to appear

Reading

Major Subways of Europe

(1) Public transportation[2] is an **intrinsic** part of every modern city. Many big cities have an **underground** rail system as their **centerpiece**. Three of the biggest and busiest underground rail systems in Europe are in London, Paris, and Moscow. The character of each city imprints its railways.

(2) The first of these subways was London's Underground, which opened in 1863. By that time, horses and **pedestrians** had so **clogged** the streets of London that city government ruled that no railroads could enter the city except underground. The method used for laying the first underground tracks is called "cut and cover," meaning the streets were dug up, the track was laid, a tunnel was built, and then everything was buried. Although the method was **disruptive**, it worked. Steam engines chugged under London, **releasing** steam through **vents** along the city streets. In its initial day of **operation**, the London Underground carried 30,000 passengers.

(3) This cut-and-cover method caused massive disruptions in the city and required the **destruction** of the structures above the tunnel. A better means of **expanding** the original Underground was needed, and builders did not have to look far to find it. In 1825, a pedestrian tunnel was built under the Thames River. The construction of this tunnel—the first underwater tunnel ever built—was made possible by engineer Marc Brunel. He had devised a way of supporting the tunnel while the workers dug, called the Brunel **Shield**. Two young

[1]BrE: utilise
[2]BrE: transport

engineers improved the Brunel Shield for use in expanding the London Underground. The new Harlow-Greathead Shield carved a circular tube more than seven feet in diameter, which is why the London Underground is called the Tube. By then, the tunnels could be deeper than the original ones because electric train engines had become available. These trains did not have to be close to the **surface** to release steam. The shield could be used to dig deeper tunnels without destroying the surface structures above them.

(4) Paris started designing an underground rail service to **rival** London's. The first part of its system was not opened until the World's Fair and Olympics were held in that city in 1900. The Paris Metro is shorter than London's, but it carries more passengers every day, second in Europe only to Moscow. Whereas London's Underground is known for its engineering, Paris's Metro is known for its beauty. The stations and entrances are examples of art nouveau **architecture**, and they are **decorated** with mosaics, sculptures, paintings, and innovative doors and walls.

(5) The Moscow Metro opened in 1935. It was based on the design of the London Tube, except much of the track is above ground. When Stalin came to power, he used the stations as **showcases** of Russian art, culture, and engineering. The underground Moscow stations are filled with statuary, painting, and mosaics.

(6) Underground railways are not only for transportation. During World War II, all three underground systems were **utilized** as bomb shelters for the populace. The Moscow subway was even used as a military **headquarters**. Stores and malls have **sprung up** by stations, something that is especially convenient in cold climates.

(7) All three systems are continuing to expand, providing service to more riders in more distant locales. This is all part of an effort to decrease greenhouse gases emitted from personal vehicles.

Answer the questions about **Major Subways of Europe**.

Questions 1–4

Do the following describe the subway system in London, Paris, or Moscow?

Write the correct letter, ***A***, ***B***, *or* ***C***.

A London
B Paris
C Moscow

.... **1** It was used as a military headquarters during World War II.

.... **2** It has a large percentage of its track above the ground.

.... **3** It was originally built for the operation of steam trains.

.... **4** It is famous for its beautiful architecture.

Questions 5–7

*Choose the correct letter, **A**, **B**, **C**, or **D**.*

5 The Paris Metro stations are decorated with
A pictures of the Olympics.
B different kinds of artwork.
C photographs of the World's Fair.
D examples of engineering.

6 The London Underground was first built because
A the underwater pedestrian tunnel had been damaged.
B a new method for digging tunnels had been developed.
C the city streets were too clogged for trains on the surface.
D the city wanted to rival the transportation system in Paris.

7 The introduction of electric train engines allowed for
A deeper tunnels.
B more pedestrians.
C innovative doors and walls.
D more art showcases in the stations.

Word Families

A

Complete each sentence with the correct word from the word family chart. Make nouns plural where necessary. Use the correct form of verbs.

noun	noun	adjective	adverb
architect	architecture	architectural	architecturally

1 Its art nouveau decorative features make Paris .... significant.

2 The .... of the stations is an important part of subway system design.

3 The .... is working on a plan for a new train station.

4 From an .... point of view, it's a very interesting building.

noun	noun	verb	adjective
decoration	decorator	decorate	decorative

5 People enjoy looking at the .... in the station while they wait for the train to arrive.

6 That column is there for .... purposes only; it has no real use.

7 The .... planned the art for the station very carefully.

8 Sometimes they .... the trains for the holidays.

noun	verb	adjective
destruction	destroy	destructive

9 It was necessary to .... some buildings in order to dig the subway tunnels.

10 The .... of buildings was part of the process of creating the subway system.

11 Digging deeper tunnels makes subway construction less .... to buildings and roads on the surface.

noun	verb	adjective
disruption	disrupt	disruptive

12 The process of building a subway can be ...., but the end result is well worth it.

13 Building a subway system can cause a lot of .... to traffic on the streets.

14 They try to .... traffic as little as possible during subway construction.

noun	verb	adjective
expansion	expand	expandable

15 The .... of the subway system cost a great deal of money.

16 By the time they were ready to .... the subway system, a new method for digging tunnels had been developed.

17 The subway system was designed to be ....

noun	noun	verb
operation	operator	operate

18 Modern subway systems use computers to .... the trains.

19 The .... of the Paris Metro began in 1900.

20 A subway train .... needs special training for the job.

Word Families

B

Choose the correct word family member from the list below to complete each blank.

1 Architecture	Architects	Architectural
2 decorates	decorations	decorative
3 destruction	destroy	destructive
4 disruption	disrupts	disruptive
5 expansion	expand	expandable
6 operation	operator	operate

The planning and construction of a subway system requires a great deal of time and effort. In addition to planning the routes, digging the tunnels, and laying the tracks, the stations have to be built. **1**.......... are hired to plan the stations. Often, the station plan includes **2**.......... features such as murals showing local scenes, or a station may be used as a showcase for the work of important local artists. Building a new subway system may require the **3**.......... of buildings on the surface, but attempts are made to cause as little **4**.......... as possible. The **5**.......... of an already-existing subway system can also be quite disruptive. Everyone looks forward to the day when the construction is over and the subway begins to **6**.......... . Often businesses spring up in and around a new subway station, contributing to the life of the neighborhood.

Paraphrases

Read the sentence from the reading passage. Then, choose the sentence that has the same meaning.

1 *By that time, horses and pedestrians had so clogged the streets of London that the city government ruled that no railroads could enter the city except underground.* (paragraph 2)

A By then, London's streets were so dirty that no one wanted to use them.

B By then, London's streets were filled with traffic, so the government banned aboveground trains from the city.

C By then, the lack of traffic rules made it difficult to control the people, horses, and trains using London's streets.

2 *The stations and entrances are examples of Art Nouveau architecture, and they are decorated with mosaics, sculptures, paintings, and innovative doors and walls.* (paragraph 4)

A The stations represent a certain building style and are beautified with art.

B Many artists have used the beauty of the stations as inspiration for their artwork.

C The stations were designed to have space for art exhibits.

Word Skill

COMPOUND WORDS

When two or more words join to form a new word, that word is called a compound word. Often, the meaning of the compound word is related to the meanings of the two separate words.

underground = under + ground Meaning: below the surface of the ground

Read the sentences. Write a definition for each underlined word.

1 They built an underwater tunnel for pedestrians below the Thames River.

underwater: ....

2 Before they could paint the mural in the station, they had to cover the wall with an undercoat of special paint.

undercoat: ....

3 Instead of a bridge, they built an underpass so that cars could cross the tracks from below.

underpass: ....

Listening

Track 8

Listen to the conversation. Complete the outline below. Write ***NO MORE THAN ONE WORD*** *for each answer.*

The London Underground: (1863)

Steam engines were used, so
- it had to be close to the **1**.......... .
- it had **2**.......... so engines could release steam.

Electric engines were introduced, so
- tunnels could be deeper.
- a **3**.......... was used to support the tunnel.
- digging the deeper tunnels did not **4**.......... streets and buildings.

Writing (Task 1)

The chart[1] below shows information about subway systems in three major European cities.

Summarize[2] the information by selecting and reporting the main information and making comparisons.

Write at least 150 words.

Size of Subway Systems

	Total track length (both underground and on the surface)	Number of stations in operation	Number of daily passengers
London Underground	408 km	275	3 million
Paris Metro	214 km	300	4.5 million
Moscow Metro	300 km	182	6.5 million

Speaking

Talk about the following topics.

Are there any subway or train stations or other buildings in your city that have especially beautiful architecture? Describe them.

Are there any public spaces in your city that are used to showcase the work of local or national artists? Do you think it is a good idea to use public spaces in this way? Why or why not?

[1]BrE: table
[2]BrE: summarise

ELECTRIC CARS AROUND THE GLOBE

Words

Write the letter of each definition with the word it defines. If you don't know the definition, use the context of the reading passage to help you. Look for the words in bold as you read the passage.

PARAGRAPH 1

Words	Definitions
1 .... span **2** .... urban **3** .... rural **4** .... suburban **5** .... sprawl	**A** adj., related to the countryside **B** n., an area of spreading growth **C** adj., related to the area just outside of a city **D** v., to cross **E** adj., related to the city

PARAGRAPHS 1–2

Words	Definitions
6 .... consume **7** .... fume **8** .... hamper **9** .... standard **10** .... plodding	**F** v., to use **G** v., to make things difficult; get in the way **H** adj., slow **I** n., harmful gas or smoke in the air **J** n., the normal or common thing

PARAGRAPHS 3–4

Words	Definitions
11 .... monetary **12** .... incentive **13** .... embrace **14** .... appeal **15** .... charge	**K** v., to be of interest **L** n., the amount of power a battery can store **M** v., to accept something enthusiastically **N** n., reason to do something; reward **O** adj., related to money

PARAGRAPHS 4–6

Words	Definitions
16 .... markedly	**P** v., to gain speed
17 .... accelerate	**Q** v., to divide into groups by type
18 .... commuter	**R** n., a person who travels regularly between home and work
19 .... classify	**S** n., elegant style
20 .... flair	**T** adv., noticeably

Reading

Electric Cars Around the Globe

(1) Cars have reshaped our world since they first rolled off mass-production lines in the early twentieth century. One- and two-thousand-year-old Roman roads have been replaced by highways. Longer and wider bridges **span** rivers. The sharp division between **urban** and **rural** landscapes has been replaced by **suburban sprawl**, town and country linked by eight-lane expressways with stop-and-go traffic. Gas[1] stations are everywhere. After a century, our love of gas-powered automobiles is diminishing. As the price of oil rises, the reserves of irreplaceable oil are **consumed**, and exhaust **fumes** **hamper** life in urban areas, alternatives to gas-powered vehicles are becoming more attractive.

(2) In the early twentieth century in North America, electric cars shared the roads with gas-fueled cars, but after a short time, gas-fueled cars became the **standard**. Although electric cars were quieter, cleaner, and easier to start, they were not able to travel the required distances, and their **plodding** speed failed to capture the imagination.

(3) Lately, in Europe and in Asia, where commuting distances are shorter and gas is more expensive than in the United States, electric cars have grown in popularity. Electric recharging stations are appearing in cities. The government of China has offered **monetary incentives** to car manufacturers for each electric car they manufacture as well as to the people who purchase the electric cars. Taxi drivers in Tokyo have **embraced** electric vehicles. Major car manufacturers, including Mitsubishi, Nissan, Toyota, and Mercedes Benz, all offer electric cars everywhere but in North America.

[1]BrE: Petrol

Unit 3

(4) In North America, slow, short-ranged electric vehicles with a high initial cost have thus far **appealed** to a limited audience. An American electric car that appeared briefly in the 1990s had a cruising speed of twenty-five miles per hour and could travel eighty-five miles on a single **charge**. Since then, battery technology has improved **markedly**. More recently, a North American company introduced an electric sports car that can travel 300 miles on a single charge and **accelerate** from 0 to 60 mph in 3.7 seconds, similar to the best sports car. The hope is that North Americans will embrace the new technology when they see an electric car as appealing as a conventional sports car.

(5) Other American auto manufacturers are marketing electric cars as they do in Europe, as **commuter** cars. The design of many of these cars is innovative: Some are made of light composites and seat only two people. One is a three-wheeler that is **classified** as a motorcycle. Another electric car, the Tango, is five inches narrower than a large motorcycle and seats two, one behind the other. Four of these vehicles fit in a single parking space. The vehicle is marketed as a great way to drive between lanes of stopped traffic.

(6) All electric cars will help to reduce exhaust and greenhouse gases; some will do it with greater **flair** than others.

Answer the questions about **Electric Cars Around the Globe**.

Questions 1–7

Complete the summary using words from the list below.

accelerated	embraced	incentives	suburban
commuters	fumes	plodding	urban
consumed	hampered	standard	

Cars have had enormous effects on the way our world looks. The landscape is now covered with highways and big bridges. New **1**.......... neighborhoods have developed between the cities and the rural areas. Cars are also causing serious problems. Oil is expensive, and we have already **2**.......... a lot of oil that cannot be replaced. Gas-powered cars also pollute the air with their **3**........... . In the early days, both electric and gas-powered cars were common, but people felt that electric cars did not have the flair that gas-powered cars had. For example, electric cars traveled at a more **4**.......... speed. Gas-powered cars became more popular, and now they are the **5**.......... . However, there is a renewed interest in electric cars, and they have been **6**.......... by people in many countries around the world. Manufacturers are developing electric cars to sell to **7**.......... in both Europe and North America, because these cars are a good way to get to work.

Word Families

A

Complete each sentence with the correct word from the word family chart. Make nouns plural where necessary. Use the correct form of verbs.

noun	verb	adjective
appeal	appeal	appealing

1 A car that uses less gasoline would .... to commuters.

2 Electric cars are .... to many people.

3 The .... of an electric car is that it doesn't cause pollution.

noun	noun	verb
class	classification	classify

4 The new .... of electric cars is very different from the electric cars of the early twentieth century.

5 If you .... your car as a commercial vehicle, you will need to get a special license[1].

6 The .... of a car as a sports car can make it more appealing to certain people.

[1]BrE: licence

noun	noun	verb
commuter	commute	commute

7 .... are worried about the increase of traffic on the highways.

8 I have a thirty-minute .... to work every day.

9 Many people .... from the suburbs to their jobs in the city.

noun	noun	verb
consumer	consumption	consume

10 Electric cars are attractive because they don't .... gasoline.

11 As the price of oil increases, ... may go down.

12 .... of gasoline are paying higher prices everyday.

noun	verb	adjective	adverb
mark	mark	marked	markedly

13 The popularity of electric cars has grown .... over the past few years.

14 In the past, before cars became common, the difference between urban and rural areas was more ....

15 The twenty-first century .... a new interest in electric cars.

16 The new hybrid vehicles have made their .... with consumers.

noun	adjective	adverb
money	monetary	monetarily

17 More people will be interested in buying electric cars for .... reasons as gasoline becomes more expensive.

18 While owning an electric car has certain advantages, it is not necessarily the best choice for the average person, ... speaking.

19 Many people own cars even though they cost a great deal of ....

Word Families

B

Choose the correct word family member from the list below to complete each blank.

1 class	classification	classify
2 commuters	commutes	commute
3 consumer	consume	consumption
4 appeal	appeals	appealing
5 monetarily	monetary	money
6 marked	markedly	mark

Car manufacturers are developing a **1**.......... of electric car especially for **2**.......... . These cars are quite small and may have room for only one or two people. They are not intended for carrying large loads or many passengers. Their main purpose is to get the driver to and from work. Because of their small size, they **3**.......... little energy. They are **4**.......... because they cost much less **5**.......... than larger cars to run. In fact, there is a **6**.......... difference in fuel costs between these new small cars and the larger cars that we are used to seeing.

Paraphrases

Read the sentence from the reading passage. Then, choose the sentence that has the same meaning.

1 *In the early twentieth century in North America, electric cars shared the roads with gas-fueled cars, but in a short time, the gas-fueled cars became the standard.* (paragraph 2)

A People preferred gas-fueled to electric cars because they could go faster and farther.

B As roads improved, traveling in gas-fueled cars became more comfortable.

C At first, people drove both electric and gas-fueled cars, but gas-fueled cars soon became more common.

2 *In North America, slow, short-ranged electric vehicles with a high initial cost have thus far appealed to a limited audience.* (paragraph 4)
A Electric vehicles have interested few North Americans because of their limitations.
B North American interest in electric vehicles has not lasted for very long.
C Electric vehicles are slowly beginning to appear on North American roads.

Dictionary Skill

DIFFERENT MEANINGS

Many words have more than one meaning.

Read the definitions below. Then read the sentences and write the letter of the correct definition for each sentence.

QUESTIONS 1–2

ap-peal [a-PEEL]
A *verb.* to be of interest
B *verb.* to ask a court of law to hear a case again

.... **1** The driver didn't agree that he was guilty of speeding and planned to *appeal* to the court to change the decision.

.... **2** A car that is inexpensive to buy and easy to maintain would *appeal* to many people.

QUESTIONS 3–4

charge [CHARJ]
A *noun.* the amount of power a battery can store
B *noun.* the price of a service or purchase

.... **3** The *charge* for car repairs is often quite high.

.... **4** This car can travel about 100 miles on one battery *charge.*

Listening

Track 9

*Listen to the talk. Look at the map labeled **1–4**. Complete the labels.*

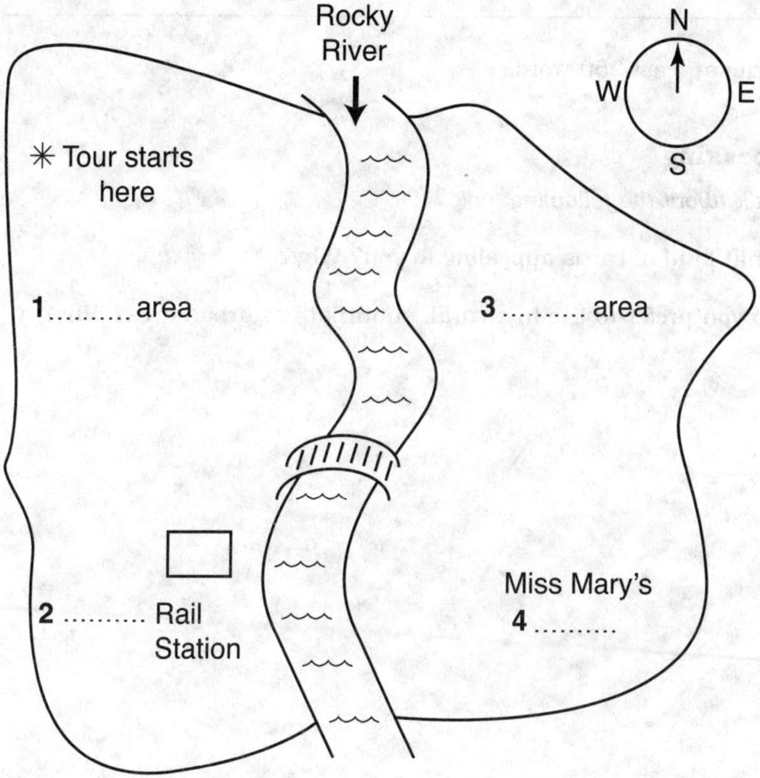

Writing
(Task 2)

In your opinion, what incentives could be offered that would persuade more people to embrace electric cars?

Support your answer with reasons and examples from your own knowledge or experience.

Write at least 250 words.

Speaking

Talk about the following topics.

What kind of car is appealing to you? Why?

Do you prefer to live in a rural, suburban, or urban area? Why?

Unit 4: Culture

ORIGINS OF WRITING

Words

Write the letter of each definition with the word it defines. If you don't know the definition, use the context of the reading passage to help you. Look for the words in bold as you read the passage.

PARAGRAPHS 1–2

Words	Definitions
1 .... civilization[1]	**A** v., to give credit for or see as the origin of something
2 .... attribute	**B** n., human society, its organization[2] and culture
3 .... creator	**C** n., the first maker of something
4 .... mythology	**D** n., person who has a great deal of knowledge about a particular subject
5 .... settle	**E** n., set of traditional stories used to explain the origins of things
6 .... scholar	**F** v., to establish a permanent place to live

PARAGRAPH 3

Words	Definitions
7 .... agricultural	**G** v., to accept or start to use something new
8 .... property	**H** adj., related to farming
9 .... token	**I** n., an area of digging, especially to find objects from past cultures
10 .... tablet	**J** n., something that is owned
11 .... excavation	**K** n., a thin, flat piece of material to write on
12 .... adopt	**L** n., an object used to represent something else

[1] BrE: civilisation
[2] BrE: organisation

Unit 4

PARAGRAPHS 4–5

Words	Definitions
13 .... carve	**M** v., to cut and shape hard material
14 .... encompass	**N** v., to mark a surface with words or letters
15 .... inscribe	**O** n., something that is built, such as a building or bridge
16 .... structure	**P** v., to include

PARAGRAPHS 5–6

Words	Definitions
17 .... deed	**Q** n., an act, especially a good or bad one
18 .... specialized[1]	**R** n., the ability to read and write
19 .... literacy	**S** adj., relating to a particular area or type of work
20 .... function	**T** v., to perform well

Reading

Origins of Writing

(1) Ancient **civilizations attributed** the origins of writing to the gods. For the ancient Egyptians, their god Thoth was the **creator** of writing and, in some stories, also the creator of speech. The ancient Sumerians and Assyrians also believed that writing originated with certain gods, as did the ancient Maya. In Chinese **mythology**, the creation of writing is attributed to an ancient sage and was used for communication with the gods. Clearly, writing was highly valued even by ancient peoples.

(2) Humans began painting pictures on cave walls 25,000 years ago or more, but writing systems did not develop until groups of people began **settling** in farming communities. **Scholars** say that writing systems developed independently in at least three different parts of the world: Mesopotamia, China, and Mesoamerica.

(3) The oldest known writing system developed among the ancient Sumerians in Mesopotamia around 3000 B.C. Along with the rise of **agricultural** societies came the development of **property** ownership and the need to keep records of it. In early agricultural societ-

[1]BrE: specialised

ies, property consisted largely of land, livestock such as cattle, and grain. Originally, clay **tokens** of various shapes were used to count these possessions. From this developed a system of impressing the shapes onto clay **tablets**. One of the earliest clay tablets of this type was found in **excavations** in Mesopotamia and dates from the time of the Sumerian culture. Scribes then began using reeds instead of tokens to mark the clay, developing a system of wedgelike shapes to represent the tokens. This system of writing using wedge shapes is known as cuneiform. It was later **adopted** by other cultures and became the basis for other writing systems. Originating in a system that used pictures to represent objects, cuneiform writing eventually developed into systems that used symbols to represent the sounds of language.

(4) The oldest form of Chinese writing dates from around 1500 B.C. It is called oracle bone script because it was **carved** on animal bones and shells that were used for predicting the future. At a later period, Chinese writing appeared on bronze vases and later still developed into a system that was used to record government affairs. The Chinese writing system was also the original basis for both the Japanese and Korean writing systems.

(5) In Mesoamerica, a region that **encompasses** parts of Mexico and Central America, it is the ancient Mayans who are famous for the writing they **inscribed** on temple walls and other religious **structures**. However, scholars believe that writing in that part of the world may have begun before the rise of the Mayan civilization. The Zapotec culture, centered[1] on Oaxaca, Mexico, was already using writing around 400 B.C., or possibly earlier. The Olmec culture may have developed a writing system even earlier than that. Recent discoveries show that the Mayans may have begun writing around 2,300 years ago. They used a system of symbols that represented words and syllables to record information about the **deeds** of their rulers as well as information connected to their calendar and astronomy. Their system of writing survived until the time of the Spanish Conquest in the 1500s.

(6) In ancient times, only **specialized**[2] people such as scholars, priests, or government officials used writing. Today, close to three-quarters of the world's adult population can read and write, and **literacy** is considered a basic skill necessary to **function** in the modern world.

---

[1]BrE: centred
[2]BrE: specialised

Answer the questions about **Origins of Writing**.

Questions 1–7

Do the following describe the ancient Sumerians, the ancient Chinese, or the ancient Maya?
Write the correct letter, ***A***, ***B***, *or* ***C***.

A Ancient Sumerians

B Ancient Chinese

C Ancient Maya

.... **1** inscribed symbols on bones

.... **2** inscribed symbols on religious structures

.... **3** inscribed symbols on clay tablets

.... **4** used tokens to keep records of their property

.... **5** used writing to record the deeds of their rulers

.... **6** wrote on metal

.... **7** used reeds as a writing tool

Questions 8–10

Do the following statements agree with the information in the reading passage?
Write

TRUE *if the statement agrees with the information.*
FALSE *if the statement contradicts the information.*
NOT GIVEN *if there is no information on this in the passage.*

.... **8** The ancient Mayans attributed the origin of writing to the gods.

.... **9** Scholars have discovered similarities between Zapotec and Mayan writing.

.... **10** Literacy was common in most ancient civilizations.

Word Families

A

Complete each sentence with the correct word from the word family chart. Make nouns plural where necessary. Use the correct form of verbs.

noun	adjective	adverb
agriculture	agricultural	agriculturally

1 Wheat was one of the first .... products.

2 People settled in Mesopotamia because it was a good area for ....

3 .... Mesopotamia was an important part of the world.

noun	noun	verb	adjective	adverb
creator	creation	create	creative	creatively

4 Some ancient peoples recorded information ...., using pictures to represent words.

5 Ancient peoples developed .... ways to record information.

6 The ancient Sumerians used clay and reeds for the .... of property records.

7 The ancient Maya were the .... of temples and other beautiful structures.

8 The ancient Sumerians .... tokens out of clay.

noun	noun	verb
excavation	excavator	excavate

9 .... found a clay tablet that dates from the time of the ancient Sumerians.

10 When they .... the area, they found some ancient oracle bones.

11 Early clay tablets and clay tokens have been found in .... in Mesopotamia.

noun	noun	adjective	adjective
literacy	illiteracy	literate	illiterate

12 .... was not considered necessary before modern times.

13 Few people were .... in the ancient world.

14 An .... person cannot read or write.

15 .... is a problem throughout the modern world.

noun	noun	adjective
mythology	myth	mythological

16 The Maya included .... creatures in their writing system.

17 Today we read the .... that were told in ancient times.

18 .... was very important in ancient civilizations.

noun	noun	verb	adjective
specialty	specialization	specialize	specialized

19 With the growth of agriculture, came the .... of work.

20 That scholar's .... is ancient Mayan culture.

21 Scholars with .... skills can identify ancient objects found in excavations.

22 Some scholars .... in ancient studies.

Word Families

B

Choose the correct word family member from the list below to complete each blank.

1 Excavations	Excavators	Excavates
2 agriculture	agricultural	agriculturally
3 creation	creators	created
4 specialty	specializes	specialized
5 literacy	illiterate	literate
6 mythology	myths	mythological

1.......... working at ancient sites uncover objects that give us clues about life in the past. Household objects and tools that were used for **2**.......... can tell us a lot about how people lived long ago. Ancient people used a variety of materials to make the objects they used in daily life. Tools that were carved from wood, stone, and bone, and jars that were **3**.......... from clay are some examples of objects that have been found. Some of these objects are quite beautiful, and it is clear that they were made by people with **4**.......... skills. In ancient times, most people were not **5**.......... . However, traditional stories were an important part of ancient civilizations, and people told the **6**.......... of their culture to their children and grandchildren.

Paraphrases

Read the sentence from the reading passage. Then, choose the sentence that has the same meaning.

1 *In early agricultural societies, property consisted largely of land, livestock such as cattle, and grain.* (paragraph 3)

A In early societies, people ate mostly meat and grain.

B The first farmers mostly owned things such as land, animals, and grain.

C Ancient farmers needed large areas of land to raise animals and grain.

2 *In Mesoamerica, a region that encompasses parts of Mexico and Central America, it is the ancient Mayans that are famous for the writing they inscribed on temple walls and other religious structures.* (paragraph 5)

A Most ancient temples in Mexico and Central America were built by the Mayans.

B The ancient Mayans wrote about their journeys to the temples of Mesoamerica.

C The ancient Mayans of Mexico and Central America wrote on the walls of their buildings.

Dictionary Skill

PARTS OF SPEECH

The word *function* can be a verb or a noun.

Read the definitions below. Then read the sentences and write the letter of the correct definition for each sentence.

func-tion [FUNGK-shun]
A *verb.* to perform well
B *noun.* purpose, role

.... **1** The skills needed to *function* in modern society are very different from those needed in the ancient world.

.... **2** Mythology had an important *function* in ancient cultures.

Listening

Track 10

Listen to the talk. Look at the map below labeled A–E. Look at the list of places and write the correct letter, ***A–E****, next to numbers* ***1–5****.*

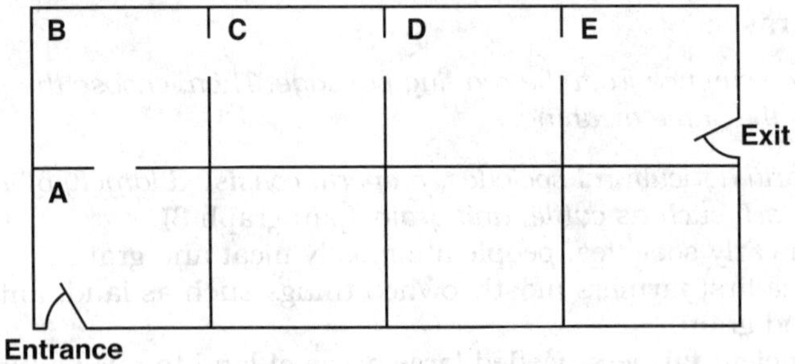

.... **1** Visiting Scholars' Room

.... **2** Agricultural Tools Exhibit

.... **3** Recent Excavations Exhibit

.... **4** Mythology Exhibit

.... **5** Gift Shop

Writing (Task 1)

The chart[1] below shows literacy rates in several different countries around the world.

Summarize[2] the information by selecting and reporting the main information and making comparisons

Write at least 150 words.

Adult Literacy Rates (age 15 and over)

Country	Total Population	Male	Female
Country A	47.8%	63.5%	32.7%
Country B	50%	70.5%	30%
Country C	90.3%	93.9%	86.9%
Country D	99%	99%	99%
World	82%	87%	77%

Speaking

Talk about the following topics.

Do you believe that it is better to have a teacher who specializes in the subject he or she teaches or a teacher who is highly skilled at teaching? Why?

What skills do you think are necessary to teach today's children to help them function in a society where technology is changing so rapidly?

[1]BrE: table
[2]BrE: summarise

HULA DANCING IN HAWAIIAN CULTURE

Words

Write the letter of each definition with the word it defines. If you don't know the definition, use the context of the reading passage to help you. Look for the words in bold as you read the passage.

PARAGRAPH 1

Words	Definitions
1 .... evoke **2** .... image **3** .... sway **4** .... benefit **5** .... stereotype **6** .... tradition	**A** n., the use, advantage of **B** v., to bring to mind **C** n., a mental picture **D** n., a fixed idea people have, especially one that is wrong **E** v., to move back and forth **F** n., the custom or belief of a group of people

PARAGRAPH 2

Words	Definitions
7 .... altar **8** .... accompany **9** .... ritual **10** .... evidence	**G** v., to go with; happen at the same time **H** n., a table or similar structure for religious ceremonies **I** n., signs; proof something is or is not true **J** n., a set of actions used as part of a ceremony

PARAGRAPH 3

Words	Definitions
11 .... discourage **12** .... revive **13** .... reign **14** .... celebration	**K** n., a social event to mark a special day or occasion **L** v., to try to stop or prevent something **M** n., the period of time that a king or queen is in power **N** v., to bring back to life

PARAGRAPHS 4–5

Words	Definitions
15 .... influence	**O** adj., having a lot of detail and decoration
16 .... energetic	**P** adj., having a lot of energy
17 .... graceful	**Q** adj., related to flowers
18 .... elaborate	**R** n., a decorative rope of flowers or leaves
19 .... floral	**S** adj., having beauty of movement
20 .... garland	**T** n., an effect; power

Reading

Hula Dancing in Hawaiian Culture

(1) Many people dream of visiting the beautiful Hawaiian Islands. Mention of this Pacific paradise **evokes images** of women in grass skirts **swaying** their hips as they perform graceful island dances for the **benefit** of tourists. Although this image is a common **stereotype** of Hawaii, it has its roots in a real **tradition** that continues to play an important role in Hawaiian culture.

(2) Hula dancing has always been part of Hawaiian life. Hawaiian mythology includes various stories that explain the origins of hula, each story attributing its creation to a different god or goddess and its first appearance to a different location. In reality, hula dancing is such an ancient tradition that it is impossible to say when or where it first appeared. It was most likely originally performed in front of an **altar** in honor of gods and **accompanied by** great **ritual**. It is a common belief that the ancient hula was danced only by men, but some scholars point to **evidence** suggesting that hula was traditionally danced by both men and women.

(3) The English explorer Captain James Cook's visit to the islands in the eighteenth century caused many changes to Hawaiian society as a result of the contact with European culture. Although hula did not completely disappear after contact, it was **discouraged**. King David Kalakaua is credited with **reviving** hula dancing during his **reign** in the late nineteenth century. He was interested in reestablishing lost traditions, and hula was performed at **celebrations** held in his honor[1].

[1]BrE: honour

Unit 4

(4) In the 1960s, a Hawaiian cultural festival was established as part of an effort to attract more tourists to the islands. A major part of this festival consisted of hula competitions, which were organized into categories of *hula kahiko*, or hula danced in the ancient style, and *hula auana*, or modern hula. This festival, called the Merrie Monarch Festival in honor of King David Kalakaua, has become a major annual cultural event. The hula competition is a central part of the festival and has had a significant **influence** on modern hula dancing.

(5) Hula continues to be danced in both the ancient and modern styles. Traditional hula is an **energetic** dance performed to the accompaniment of chants and the beating of drums. The dancers wear traditional costumes consisting of garlands of leaves, skirts of tapa (a type of bark), and anklets made of animal bone. Many of the movements of modern hula are based on the ancient hula, but the modern style is slower and more **graceful**. It is danced to flowing guitar and ukulele music, and the dancers wear **elaborate** costumes, including the famous Hawaiian **floral garlands** known as *leis*.

(5) Hula has attracted the interest of people outside the islands, and hula schools can be found in many parts of the world. Although people of other nationalities learn to dance some form of hula, it is also danced by Hawaiians who live away from the islands, on the mainland United States, in Europe, and elsewhere. It has become a way for native Hawaiians to maintain their cultural identity even while living away from their island homeland. What was once a religious ritual has become a form of entertainment, not only for tourists, but also for native Hawaiians who seek to maintain connections with their cultural heritage.

Answer the questions about **Hula Dancing in Hawaiian Culture**.

Questions 1–4

*Choose the correct letter, **A**, **B**, **C**, or **D**.*

1 Originally, hula was danced

A by dancers wearing floral garlands.
B for the benefit of kings.
C in competitions.
D near an altar.

2 Hula dancing was discouraged
- **A** in certain ancient rituals.
- **B** after contact with Europeans.
- **C** in the 1960s.
- **D** during traditional celebrations.

3 Hula was revived in the nineteenth century by
- **A** a Hawaiian king.
- **B** an English explorer.
- **C** Hawaiians in Europe.
- **D** the tourist industry.

4 Modern hula dances are accompanied by
- **A** drums.
- **B** guitars.
- **C** chants.
- **D** violins.

Questions 5–7

Complete the summary using words from the list below.

elaborate	evidence	influence
energetic	graceful	reign

Hula dancing has been part of Hawaiian culture since ancient times, although the styles of dancing have changed over time. The traditional style of hula dancing, which is still performed, is fast, whereas modern hula is more **5**.......... and flowing. Dancers of modern hula wear costumes that are **6**.........., while dancers of ancient hula wear simpler traditional costumes. People everywhere are interested in hula, including Hawaiians living in other parts of the world. The fact that hula is danced by Hawaiians living away from their homeland is **7**.......... of its importance to Hawaiian culture.

Word Families

A

Complete each sentence with the correct word from the word family chart. Make nouns plural where necessary. Use the correct form of verbs.

noun	verb
accompaniment	accompany

1 Guitars often .... modern hula dances.

2 The .... of drums and chants helps the hula dancers maintain their energy.

noun	verb	adjective
benefit	benefit	beneficial

3 Tourism is .... to the economy of Hawaii.

4 Hawaii .... from the large numbers of tourists who visit the islands.

5 A .... of visiting Hawaii in the off season is the lower hotel prices.

noun	verb	adjective
celebration	celebrate	celebratory

6 People like to .... important events by dancing.

7 Hula dances are often performed at cultural ....

8 .... dances were performed in honor of the king.

noun	verb	adjective	adverb
energy	energize[1]	energetic	energetically

9 The dancers performed .... all evening.

10 It takes a great deal of .... to dance hula.

11 .... chants and drumming accompany the hula dancers.

12 The beating of the drums .... the crowd.

noun	verb	adjective
influence	influence	influential

13 The .... of other cultures has changed the way hula is danced.

14 Ancient hula .... the modern style of hula dancing.

15 King David Kalakaua was .... in the return to old traditions.

noun	adjective	adverb
tradition	traditional	traditionally

16 Hula was .... performed in honor of the gods.

17 Hula dancing is an ancient ....

18 Hula is the .... dance of Hawaii.

Unit 4

[1]BrE: energise

Word Families

B

Choose the correct word family member from the list below to complete each blank.

1 tradition	traditional	traditionally
2 energy	energetic	energetically
3 accompaniment	accompany	accompanies
4 influences	influenced	influential
5 celebrations	celebrates	celebratory
6 benefits	benefited	beneficial

Hula is a **1**.......... dance from Hawaii. Originally, it was performed as part of religious rituals. It was danced **2**.......... to the **3**.......... of drums and chants. Over time it has been **4**.......... in different ways, and styles have changed. Modern hula is a more graceful dance performed to guitar and ukulele music. It is performed for tourists and also as part of **5**.......... . The wide interest in hula dancing is **6**.......... for Hawaii because it helps attract tourists to the islands.

Paraphrases

Read the sentence from the reading passage. Then, choose the sentence that has the same meaning.

1 *Although this image is a common stereotype of Hawaii, it has its roots in a real tradition that continues to play an important role in Hawaiian culture.* (paragraph 1)

A Many people don't realize that hula is an old and important tradition.
B People enjoy seeing photographs of traditional hula dancers.
C Hula dances are traditionally performed for visitors to Hawaii.

2 *It is a common belief that the ancient hula was danced only by men, but some scholars point to evidence suggesting that hula was traditionally danced by both men and women.* (paragraph 2)

A Contrary to common opinion, there are signs that women, as well as men, danced the ancient hula.

B The ancient hula was originally danced by men, but later women started dancing it, too.

C Some scholars have pointed out that women may have danced the ancient hula more skillfully than men.

Dictionary Skill

DIFFERENT MEANINGS

Many words have more than one meaning.

Read the definitions below. Then read the sentences and write the letter of the correct definition for each sentence.

im-age [IM-mij]
A *noun.* a mental picture
B *noun.* impression, appearance

.... 1 The word *Hawaii* carries *images* of sunny beaches, volcanoes, and hula dancing.

.... 2 King David Kalakaua was known as the Merrie Monarch because of his *image* as a happy party host.

Listening

Track 11

*Listen to the conversation. Choose **FOUR** letters, **A–G**.*

Which **FOUR** of the following will be included in the hula demonstration?

A floral decorations

B elaborate costumes

C garlands of leaves

D an altar

E energetic dances

F graceful movements

G traditional music

Writing (Task 2)

Most countries have traditional celebrations that occur annually. In your opinion, what benefits do these celebrations have for society?

Support your opinion with reasons and examples from your own knowledge or experience.

Write at least 250 words.

Speaking

Talk about the following topics.

What are some important traditional celebrations in your country?

What are some rituals connected with traditional celebrations in your country?

THE ART OF MIME

Words

Write the letter of each definition with the word it defines. If you don't know the definition, use the context of the reading passage to help you. Look for the words in bold as you read the passage.

PARAGRAPH 1

Words	Definitions
1 .... gesture	**A** v., to result in; end with
2 .... portray	**B** n., a movement to express a feeling or idea
3 .... prop	**C** v., to represent; act out
4 .... culminate	**D** n., object used by actors

PARAGRAPH 2

Words	Definitions
5 .... abstract	**E** adj., not concrete; related to ideas or feelings
6 .... literal	**F** n., difficulty; opposition
7 .... conflict	**G** adj., funny; entertaining
8 .... humorous[1]	**H** adj., following the exact meaning

PARAGRAPH 3

Words	Definitions
9 .... exaggerated	**I** adv., well; successfully
10 .... sharpen	**J** adj., made to seem more or bigger
11 .... effectively	**K** n., weakness and lack of strength
12 .... frailty	**L** v., to improve; perfect

[1]BrE: humourous

PARAGRAPHS 4–5

Words	Definitions
13 .... renowned	**M** v., to appear; develop
14 .... prominent	**N** n., appearance of being real; false impression
15 .... emerge	**O** adj., important; major
16 .... illusion	**P** adj., famous

PARAGRAPHS 5–6

Words	Definitions
17 .... reminiscent	**Q** n., the feeling of a place
18 .... considerably	**R** adv., a great deal; noticeably
19 .... atmosphere	**S** v., to combine
20 .... merge	**T** adj., similar to; reminding of something

Reading

The Art of Mime

(1) Miming dates back to the theaters[1] of ancient Greece and Rome. Mimes use movements, **gestures**, and facial expressions to **portray** a character or an emotion or to tell a story—all without words. Over the centuries, the art of miming grew to include acrobatics, **props**, and costumes, **culminating** in the fine-tuned art form that people recognize[2] today.

(2) Miming can be **abstract**, **literal**, or a combination of the two. Abstract miming usually has no plot or central character but simply expresses a feeling such as sorrow or desire. Literal miming, on the other hand, tells a story and is often comedic, using body gestures and facial expressions to present a main character facing some type of **conflict** in a **humorous** way, for example, acting out a tug-of-war without the aid of rope or other props.

---

[1]BrE: theatres
[2]BrE: recognise

(3) The twentieth-century style of miming reflects outside influences of the period, most notably silent films, in which actors relied on their ability to communicate thoughts and stories through facial expressions and **exaggerated** gestures. Two superstars of the silent movie era, Buster Keaton and Charlie Chaplin, **sharpened** their miming skills in the theater before using them in movies. Both were so successful that they have continued to influence mimes and other live performers long after their deaths. People still consider Chaplin a master of the miming technique, in particular, his tragicomic "little tramp" character, who so **effectively** portrays human **frailty** through physical comedy, also known as slapstick.

(4) Another twentieth-century influence on modern miming involves a **renowned** French mime and acting teacher named Etienne Decroux, who developed what was known as corporeal mime. This art form focused on the body, showing thought through movement, and became the **prominent** form of the modern mime era. In the 1930s, Decroux founded a mime school in Paris based on corporeal mime. One of his students, a young Frenchman named Marcel Marceau, **emerged** as what many consider the master of modern mime.

(5) Marceau added his personal touch to the art of miming and presented it to the world for half a century on television and in theaters. Among his well-known **illusions** are portrayals of a man walking against the wind and a man trapped inside a shrinking box. Marceau also created his own special character, Bip the Clown. White-faced and dressed in a striped shirt and floppy top hat with a red flower, Bip is **reminiscent** of both Chaplin's Little Tramp and Pierrot, the traditional downtrodden mime character from centuries earlier.

(6) Miming is still taught in dance, drama, and acting schools worldwide, although it has changed **considerably** since the ancient Greek plays and even since the solo performances of Marceau. Group miming is now in fashion, and sounds, lighting, and other special effects are included to help create the desired **atmosphere**. Current examples include the U.S. dance troupe Pilobolus, which **merges** modern dance, acrobatics, gymnastics, and mime to create elaborate geometric shapes with their bodies, and the Canadian Cirque du Soleil, which uses lighting, spectacular costumes, and special effects to produce striking illusions.

Answer the questions about **The Art of Mime.**

Questions 1–7

Complete the summary using words from the list below.

abstract	gestures	literal	renowned
conflicts	humorous	merged	sharpened
emerged	illusion	props	

Mime is a type of theater performance that uses **1**.......... and expressions to tell a story or show a character. There are two types of mime. The first is **2**.......... mime, which tells a story and is often **3**.......... . It makes people laugh. The second is **4**.......... mime, which portrays feelings. Two influential actors **5**.......... during the silent film era. They were Charlie Chaplin and Buster Keaton, whose years of experience in the theater culminated in miming skills that they were able to use effectively in silent films. Their techniques influenced mimes for many years. The French mime Etienne Decroux developed the form known as corporeal mime. One of his students, Marcel Marceau, became a prominent modern mime. Marceau's **6**.......... illusions include a man walking against the wind and a man trapped in a box. Now mimes often perform in groups. They have **7**.......... a variety of skills, such as dance, acrobatics, and gymnastics, as well as mime, in their performances.

Word Families

A

Complete each sentence with the correct word from the word family chart. Make nouns plural where necessary. Use the correct form of verbs.

adjective	adverb
considerable	considerably

1 It takes .... skill to perform mime.

2 The mime's audiences grew .... as word of his skill spread.

noun	verb	adjective	adverb
effect	effect	effective	effectively

3 He worked hard to .... change.

4 A really .... mime performance makes the audience believe in the illusion.

5 His skilled performance was the .... of years of experience.

6 A skilled mime can .... perform a variety of illusions.

noun	verb	adjective
exaggeration	exaggerate	exaggerated

7 The .... gestures of a mime are used for humorous effect.

8 A mime uses .... to create illusions.

9 A mime may .... certain gestures.

noun	adjective
frailty	frail

10 Humans are ...., and mimes can make us laugh at this.

11 Mimes can make us laugh at our own ....

noun	noun	verb
portrayal	portrayer	portray

12 Marcel Marceau was the .... of Bip the Clown.

13 Charlie Chaplin is renowned for his .... of the Little Tramp character.

14 Mimes .... common situations in humorous ways.

noun	verb	adjective
reminiscence	reminisce	reminiscent

15 Marcel Marceau's clown character was .... of characters performed by earlier mimes.

16 People like to .... about the great performers of the past.

17 .... of the early days of film would include stories of stars such as Charlie Chaplin and Buster Keaton.

Word Families

B

Choose the correct word family member from the list below to complete each blank.

1 exaggeration	exaggerate	exaggerated
2 effect	effective	effectively
3 considerable	considerably	
4 portrayal	portrayer	portray
5 frailties	frail	
6 reminiscence	reminisce	reminiscent

Everyone enjoys watching mimes perform. A really good mime makes the job look easy, but in reality it is impossible to **1**.......... the skill required to perform mime **2**.......... . It takes a **3**.......... amount of time to develop techniques and learn to perform them well. Mimes need to be able to **4**.......... characters who will interest their audience, as well as perform a variety of illusions. The best mimes can show us our **5**.......... while making us laugh at ourselves at the same time. Although mime has changed over the years, people still **6**.......... about some of the popular mimes of the past, who have inspired today's performers.

Paraphrases

Read the sentence from the reading passage. Then, choose the sentence that has the same meaning.

1 *White-faced and dressed in a striped shirt and floppy top hat with a red flower, Bip is reminiscent of both Chaplin's little tramp and Pierrot, the traditional down-trodden mime character from centuries earlier.* (paragraph 5)

A Bip brought back interest in the old tradition of mime.
B Bip was more successful than the characters that came before him.
C Bip reminds us of famous mime characters from the past.

2 *Miming is still taught in dance, drama, and acting schools worldwide, although it has changed considerably since the ancient Greek plays and even since the solo performances of Marceau.* (paragraph 6)

A Dancers and actors around the world also learn how to perform mime.
B People are still interested in mime, although it is very different from the mime of the past.
C Opinions about mime have changed over time, and it has become very popular.

Dictionary Skill

DIFFERENT MEANINGS

Many words have more than one meaning.

Read the definitions below. Then read the sentences and write the letter of the correct definition for each sentence.

QUESTIONS 1–2

at-mo-sphere [AT-mu-sfeer]
A *noun.* the feeling of a place
B *noun.* the mixture of gases surrounding some planets

.... **1** Earth's *atmosphere* helps hold warmth from the sun.

.... **2** The bright lighting in the theater created a happy *atmosphere.*

QUESTIONS 3–4

ef-fect [i-FEKT]
A *noun.* result
B *noun.* special sound or lighting in a theater or movie

.... **3** The *effect* of watching Charlie Chaplin's Little Tramp character is a mixture of sadness and laughter.

.... **4** Modern mime performances often include special *effects* as part of the illusions they create.

Listening

Track 12

Listen to the talk. Complete the notes below.
*Write **NO MORE THAN ONE WORD** for each answer.*

Mime

Performed without **1** ....

2 .... of everyday activities
- climbing stairs
- opening a window

Use **3** .... to show presence of objects

Act out stories
- **4** .... different characters
- Show the characters in **5** ....

Writing (Task 1)

The chart[1] below shows information about ticket sales for performances at the National Theater over a six-month period.

Summarize[2] the information by selecting and reporting the main information and making comparisons.

Write at least 150 words.

National Theater
Ticket Sales: January–June

Performers	Performance title	Number of tickets sold
National Mime Troupe	"Humorous Situations"	5,000
City Opera	*Carmen*	2,500
National Symphony Orchestra	"Works of Beethoven"	3,000
City Ballet	*Swan Lake*	4,750
Rock Stars Rock Band	"Rock Stars Live!"	4,750

Speaking

Talk about the following topics:

When you see a live performance, do you prefer humorous types of performances or more serious types? Why?

Who are some of the more renowned performers in your country?

Do you enjoy movies that portray real people and events, or do you prefer movies with made-up stories?

[1]BrE: table
[2]BrE: summarise

Unit 5: Health

NURSE MIGRATION

Words

Write the letter of each definition with the word it defines. If you don't know the definition, use the context of the reading passage to help you. Look for the words in bold as you read the passage.

PARAGRAPHS 1–2

Words	Definitions
1 .... shortage **2** .... cripple **3** .... complex **4** .... vacancy	**A** adj., not simple **B** n., a position or job that needs to be filled **C** n., a situation where there is not enough of something **D** v., to cause serious damage; weaken

PARAGRAPHS 3–4

Words	Definitions
5 .... abroad **6** .... standpoint **7** .... lure **8** .... primary **9** .... decline **10** .... estimate	**E** adv., in a foreign country **F** v., to gradually go lower; become smaller **G** v., to guess based on information **H** v., to attract **I** adj., main; most important **J** n., point of view

PARAGRAPHS 4–5

Words	Definitions
11 .... bulk **12** .... rudimentary **13** .... epidemic **14** .... rampant **15** .... administer	**K** v., to give medicine or medical treatment **L** n., the largest part **M** n., rapid spread of a disease **N** adj., basic; not well developed **O** adj., spreading out of control

PARAGRAPHS 6–7

Words	Definitions
16 .... stem	**P** n., period of ten years
17 .... supply	**Q** adj., skilled; able to do a job
18 .... decade	**R** v., to keep
19 .... qualified	**S** v., to come from; originate
20 .... retain	**T** n., the total amount available

Reading

Nurse Migration

(1) There are more nurses today than at any time in history, yet a global nursing **shortage** threatens to **cripple** health care systems worldwide. Because the underlying causes of a shortage are **complex** and vary in different regions, a simple, short-term fix will not remedy the situation.

(2) In developing nations—particularly in sub-Saharan Africa, South Asia, and Latin America—a major reason for the shortage is nurse migration to developed countries in Europe and North America as well as Australia to help fill **vacancies** there.

(3) Nurse migration is hardly a recent phenomenon. For years the Philippines has trained many more nurses than the country needs, with thousands working **abroad** and sending money to relatives back home (nearing $1 billion annually). From that **standpoint**, migration of nurses from poorer to wealthier countries would appear to benefit all involved. But there is another side to the story. Today, even the Philippines feels the effects of the nursing shortage, with nurses continuing to migrate abroad while positions at home go unfilled.

(4) **Lured** by the higher salaries and better quality of life available in wealthier countries, nurses from developing countries frequently leave behind already overburdened health care systems, where nurses are often the **primary** caregivers because doctors, too, are in short supply. Conditions then deteriorate further as the nurse-to-population ratio **declines**, a number that is **estimated** to be ten times higher in European than in African countries. Some Latin American countries are experiencing such a shortage of nurses that doctors actually outnumber them, leaving the **bulk** of health care up to assistant nurses, who have only **rudimentary** training.

(5) Routine immunizations and prenatal care fall victim to the nursing shortage in developing countries, and in many cases the results can be life threatening. In African countries where the HIV/AIDS

epidemic is **rampant**, some patients go untreated not because lifesaving drugs are unavailable but because there are not enough nurses to **administer** them.

(6) In developed countries in Europe and North America, the nursing shortage largely **stems** from an aging population, who require more health care services, coupled with a dwindling **supply** of nurses, many of whom are likewise nearing retirement age, with fewer young people preparing to replace them.

(7) A common thread among nurse-importing countries—underinvestment in nursing education dating back two or more **decades**—has prevented them from creating a stable workforce to meet current and future needs. The United Kingdom, for example, still feels the effects of a cutback in nurse training some twenty years ago. In the United States, nursing schools turn down thousands of **qualified** applicants every year because of their own shortages of nursing faculty. Developed countries need to invest in nursing education and focus on **retaining** and rewarding nurses appropriately, both financially and through high-quality working conditions.

(8) Widespread nurse migration helps neither the host country nor the country of origin in the long run, does nothing to remedy the underlying cause of the shortage, and results in millions of people being deprived of the health care they need.

Answer the questions about **Nurse Migration**.

Questions 1–6

Complete the summary using the list of words below.

abroad	complex	qualified
administered	cripple	rudimentary
bulk	lure	shortage

The **1**.......... of nurses in developing nations is largely caused by nurses leaving their countries to work **2**.......... . It is difficult for poorer nations to retain their nurses because better salaries and living conditions **3**.......... many nurses to work in wealthier countries. When nurses migrate to other countries, there are fewer **4**.......... health care givers left in their own countries. The lack of trained doctors as well as nurses means that health care is often **5**.......... by workers who have only **6**.......... skills.

Questions 7–9

Do the following statements agree with the information in the reading passage?
Write

TRUE	*if the statement agrees with the information.*
FALSE	*if the statement contradicts the information.*
NOT GIVEN	*if there is no information on this in the passage.*

.... **7** A primary reason for the nursing shortage in developed countries is the health care needs of the aging population.

.... **8** There is not a large enough supply of qualified applicants for nursing schools in the United States.

.... **9** In the United Kingdom, a high percentage of nurses have retired during the past two decades.

Word Families

A

Complete each sentence with the correct word from the word family chart. Make nouns plural where necessary. Use the correct form of verbs.

noun	**adjective**
complexity	complex

1 The .... of the nursing shortage problem makes it difficult to solve.

2 The reasons for the world-wide nursing shortage are ....

noun	**verb**	**adjective**
qualification	qualify	qualified

3 A nurse who has the right .... will have no trouble finding a job.

4 .... nurses are needed everywhere.

5 At nursing school, a student learns the skills to .... for a career in nursing.

adjective	adverb
rampant	rampantly

6 The .... spread of the epidemic made it difficult to control.

7 The disease spread .... throughout the region.

noun	verb	adjective
shortage	shorten	short

8 Lack of proper medical care can .... a patient's life.

9 Both nurses and doctors are in .... supply in many places.

10 The nursing .... is affecting countries around the world.

noun	verb	adjective
vacancy	vacate	vacant

11 A .... position at a hospital will be filled quickly if the salary and benefits are attractive.

12 When a nurse leaves a job, it is not always easy to fill the ....

13 Many nurses .... their jobs in their native countries in favor of better positions elsewhere.

Word Families

B

Choose the correct word family member from the list below to complete each blank.

1	shortage	shorten	short
2	complexities	complex	complexes
3	ramp	rampant	rampantly
4	vacancies	vacate	vacant
5	qualifications	qualifies	qualified

Nurses are in **1**.......... supply in many parts of the world. There are many reasons for this lack of nurses; the issue is filled with **2**.......... . A solution needs to be found soon, because the problem has become **3**.......... . When nurses **4**.......... their positions at hospitals and health care centers, it is not easy to find other nurses to replace them. The ability to administer health care where it is needed is crippled when there are not enough **5**.......... nurses.

Paraphrases

Read the sentence from the reading passage. Then, choose the sentence that has the same meaning.

1 *There are more nurses today than at any time in history, yet a global nursing shortage threatens to cripple health care systems worldwide.* (paragraph 1)

A Many nurses around the world have difficulty finding good jobs.

B The lack of nurses is harming health care systems around the world.

C Nurses need better training to meet the needs of health care systems.

2 *Some Latin American countries are experiencing such a shortage of nurses that doctors actually outnumber them, leaving the bulk of health care up to assistant nurses, who have only rudimentary training.* (paragraph 4)

A In parts of Latin America, the lack of nurses means that most care is provided by assistants with only basic training.

B Many Latin American nurses leave their countries to get better training elsewhere.

C Some Latin American nurses have difficulty providing care because they don't have assistants.

Word Skill

COMPOUND WORDS

When two or more words join to form a new word, that word is called a compound word. Sometimes, the meaning of the compound word is related to the meanings of the two separate words.

> standpoint = stand + point
> Meaning: the place where you stand, the position from which you see and understand things.

Read the sentences. Write a definition for each underlined word.

1 Work at the health care center came to a standstill because there was not enough money to pay the staff.

standstill: ....

2 The new nurse has been a real standout with excellent reviews from doctors and patients alike.

standout: ....

Listening

Track 13

Listen to the talk. Complete the sentences below.
*Write **ONE NUMBER ONLY** for each answer.*

1 In the United States, the bulk of nursing school programs take .... years.

2 In the United Kingdom, ... percent of nurses have degrees.

3 There has been a decline of .... percent or more of people applying to nursing schools in the United States.

4 By 2015, there may be as many as .... vacancies for nurses in the United States.

Writing (Task 1)

The chart[1] below shows information about wages for health care professionals in four different countries.

Summarize[2] the information by selecting and reporting the main information and making comparisons.

Write at least 150 words.

Average Monthly Salaries for Qualified Health Care Professionals

	Nurses	Doctors
Country A *	$35	$64
Country B *	$350	$700
Country C **	$2,900	$5,500
Country D **	$3,420	$10,200

*Source countries: supply health care professionals to other countries
**Destination countries: receive health care professionals from abroad

Speaking

Talk about the following topics.

What profession do you work in or plan to work in? What were your primary reasons for choosing this profession?

What are your professional goals for the next decade?

What kinds of opportunities does your profession offer for working abroad?

---

[1]BrE: table
[2]BrE: summarise

AEROBIC EXERCISE AND BRAIN HEALTH

Words

Write the letter of each definition with the word it defines. If you don't know the definition, use the context of the reading passage to help you. Look for the words in bold as you read the passage.

PARAGRAPH 1

Words	Definitions
1 .... aerobic	**A** adj., relating to energetic exercise
2 .... mood	**B** n., the use of mental processes
3 .... cognition	**C** n., a disease or illness
4 .... disorder	**D** n., a feeling; a state of mind

PARAGRAPH 2

Words	Definitions
5 .... stimulate	**E** n., a large amount of something in the same place
6 .... regulate	**F** n., the loss of intellectual functioning of the brain
7 .... rodent	**G** v., to control
8 .... concentration	**H** n., the group of small animals that includes mice and rats
9 .... dementia	**I** adj., of or relating to space
10 .... spatial	**J** v., to cause a response

PARAGRAPH 3

Words	Definitions
11 .... stave off	**K** n., total amount available
12 .... gravity	**L** n., the process of becoming worse
13 .... capacity	**M** n., seriousness
14 .... deterioration	**N** v., to prevent for a period of time

PARAGRAPHS 4–5

Words	Definitions
15 .... diagnose	**O** v., to work against
16 .... indicate	**P** adv., before
17 .... counteract	**Q** v., to identify an illness
18 .... link	**R** adj., damaged or weakened
19 .... impaired	**S** v., to show
20 .... previously	**T** n., connection

Reading

Aerobic Exercise and Brain Health

(1) The disease-fighting, weight-controlling benefits of physical exercise, especially **aerobic** exercise, have long been known. Now, researchers have discovered another advantage: Physical exercise has a powerful effect on brain health, and the benefits go beyond the release of endorphins, the chemical in the brain that improves **mood**. Exercise affects the brain's plasticity—that is, its ability to reorganize[1] itself—and can reduce the age-associated loss of brain tissue that decreases **cognition** in the elderly and in those who have **disorders** such as Alzheimer's disease.

(2) Recent studies have found that exercise activates a number of factors in the brain, including a protein known as *brain-derived neurotrophic factor* (BDNF), that **stimulate** the growth and development of brain cells. BDNF **regulates** the production of synapses, the connections between neurons that are essential for transmitting signals from one nerve cell to the next, and may also be involved in producing new nerve cells. Using **rodent** models, researchers found increased **concentrations** of BDNF in the hippocampus, an area of the brain involved in learning and memory and associated with **dementia**, after only one week of regular exercise. A study in older humans found a correlation between aerobic fitness, the size of the hippocampus, and performance on **spatial** memory tests. Other human studies noted that aerobic exercise increased the volume of gray[2] matter in some parts of the brain.

---

[1]BrE: reorganise

[2]BrE: grey

(3) Regular exercise can help **stave off** some effects of normal aging and delay or diminish the **gravity** of conditions such as Alzheimer's disease, depression, and multiple sclerosis. Even over a relatively short time, exercise can repair some of the loss in brain **capacity** associated with aging. The greatest effects have been found in processes such as decision-making. Aerobic exercise can also improve short-term memory in the elderly. Exercise has been found to lower the risk of Alzheimer's disease in mice by decreasing the buildup of a protein known as beta-amyloid, which forms the brain plaques that precede Alzheimer's. The mice also outperformed non-exercising mice in a memory test. In a study of multiple sclerosis patients, those who exercised regularly fared better than those who exercised less. The exercise group scored better on tests of cognitive function, and their brain scans showed less **deterioration** and more gray matter.

(4) In addition to increasing brainpower, exercise can help relieve depression. Although it is well known that endorphins help relieve stress and reduce anxiety and depression, BDNF plays a role as well. Human studies have shown people who have been **diagnosed** with major depression typically have lower concentrations of BDNF in their blood. Animal studies **indicate** that corticosteroids, which the body produces in response to stress, decrease the availability of BDNF in the hippocampus. Exercise can **counteract** this effect. Exercise also lessens depression by increasing blood flow to the brain.

(5) The **link** between aerobic exercise and improved brain function in the elderly and in people with **impaired** cognition could lead to new ways to prevent and treat brain disorders. Meanwhile, people may have more control over their own brain health than was **previously** believed.

Answer the questions about **Aerobic Exercise and Brain Health**.

Questions 1–8

Complete the sentences below.
Choose ***NO MORE THAN ONE WORD*** *from the text for each answer.*

1 Exercise helps people feel good mentally because it releases endorphins, which put people in a better ....

2 BDNF improves the connections between nerve cells in the brain because it .... how those connections, or synapses, are made.

3 Studies on rodents showed that there were larger .... of BDNF in the brain after just one week of exercise.

4 Exercise may lessen the .... of Alzheimer's disease and other disorders that affect the brain.

5 As people age, they may not function as well because they lose some brain ...., but exercise can repair some of this lost ability.

6 A study with multiple sclerosis patients showed that those who exercised more had less .... of the brain.

7 Usually, smaller amounts of BDNF are found in the blood of people .... with depression.

8 Exercise may lessen the effects of stress because it can .... the effects of corticosteroids, which are produced by stress.

Word Families

A

Complete each sentence with the correct word from the word family chart. Make nouns plural where necessary. Use the correct form of verbs.

noun	noun	verb	adjective
diagnosis	diagnostician	diagnose	diagnostic

1 The doctor is an outstanding ....

2 Doctors use different .... tests to identify diseases.

3 The doctor asks the patient a series of questions in order to make a ....

4 It is not always easy to .... a disease.

noun	adjective	adverb
gravity	grave	gravely

5 The patient was .... ill.

6 The patient arrived at the hospital in .... condition.

7 Because of the .... of her condition, the patient was kept in the hospital.

noun	noun	verb	adjective
indication	indicator	indicate	indicative

8 Forgetfulness may be an .... that a patient is entering the early stages of dementia.

9 Studies .... that exercise helps increase brain power.

10 Memory loss may be .... of a more serious condition.

11 There are several key .... that doctors look for in their diagnoses.

noun	verb	adjective
impairment	impair	impaired

12 Multiple sclerosis patients suffer many physical ....

13 Aging can .... short-term memory.

14 .... memory can be improved by regular exercise.

noun	noun	adjective	adverb
mood	moodiness	moody	moodily

15 The patient replied .... when asked if he was feeling much pain.

16 A person who suffers from .... may be helped by regular exercise.

17 People are often in a good .... after exercising.

18 If you are feeling ...., get some exercise.

Word Families

B

Choose the correct word family member from the list below to complete each blank.

1 mood	moodiness	moody
2 indication	indicate	indicative
3 diagnosis	diagnose	diagnostic
4 gravity	grave	gravely
5 impairment	impair	impaired

If you are suffering from a bad **1**.......... that won't go away, it is important to see a doctor. Mild depression may be a temporary response to the normal stresses of life, but ongoing depression could **2**.......... a more serious condition. The doctor will ask you a series of questions and may recommend some tests to come up with a **3**.......... . If your condition is **4**.........., the doctor may give you medication. If, on the other hand, you are not suffering any serious disorder or **5**.........., the doctor may recommend something as simple as regular exercise.

Paraphrases

Read the sentence from the reading passage. Then, choose the sentence that has the same meaning.

1 *Using rodent models, researchers found increased concentrations of BDNF in the hippocampus, an area of the brain involved in learning and memory and associated with dementia, after only one week of regular exercise.* (paragraph 2)

A Research with mice and rats showed that exercise raised levels of BDNF in a certain area of the brain.
B Researchers found that after exercise, mice and rats had increased intelligence.
C Mice and rats with higher levels of BDNF were able to learn exercise routines more quickly.

2 *Regular exercise can help stave off some effects of normal aging and delay or diminish the gravity of conditions such as Alzheimer's disease, depression, and multiple sclerosis.* (paragraph 3)

A The ability to exercise regularly is affected by age and by certain serious conditions.

B The effects of exercise are less in the elderly and in those who suffer from certain conditions.

C Exercise may delay conditions of aging and the seriousness of certain medical disorders.

Dictionary Skill

DIFFERENT MEANINGS

Many words have more than one meaning.

Read the definitions below. Then read the sentences and write the letter of the correct definition for each sentence.

QUESTIONS 1–2

gra-vi-ty [GRA-vuh-tee]
A *noun.* seriousness
B *noun.* the force that holds objects on the Earth

.... **1** *Gravity* makes it easier to walk downhill than uphill.

.... **2** Because of the *gravity* of his injury, the doctor told him not to exercise for several months.

QUESTIONS 3–4

dis-or-der [dis-OR-der]
A *noun.* a disease or illness
B *noun.* confusion; lack of order

.... **3** The doctor's office was in such *disorder* that she couldn't find the test results.

.... **4** Depression is a serious *disorder*, but there are ways to treat it.

Listening

Track 14

*Listen to the conversation. Complete the form below. Write **NO MORE THAN ONE WORD** for each answer.*

Hospital Fitness Center[1]

New Patient Information

Patient Name: *Amanda* **1**..........

Interests: **2** .... *exercise classes*

Level: *beginner, but previously took* **3**.......... *classes*

Referral? *Yes, recommended by doctor in order to improve* **4**.......... *and stave off* **5** .... *gain.*

[1]BrE: Centre

Unit 5

Writing
(Task 1)

The charts[1] below show changes in mental capacity in patients who have been given a diagnosis of mild cognitive impairment, a condition that can develop into Alzheimer's disease or other types of dementia.

Summarize[2] the information by selecting and reporting the main information and making comparisons.

Write at least 150 words.

Group A (followed a program of 1 hour of aerobic exercise daily for 6 months)

Memory	Thinking Speed	Word Fluency
=	+	+

Group B (followed a program of 1 hour of nonaerobic [stretching and balancing] exercise daily for 6 months)

Memory	Thinking Speed	Word Fluency
–	–	–

Key:
– .... deteriorated
= .... no change
+ .... improved

---

[1]BrE: tables
[2]BrE: summarise

Speaking

Talk about the following topics.

Do you find that exercise improves your mood? What other things do you do to feel better when you are in a bad mood?

Now that researchers have found links between exercise and improved brain capacity, do you think exercising will become more popular? Why or why not?

What can be done to stimulate people to exercise more?

HOW DRUGS ARE STUDIED

Words

Write the letter of each definition with the word it defines. If you don't know the definition, use the context of the reading passage to help you. Look for the words in bold as you read the passage.

PARAGRAPHS 1–2

Words	Definitions
1 .... theoretical **2** .... investigation **3** .... fraction **4** .... target	**A** n., a small part **B** v., to focus on **C** n., a study **D** adj., abstract; based on theory

PARAGRAPH 2

Words	Definitions
5 .... manufacture **6** .... culture **7** .... desirable **8** .... enhance **9** .... outcome	**E** v., to improve **F** v., to produce **G** n., result **H** n., organic materials grown in a laboratory setting **I** adj., wanted; worth having

PARAGRAPHS 3–4

Words	Definitions
10 .... absorb **11** .... toxic **12** .... deem **13** .... recur **14** .... chronic	**J** v., to take in **K** adj., long-lasting **L** adj., poisonous **M** v., to believe; judge **N** v., to happen or occur again

PARAGRAPHS 6–8

Words	Definitions
15 .... ascertain	**O** v., to lessen; ease
16 .... combat	**P** v., to determine; find out
17 .... monitor	**Q** v., to watch; observe
18 .... interval	**R** n., the period between two times or events
19 .... alleviate	**S** n., material
20 .... substance	**T** v., to fight against

Reading

How Drugs Are Studied

A

It takes years, and sometimes decades, for a drug to move from the **theoretical** stage to the pharmacy shelf. Of the thousands of drugs under **investigation** at any one time, only a small **fraction** will produce the desired result without unacceptable side effects.

B

First, scientists **target** a step in the disease process where they believe a drug can have an effect. Then they **manufacture** compounds or take them from organisms such as viruses and fungi and test them in laboratory **cultures**. Once scientists isolate a chemical that produces a **desired** effect, they analyze[1] its structure and alter it as necessary to **enhance** the **outcome**.

C

The next step involves testing the drug on animals. Scientists look at how much of the drug is **absorbed** into the bloodstream, how it spreads to different organs, how quickly it is excreted, or leaves the body, and whether it has any **toxic** by-products. Researchers usually test at least two animal species because the same drug may affect species differently.

[1]BrE: analyse

Unit 5

D

If a chemical passes laboratory and animal testing and is **deemed** appropriate to analyze in human volunteers, it is ready for clinical trials. Researchers follow a protocol that describes who may participate in the study, tests and procedures to follow, the length of the study, and outcomes to be measured. Drug trials may focus on treating a disease, preventing a disease from occurring or **recurring**, or enhancing the quality of life for people living with incurable, **chronic** conditions.

E

There are four phases of clinical trials; the first three phases study whether the drug is effective and can be safely administered to patients, and the fourth phase evaluates long-term safety and use once a drug is on the market.

F

Phase I clinical trials test a drug in small groups of healthy volunteers (fewer than 100) to **ascertain** its safety and the appropriate dose range. These studies last for six months to one year.

G

Phase II clinical trials test several hundred volunteers to determine how effectively the drug **combats** the disease being studied. These trials continue to evaluate safety, side effects, and optimal dose. Phase II studies also last for six months to one year.

H

Phase III trials test thousands of volunteers for several years, with researchers closely **monitoring** study participants at regular **intervals**. These studies typically compare the drug under investigation with a control: either a drug known to cure or **alleviate** a specific disease or, if one does not exist, a **substance** that has no medicinal effects, known as a placebo. Phase III trials are typically blind studies (participants do not know which drug they are receiving) or double-blind studies (neither participants nor researchers know which drug an individual is receiving until the trial is completed).

I

Once a drug passes the first three phases and is found to be safe and effective, drug companies may apply for the right to market the product. After a drug is approved and on the market, Phase IV trials may investigate longer-term effects, effects in different groups of patients such as the elderly, or use of the medication for a different condition such as using a cancer drug to treat AIDS.

Answer the questions about **How Drugs Are Studied**.

Questions 1–4

The reading passage contains nine paragraphs, ***A–I***.

Which paragraph discusses the following information?
Write the correct letter, ***A–I***.

.... **1** Drug tests that involve growing biological material in a laboratory

.... **2** Investigations of the effects of drugs on animals

.... **3** Studies to determine how safe a drug is and how much a patient should take

.... **4** Studies to monitor how well a drug fights a disease

Questions 5–7

Choose the correct letter, ***A***, ***B***, ***C***, *or* ***D***.

5 Drug tests on animals look at
A how the drug is absorbed by the body.
B how effective the drug is for chronic conditions.
C how well the drug prevents a disease from recurring.
D how quickly the drug alleviates the disease.

6 During Phase II clinical trials, study participants are monitored for
A chronic conditions.
B toxic doses.
C speed of cure.
D possible side effects.

7 After a drug is deemed safe and effective, a drug company may do further tests to ascertain
A the best way to market it.
B possible effects over time.
C how it compares with other drugs.
D the best group of people to use it.

Word Families

A

Complete each sentence with the correct word from the word family chart. Make nouns plural where necessary. Use the correct form of verbs.

noun	verb	adjective
absorption	absorb	absorbent

1 Cotton makes a good cleaning material because it is so ....

2 As part of their research, scientists look at the .... of a drug into the bloodstream.

3 The body .... some drugs very quickly.

noun	verb	adjective
desire	desire	desired

4 Even when a certain treatment is generally successful, it may not produce the .... outcome in all patients.

5 The .... to help others attracts many people to medical professions.

6 Patients .... drugs that will treat their conditions effectively.

noun	noun	verb	adjective
investigation	investigator	investigate	investigative

7 An .... report showed the drug to be ineffective in fighting the disease.

8 Researchers may .... several possible uses of a new drug.

9 The .... of a potential new drug costs a great deal of money and takes a long time.

10 The .... submitted a report about the crime.

noun	verb	adjective	adverb
theory	theorize	theoretical	theoretically

11 Scientists .... that a substance will have a certain medical effect, and then they set up a research study.

12 It was a good idea ...., so they decided to test it.

13 Ideas are .... before they are tested.

14 The scientists set up the study in order to test the ....

noun	noun	adjective	adverb
toxin	toxicity	toxic	toxically

15 Potential drug .... is a part of every study.

16 Part of drug research involves testing for .... effects.

17 If one drug reacts .... with another, you cannot take them both together.

18 Some substances can release .... into the blood.

Word Families

B

Choose the correct word family member from the list below to complete each blank.

1 investigation	investigator	investigate
2 theory	theorize	theoretical
3 absorption	absorb	absorbent
4 toxins	toxic	toxically
5 desires	desire	desirably

A good deal of time, effort, and money is required to thoroughly **1**.......... a new drug before it can be put on the market. Scientists develop a **2**.......... about the ability of a certain substance to combat a specific disease or medical condition. Then they have to test their idea. After manufacturing the drug in the laboratory, they test it first on animals and then on people. They monitor the **3**.......... of the drug by the body, and they look for any **4**.......... that may be produced as the drug moves through the body. Then they test the drug's ability to combat the disease. If they get the outcome that they **5**.......... and the drug cures the disease or alleviates the condition, then it's time to work on marketing the product.

Paraphrases

Read the sentence from the reading passage. Then, choose the sentence that has the same meaning.

1 *Of the thousands of drugs under investigation at any one time, only a small fraction will produce the desired result without unacceptable side effects.* (paragraph 1)

A Many drugs are studied, but only a few are found to be useable.
B It may be hard to choose the right drug among the many that are available.
C Although drugs are helpful to most people, a small number of people get no effects from them.

2 *Scientists look at how much of the drug is absorbed into the bloodstream, how it spreads to different organs, how quickly it is excreted or leaves the body, and whether it has any toxic by-products.* (paragraph 3)

A Scientists try to find out which parts of the body are most affected by a drug.
B Researchers want to know how much of a drug is needed to treat a specific condition without causing side effects.
C Researchers study how a drug moves through the body, and whether it is poisonous in any way.

Dictionary Skill

DIFFERENT MEANINGS

Many words have more than one meaning.

Read the definitions below. Then read the sentences and write the letter of the correct definition for each sentence.

cul-ture [KUL-cher]
A *noun.* organic materials grown in a laboratory setting
B *noun.* a shared system of beliefs, customs, and language
C *noun.* the arts

.... **1** It is always interesting to learn about the *culture* of another country.

.... **2** A clinic might use a *culture* from the patient to diagnose a disease.

.... **3** Because of their museums, theaters, and libraries, cities have a lot more to offer in terms of *culture* than small towns do.

Listening

Track 15

*Listen to the conversation. Complete the notes below. Write **NO MORE THAN ONE WORD** for each answer.*

Laboratory Research Project

Steps to follow:

- Grow **1** .... in the laboratory.
- Introduce different substances.
- **2**............ at regular intervals.
- **3**............ if there are changes.
- Describe the **4**............ in the final report.

Writing (Task 2)

Modern medical science has made it possible to combat many diseases. This is one reason that people are living longer lives now than they did in the past. Discuss the effects this might have on society.

Support your answer with reasons and examples from your own knowledge or experience.

Write at least 250 words.

Speaking

Talk about the following topics.

A lot of money is spent on investigating drugs. Do you think it is desirable to spend so much money on developing new drugs, or should more money be spent on other areas of health care?

What do you think are some of the most important health issues to target?

What do you think is the best way to combat common but potentially dangerous diseases such as influenza?

Unit 6: Tourism

HIKING THE INCA TRAIL

Words

Write the letter of each definition with the word it defines. If you don't know the definition, use the context of the reading passage to help you. Look for the words in bold as you read the passage.

PARAGRAPH 1

Words	Definitions
1 .... imagination	**A** adj., related to traditional or formal practices
2 .... archeologist[1]	**B** v., to build
3 .... native	**C** adj., original to a place
4 .... site	**D** n., place
5 .... ceremonial	**E** adv., exactly
6 .... construct	**F** n., the ability to think creatively or form pictures in the mind
7 .... precisely	**G** n., a person who studies ancient cultures

PARAGRAPHS 2–3

Words	Definitions
8 .... spectacular	**H** n., a wonderful thing
9 .... mystery	**I** v., to attract; pull
10 .... draw	**J** adj., daring; willing to try new or dangerous activities
11 .... adventurous	**K** n., a system of various parts that work together
12 .... network	**L** adj., wonderful to see
13 .... marvel	**M** n., something strange, unknown, or difficult to understand

[1]BrE: archaeologist

PARAGRAPH 4

Words	Definitions
14 .... institute	N n., something expensive and desirable but unnecessary
15 .... restriction	O adj., reachable; easy to get
16 .... preserve	P n., advantage; good part
17 .... pertain	Q n., an official limit on something
18 .... luxury	R v., to start; put in place
19 .... accessible	S v., to protect; save
20 .... upside	T v., be related to something

Reading

Hiking the Inca Trail

(1) Sitting high in the Andes Mountains in Peru, the ancient ruins of Machu Picchu have captured the **imaginations** of travelers[1] ever since they were rediscovered by **archeologist** Hiram Bingham in 1911. The name Machu Picchu means "old peak" in the **native** Incan language, and the **site** had probably been considered a sacred place since long before the ancient Incas arrived there. The Incas built a **ceremonial** city on the site that included palaces, temples, storage rooms, baths, and houses, all **constructed** from heavy blocks of granite fitted **precisely** together. Although little is known about the activities that took place in the ancient city, it appears that one of its functions was as an astronomical observatory. The so-called Intihuatana stone, located at the site, was used to mark the autumn and spring equinoxes as well as other astronomical events.

(2) The **spectacular** natural setting, the wonders of architectural and engineering skills embodied in the well-preserved buildings, and the **mysteries** of the ancient culture **draw** thousands of tourists from around the world every year. The nearest city is Cuzco, about thirty miles away. From there, tourists can take trains and buses to the ruins. A popular route for the more **adventurous** is to hike along the Inca Trail. The ancient Inca created a **network** of trails throughout the mountains, some of which are still in existence. The Inca Trail to Machu Picchu, used by hikers today, was likely considered a sacred route in its time, used by travelers making pilgrimages to that ceremonial site.

[1]BrE: travellers

(3) While the Inca Trail leads to the wonders of Machu Picchu, it offers many **marvels** of its own. Hikers are treated to magnificent views of glacier-covered peaks above and tropical valleys below in their journey over high mountain passes. Many species of orchids can be seen, as well as all kinds of birds, from tiny hummingbirds to the splendid Andean condor. The Inca Trail also passes by ruins of other ceremonial sites on the way to the grand destination of Machu Picchu.

(4) Tourists have been hiking the Inca Trail since the early part of the twentieth century, and for much of that time there were no regulations. Hikers could travel when they pleased and camp wherever they chose. However, the trip has become so popular that in 2005, the Peruvian government **instituted** a set of **restrictions** on the use of the trail. To protect the natural environment and **preserve** the ruins, no more than 500 people a day are allowed to enter the trail. Because each group that sets out includes guides and porters, the number of tourists entering the trail each day is probably closer to 200. In addition, both tour companies and individual guides must be licensed. There are also legal requirements that **pertain** to the minimum wage that porters must be paid as well as the maximum weight load they can be required to carry. Fees for trail use help pay for upkeep of the trail and the ruins. All these regulations and fees combine for a more expensive trip, and this has made it a **luxury accessible** to fewer people. The **upside** is that the environment and the workers are protected.

Answer the questions about **Hiking the Inca Trail**.

Questions 1–9

Complete the summary below.
Choose **NO MORE THAN ONE WORD** *from the text for each answer.*

Machu Picchu is an ancient **1**.......... city in the Andes Mountains of Peru. It was rediscovered by an **2**.......... in 1911. It is not precisely clear how the ancient Inca used the site, but experts believe that at least some of its **3**.......... pertained to astronomy. The wonders of Machu Picchu **4**.......... visitors from all around the world. Many visitors like to reach the site by hiking the Inca Trail, part of a **5**.......... of trails originally made by the ancient Inca. This is a trip for **6**.......... people. Along the way, hikers can enjoy many **7**.......... such as spectacular views and interesting flowers and birds. Because such large numbers of people use the Inca Trail, the Peruvian government has had to take steps to **8**.......... the ruins and the environment. It has instituted a number of restrictions as well as fees. Because of this, hiking the trail has become an expensive **9**.......... that many people cannot afford.

Word Families

A

Complete each sentence with the correct word from the word family chart. Make nouns plural where necessary. Use the correct form of verbs.

noun	noun	verb	adjective	adjective
access	accessibility	access	accessible	inaccessible

1 Machu Picchu is .... by plane, train, or hiking.

2 Machu Picchu was .... to most people before they built the train from Cuzco.

3 Nowadays, fewer people can .... the site because the trip has become so expensive.

4 The train from Cuzco increases .... to Machu Picchu.

5 The Inca Trail provides one way to gain .... to Machu Picchu.

noun	noun	adjective	adverb
adventure	adventurer	adventurous	adventurously

6 Our trip to Machu Picchu was a great ....

7 .... people enjoy hiking in the Andes Mountains.

8 We felt like modern-day .... as we hiked the Inca Trail.

9 We hiked .... over tall peaks and steep cliffs.

noun	noun	adjective
archeologist	archeology	archeological

10 The field of .... has taught us a great deal about the ancient world.

11 Machu Picchu is one of the most visited .... sites in the world.

12 An .... is interested in ancient cultures.

noun	verb	adjective	adjective
luxury	luxuriate	luxurious	luxuriously

13 A simple bed felt .... after a week-long hiking trip.

14 After we returned from a week of hiking in the mountains, we .... in the comfort of our beds.

15 We dined .... on champagne and chocolate.

16 Hiring porters to carry your equipment on a hiking trip is quite a ....

noun	verb	adjective
restriction	restrict	restrictive

17 .... are necessary to preserve the environment.

18 The government .... large numbers of people from entering the area.

19 The rules may seem ...., but they are meant to protect the area.

noun	adjective	adverb
precision	precise	precisely

20 Archeologists have many theories but few .... ideas about the ceremonial functions of Machu Picchu.

21 We arrived at the site at .... five o'clock.

22 The blocks were fitted together with great ....

Word Families

B

Choose the correct word family member from the list below to complete each blank.

1 access	accesses	accessible
2 restrictions	restricted	restrictive
3 luxury	luxurious	luxuriously
4 archeology	archeologist	archeological
5 precision	precise	precisely
6 adventure	adventurer	adventurous

Hiking the Inca trail is a popular way to **1**.......... Machu Picchu. However, the Peruvian government has **2**.......... use of the trail, so not everyone is able to make the trip. The upside is that hiking is not the only way to get there, and because it is not a particularly **3**.......... way to travel, other methods might be preferable. You can get to the

4.......... site by train and bus, and they will get you there much faster than hiking. When you arrive in Cuzco, you can check the schedules. You may not be able to leave at **5**.......... the time you wish, but you should be able to work out a schedule that is convenient. Whatever method you choose to get there, a trip to Machu Picchu is always a great **6**........... .

Paraphrases

Read the sentence from the reading passage. Then, choose the sentence that has the same meaning.

1 *The spectacular natural setting, the wonders of architectural and engineering skills embodied in the well-preserved buildings, and the mysteries of the ancient culture draw thousands of tourists from around the world every year.* (paragraph 2)

A The number of people who visit Machu Picchu is amazing.
B The beauties of Machu Picchu attract visitors from all over the world.
C Most people who visit Machu Picchu think it is wonderful.

2 *However, the trip has become so popular that in 2005, the Peruvian government instituted a set of restrictions on the use of the trail.* (paragraph 4)

A In 2005, the government started counting the number of people using the trail.
B The government reports that since 2005, fewer people have been using the trail.
C In 2005, the government created limits because so many people were using the trail.

Dictionary Skill

DIFFERENT MEANINGS

Many words have more than one meaning.

Read the definitions below. Then read the sentences and write the letter of the correct definition for each sentence.

QUESTIONS 1–2

in-sti-tute [IN-sti-toot]
A *verb.* to start, put in place
B *noun.* a type of organization

.... **1** The government founded an *institute* of archeology to promote the study of ancient cultures.

.... **2** The school plans to *institute* a summer program for students who are interested in archeology.

QUESTIONS 3–4

draw [DRAW]
A *verb.* to attract, pull
B *verb.* to make a picture using pencils or crayons

.... **3** People like to *draw* the beautiful mountain scenery they see around Machu Picchu.

.... **4** The interesting birds and flowers *draw* many people to the mountains around Machu Picchu.

Listening

Track 16

Listen to the talk.
Complete the information about the archeological site.
Write ***NO MORE THAN ONE WORD*** *for each answer.*

Information for Visitors

Restrictions:
Stay on the **1**.......... of paths.
2.......... the buildings between 10:00 A.M. and 4:00 P.M. only.
Enter the **3**.......... area only with a guide.

Entry Fees:

Adults:	$15
Children:	$10

4.......... crafts are available for sale in the gift shop.

Writing (Task 2)

Large numbers of visitors can endanger ancient archeological sites such as Machu Picchu. In your opinion, is it more important to try to preserve such sites or to allow public access to them?

Support your opinion with reasons and examples from your own knowledge or experience.

Write at least 250 words.

Speaking

Talk about the following topics.

What kinds of adventures are attractive to you?

What kinds of luxuries do you enjoy?

Is it important to you to have luxuries? Why or why not?

WHAT IS ECOTOURISM?

Words

Write the letter of each definition with the word it defines. If you don't know the definition, use the context of the reading passage to help you. Look for the words in bold as you read the passage.

PARAGRAPH 1

Words	Definitions
1 .... concept	**A** v., to hurt
2 .... publicity	**B** v., to work very hard to do something
3 .... practice[1]	**C** n., activity that makes something known to the public
4 .... injure	**D** n., idea
5 .... strive	**E** v., to prevent from happening; stay away from
6 .... avoid	**F** n., a custom; method

PARAGRAPH 2

Words	Definitions
7 .... category	**G** v., to work for no pay; freely offer to do something
8 .... destination	**H** n., natural region away from towns and cities
9 .... volunteer	**I** n., the place somebody or something is going to
10 .... wilderness	**J** n., a group of things that have something in common

[1]BrE: practice *n.*, practise *v.*

PARAGRAPHS 3–4

Words	Definitions
11 .... accommodations[1]	**K** n., guilty party; origin of a problem
12 .... recycling	**L** n., a place to stay such as a hotel
13 .... barrier	**M** n., something that blocks or separates
14 .... culprit	**N** v., collection and treatment of trash for reuse

PARAGRAPHS 4–5

Words	Definitions
15 .... dump	**O** v., to get rid of garbage and trash[2]
16 .... delicate	**P** adj., not completely trusting
17 .... pleasure	**Q** adj., easily hurt or broken
18 .... remote	**R** n., enjoyment
19 .... wary	**S** n., rule; basic idea behind a system
20 .... principle	**T** adj., far away

[1]BrE: accomodations

[2]BrE: rubbish

Reading

What Is Ecotourism?

(1) The **concept** of ecotourism has been gaining **publicity** over the past couple of decades. It arose out of the "green movement"—a growing interest in developing **practices** in all aspects of daily life that preserve rather than **injure** the natural environment. Ecotourists **strive** to have minimal impact on the places they visit, in terms of both the local ecology and the local culture. Some followers take the concept even further and define ecotourism as travel that aims not only to **avoid** harming the environment, but also to make a positive contribution to the local ecology and culture.

(2) The types of vacations[1] that fit into the **category** of ecotourism vary widely. Ecotourism might involve travel to a natural **destination** such as a national park or a nature preserve to learn about the natural environment and, in some cases, to **volunteer** on environmental protection projects. It could be a few weeks spent with local artisans learning how to do a traditional craft. Trips that involve hiking or rafting through **wilderness** areas with no regard for the natural habitats one passes through would not be included in the definition of ecotourism. Neither, of course, would be trips with a focus on hunting.

(3) Ecotourists seek out **accommodations** that follow environmentally friendly practices such as using renewable resources and **recycling**. Ecotourists look for hotels and tour companies that hire mainly local staff, keeping tourist dollars within the local economy. Ecotourists might choose to join a bicycling or walking tour rather than a bus tour that adds to air pollution and allows tourists to see the local area only through a **barrier** of glass windows.

(4) Ecotourists usually avoid cruise ships, because these are among the biggest **culprits** in the tourism industry in terms of environmental pollution. Massive cruise ships release large quantities of harmful emissions into the air as well as pollute the waters they sail through with fuel from their engines. The huge numbers of passengers on these ships generate many tons of garbage and wastewater, which is often **dumped** into the sea. Cruise ships also cause damage to coral reefs and other **delicate** ecosystems that they travel near. Perhaps in part because of the growing interest in ecotourism, some cruise companies are now making an effort to be more environmentally friendly. These efforts include recycling wastes and using fuel more efficiently. Vacationers who are interested in ecotourism and still get **pleasure** from cruises can travel with cruise companies that follow these practices.

---

[1]BrE: holidays

(5) Because of the growing interest in ecotourism, many companies advertise themselves as ecotourism companies, especially those that offer trips to **remote**, natural areas, the type of destination that ecotourists favor[2]. Travelers need to be **wary** and do their research carefully. Not all of these companies follow the **principles** of ecotourism. Some are simply trying to take advantage of the current interest in this type of travel. The positive side of this, however, is that it may actually be an indication that the movement is gaining in popularity.

Answer the questions about **What Is Ecotourism?**

Questions 1–7

Do the following statements agree with the information in the reading passage?

Write

TRUE *if the statement agrees with the information.*
FALSE *if the statement contradicts the information.*
NOT GIVEN *if there is no information on this in the passage.*

.... **1** Ecotourism refers only to trips made to remote wilderness destinations.

.... **2** Ecotourists are interested in preserving delicate natural areas.

.... **3** Ecotourists prefer less expensive accommodations.

.... **4** Ecotourists strive to support the local economy where they travel.

.... **5** Many large cruise ships injure the environment by dumping garbage into the sea.

.... **6** Hunting trips can be included in the category of ecotourism.

.... **7** An ecotourism trip might include volunteering to work on local projects.

.... **8** Some cruise companies are changing their practices to become more environmentally friendly.

.... **9** Cruise ships do not recycle paper and plastic because it is too expensive.

---

[2]BrE: favour

Word Families

A

Complete each sentence with the correct word from the word family chart. Make nouns plural where necessary. Use the correct form of verbs.

noun	verb	adjective
accommodations	accommodate	accommodating

1 The .... on our trip were very comfortable.

2 We found our hosts very ....

3 It's a small hotel that can only.......... about 50 guests.

noun	verb	adjective
avoidance	avoid	avoidable

4 We can .... damaging the environment if we are careful to follow certain practices.

5 Following certain environmentally friendly practices makes damage to the environment ....

6 .... of environmental damage is an important part of ecotourism.

noun	verb	adjective	adverb
concept	conceive	conceptual	conceptually

7 It is not hard to .... of ways to protect the environment.

8 Ecotourism differs .... from regular tourism.

9 Ecotourism is a .... that is growing in popularity.

10 Ecotourism has gone beyond the .... stage to become something that many people have put into practice.

noun	verb	adjective
injury	injure	injurious

11 Some practices, such as anchoring large cruise ships close to coral reefs, are .... to the environment.

12 Ecotourists try not to .... the environment.

13 Large cruise ships cause several types of .... to the environment.

noun	verb	adjective	adverb
publicity	publicize[1]	public	publicly

14 Many companies .... themselves as ecotourism companies, but not all of them follow ecotourism principles.

15 The need to protect the environment is being discussed ....

16 The more .... ecotourism gets, the more people will become interested in this type of travel.

17 Tour companies make their services .... through advertisements on the Internet and in magazines.

noun	noun	adjective	adverb
wild	wilderness	wild	wildly

18 Many tourists enjoy photographing animals in the ....

19 Some tours travel to destinations where .... animals can be observed.

20 Many people enjoy spending time in the ....

21 The tiger growled .... in its cage.

[1]BrE: publicise

Word Families

B

Choose the correct word family member from the list below to complete each blank.

1 avoidance	avoid	avoidable
2 concept	conceive	conceptual
3 accommodations	accommodate	accommodates
4 wilderness	wildly	wild
5 injury	injure	injurious
6 publicity	publicize	public

Ecotourism companies operate on the principle that **1**.......... of harm to the environment is not only possible but also an important part of pleasure trips. The basic **2**.......... of ecotourism is to respect the places you visit, in terms of both the culture and the natural environment. Ecotourism companies offer a wide range of tours. Some include stays in luxury hotels, whereas others take travelers to remote destinations where only the simplest **3**.......... are available. On some trips, travelers learn about the **4**.......... plants and animals that live in the area. On others, they learn about the local traditions. On all trips, travelers are careful not to cause any type of **5**.......... to the environment. Where environmental harm is concerned, they don't want to be among the culprits. If you are interested in ecotourism, it's easy to find out about trips being offered. Ecotourism companies **6**.......... their trips in travel magazines and on travel websites.

Paraphrases

Read the sentence from the reading passage. Then, choose the sentence that has the same meaning.

1 *Ecotourists seek out accommodations that follow environmentally friendly practices such as using renewable resources and recycling.* (paragraph 3)

A When traveling, ecotourists make sure to always recycle their trash.

B Ecotourists prefer hotels that are careful not to harm the environment.

C Ecotourists often return to the same place year after year.

2 *The huge numbers of passengers on these ships generate many tons of garbage and wastewater, which is often dumped into the sea.* (paragraph 4)

A Cruise ships throw large amounts of waste into the sea.

B Large cruise ships create much more waste than other ships.

C Often, cruise ship passengers don't know where to put their garbage.

Dictionary Skill

PARTS OF SPEECH

Volunteer can be a noun, a verb, or an adjective.

Read the dictionary definitions below. Then read the sentences and write the letter of the correct definition for each sentence.

vol-un-teer [vol-un-TEER]

A *noun.* a person who offers to do work for no pay; a person who freely offers a service

B *verb.* to work for no pay; freely offer to do something

C *adjective.* done by volunteers

.... **1** Many environmental protection projects depend on *volunteer* work.

.... **2** A *volunteer* not only provides a service but also has the opportunity to gain valuable experience.

.... **3** Many people *volunteer* to spend their vacation time helping out on environmental protection projects.

Listening

Track 17

*Listen to the conversation. Complete the form below. Write **NO MORE THAN ONE WORD** for each answer.*

Excellent Eco Tours

Customer Name: *Bob Henderson*
Trip: **1**........ *Adventure*
Dates **2**.......... *12–25*
Type of **3**.......... : *campground*
How did customer hear about us?
Saw our **4**......... *in a travel magazine*

Writing (Task 1)

The charts[1] below show information about environmentally friendly practices followed by three different cruise ship companies in two different years. **Summarize[2] the information by selecting and reporting the main information and making comparisons.**

Write at least 150 words.

[1]BrE: tables
[2]BrE: summarise

Year: 2000

	Sun Cruises	Sea Adventure	Water World Tours
Recycles at least 75% of waste	Yes	No	Yes
Has system to reduce air pollution	No	No	No
Avoids dumping waste water into the sea	Yes	No	Yes
Avoids destinations with delicate underwater ecosystems	No	No	No

Year: 2010

	Sun Cruises	Sea Adventure	Water World Tours
Recycles at least 75% of waste	Yes	Yes	Yes
Has system to reduce air pollution	Yes	No	Yes
Avoids dumping waste water into the sea	Yes	Yes	Yes
Avoids destinations with delicate underwater ecosystems	Yes	No	Yes

Speaking

Talk about the following topics.

When you travel, do you enjoy going to wilderness destinations, or do you prefer visiting cities or some other kind of place?

What kinds of places do you avoid visiting when you travel?

What kinds of accommodations do you like? Is luxury important to you when choosing accommodations?

LEARNING VACATIONS

Words

Write the letter of each definition with the word it defines. If you don't know the definition, use the context of the reading passage to help you. Look for the words in bold as you read the passage.

PARAGRAPHS 1–4

Words	Definitions
1 .... ongoing **2** .... survey **3** .... endeavor[1] **4** .... sponsor	**A** n., activity with a specific purpose; effort **B** n., a study of opinions in a sample of the population **C** adj., continuing **D** v., to organize and be responsible for

PARAGRAPH 4

Words	Definitions
5 .... hone **6** .... supervision **7** .... breeze **8** .... colorful[2] **9** .... cuisine **10** .... ingredient **11** .... acquire **12** .... enroll **13** .... residential **14** .... content	**E** n., style of cooking **F** n., direction, assistance **G** adj., interesting and unusual **H** n., light wind **I** v., to sharpen, improve **J** v., to learn something or get something **K** n., subject matter **L** adj., with living accommodations, related to housing **M** v., to sign up for a class **N** n., an item in a recipe

[1]BrE: endeavour
[2]BrE: colourful

PARAGRAPH 5

Words	Definitions
15 .... economical	**O** n., a vacation place
16 .... resort	**P** n., preference
17 .... costly	**Q** adj., inexpensive
18 .... broad	**R** adj., wide or large
19 .... taste	**S** n., a plan for spending money
20 .... budget	**T** adj., expensive

Reading

Learning Vacations

(1) A couple spends a week in Thailand learning to cook in the local style. A group flies to Turkey to join an **ongoing** archeological[1] dig for the summer. A history professor leads a tour of historical sites of Europe.

(2) The participants in these trips are all enjoying a different kind of travel: learning vacations[2]. Rather than spending their vacations relaxing on a beach or taking a bus[3] tour of ten cities in eight days, they have opted to enjoy their time off by learning something new. From attending summer camps for adults to studying botany in the rain forest, people everywhere are experiencing the value of a vacation with a purpose. According to **surveys**, close to one-third of travelers[4] each year choose learning programs over other types of vacations, and their numbers are growing.

(3) In the past, these types of vacations were generally considered to be for young people still in school. A student of French might spend the summer studying that language in Paris. A marine biology major could learn to scuba dive and spend a few months at sea assisting researchers. Now, it has become common for adults, too, to spend their vacation time in educational **endeavors**, and various types of travel programs[5] have grown up around this interest.

---

[1]BrE: archaeological
[2]BrE: holidays
[3]BrE: coach
[4]BrE: travellers
[5]BrE: programmes

(4) Art schools and writing programs **sponsor** trips to interesting parts of the world. Trip participants **hone** their creative skills under the **supervision** of professional artists and writers while at the same time enjoying, for example, the warm **breezes** of the Caribbean islands or the **colorful** villages of Spain. Cooking is a popular hobby, and tour companies have developed trips that focus on the **cuisine** of different regions of the world. Travelers may learn all about how traditional meals are prepared and what **ingredients** are used. Or, for those who want to improve their abilities in the kitchen, they may actually receive hands-on lessons, **acquiring** new skills that they can take home with them. Travelers to Britain can **enroll** in courses at any of the twenty-plus adult **residential** colleges around the country. The courses at these schools generally last just a few days and range in **content** from activities such as photography and dancing to more serious subjects such as history, philosophy, and literature.

(5) These are just a few examples of the many types of learning vacations that people enjoy every year. In addition to gaining knowledge and skills, another advantage of these types of vacations is that they can be more **economical** than traditional vacations. Camping out near an archeological site or sleeping in a college dormitory or youth hostel certainly costs less than staying at a luxury hotel or vacation **resort**. And the fact that many of these trips can be organized[6] by the travelers themselves without the services of a tour company or travel agency makes them even more economical. Of course, it all depends on the type of trip one chooses, and some companies offer learning vacations to exotic locales with expert professionals that are quite **costly**. With the **broad** range of possibilities available, there are options to suit all **tastes** and **budgets**.

Answer the questions about **Learning Vacations**.

Questions 1–3

Which of the following types of learning vacations are mentioned in the passage? Choose **three** *answers from the list below.*

A Honing cooking skills

B Working on artistic endeavors

C Enrolling in an archeology course

[6] BrE: organised

D Studying the Spanish language

E Taking classes at a residential college

F Acquiring knowledge about Thailand's history

Questions 4–7

Do the following statements agree with the information in the reading passage?

Write

TRUE *if the statement agrees with the information.*
FALSE *if the statement contradicts the information.*
NOT GIVEN *if there is no information on this in the passage.*

.... **4** Most participants in learning vacations are young people.

.... **5** Surveys show that around 30 percent of travelers take learning vacations.

.... **6** It is common for colleges to sponsor learning vacations.

.... **7** Learning vacations are generally less costly than resort vacations.

Word Families

A

Complete each sentence with the correct word from the word family chart. Make nouns plural where necessary. Use the correct form of verbs.

noun	verb
acquisition	acquire

1 It's fun to .... new skills while on vacation.

2 The .... of new skills is just one of the goals of learning vacations.

noun	verb	adjective
cost	cost	costly

3 A learning vacation could .... less than another type of vacation.

4 Learning vacations can be .... , but usually they are not.

5 The .... of a learning vacation is often lower than that of other types of vacations.

noun	verb	adjective	adverb
economy	economize[1]	economical	economically

6 Taking a learning vacation can be an .... way to travel.

7 People can .... by avoiding resort vacations.

8 By planning ...., you can save money and still have a great vacation.

9 A family that doesn't have a lot of money to spend needs to practice .... when planning a vacation.

noun	noun	verb
enrollment	enrollee	enroll

10 .... have to pay a deposit for the class.

11 If .... is low, they will cancel the class.

12 One way to take a learning vacation is to .... in a class.

noun	noun	verb	adjective
resident	residence	reside	residential

13 .... colleges are popular places for learning vacations.

14 The student .... is simple but comfortable.

---

[1]BrE: economise

15 The local .... are always helpful to visitors.

16 This place is convenient for a learning vacation because you can .... right at the college.

noun	noun	verb	adjective
supervision	supervisor	supervise	supervisory

17 You will always have the .... of an experienced art teacher during the painting trip.

18 The professor will be in a .... role on the trip.

19 Experienced art teachers will .... your work.

20 A professional artist will act as .... of the trip.

Word Families

B

Choose the correct word family member from the list below to complete each blank.

1 acquisition	acquire	acquires
2 cost	costs	costly
3 economy	economize	economical
4 Enrollment	Enroll	Enrolled
5 supervisor	supervision	supervise
6 residence	reside	residential

Many people are interested in the concept of a learning vacation because it is a fun way to **1**.......... skills while traveling. Learning vacations don't necessarily **2**.......... a great deal, so they are a good option for people on a budget. If you would like to travel to colorful[1] parts of the world,

[1]BrE: colourful

taste exotic cuisine, and learn something new at the same time, then a learning vacation might be a good choice for you. If you want to **3**....... , you can plan your vacation on your own. **4**.......... in a short course on a topic of special interest, often under the **5**.......... of a specialist in that subject, is a common way to spend a learning vacation. If the school that offers the course also has a **6**.......... for students, that will make your plans even easier. You don't need the assistance of a professional to organize your vacation. A little research online might provide you with all the information you need.

Paraphrases

Read the sentence from the reading passage. Then, choose the sentence that has the same meaning.

1 *According to surveys, close to one-third of travelers each year choose learning programs over other types of vacations, and their numbers are growing.* (paragraph 2)

A Many travelers have difficulty choosing among the different types of vacations.

B Travelers have an increasing number of vacation types available to them.

C Studies show that there is a growing number of people interested in learning vacations.

2 *Trip participants hone their creative skills under the supervision of professional artists and writers, while at the same time enjoying, for example, the warm breezes of the Caribbean islands or the colorful villages of Spain.* (paragraph 4)

A These travelers improve their artistic skills in beautiful and interesting places.

B These travelers enjoy the work of artists and writers from other countries.

C These travelers assist local artists and writers with their creative projects.

Dictionary Skill

CHANGING STRESS

The meanings of some words change when different syllables are stressed. These words are spelled the same but are pronounced with different stress. Most are also different parts of speech.

Read the definitions below. Then read the sentences and write the letter of the correct definition for each sentence.

con-tent [KON-tent]
A *noun.* subject matter

con-tent [kon-TENT]
B *adjective.* happy

.... **1** The *content* of the article was quite interesting—it was all about learning vacations.

.... **2** We were *content* to spend our vacation painting and enjoying the scenery.

Listening

Track 18

Listen to the conversation. Complete the chart[1] below. Write ***NO MORE THAN ONE WORD*** *for each answer.*

	Accommodations	**3**..........	**4**.......... ends
Painting trip	Beach **1**..........	Springfield University	June 15
Cooking trip	**2**.......... college	National Cooking Institute	July 1

[1]BrE: table

Writing
(Task 1)

The chart[1] below shows information about enrollment in courses at an adult residential college.

Summarize[2] the information by selecting and reporting the main information and making comparisons.

Write at least 150 words.

Barkford Adult Residential College
Enrollment by subject area
(percentage of total students enrolled)

SUMMER 2012		SUMMER 2013	
Art Department		**Art Department**	
Photography	25%	Photography	20%
Painting	40%	Painting	30%
Academic Department		**Academic Department**	
History	20%	History	20%
Philosophy	10%	Philosophy	15%
Science	5%	Science	15%

Speaking

Talk about the following topics.

What are some dishes that are typical of the cuisine of your country or region?

What are some common ingredients in your country or region's cuisine?

How has the cuisine of your country or region changed over the past century? How do you think it will be different in the future?

[1]BrE: table
[2]BrE: summarise

Unit 7: Business

WHAT MAKES A SMALL BUSINESS SUCCESSFUL?

Words

Write the letter of each definition with the word it defines. If you don't know the definition, use the context of the reading passage to help you. Look for the words in bold as you read the passage.

PARAGRAPH 2

Words	Definitions
1 .... particular	**A** v., to do as well as or better than others
2 .... motivation	**B** n., reason for doing something
3 .... characteristic	**C** adj., specific
4 .... niche	**D** n., position or place that is very suitable; specialized market
5 .... compete	**E** n., something that is made
6 .... product	**F** n., feature; quality

PARAGRAPHS 2–3

Words	Definitions
7 .... unique	**G** n., an advantage
8 .... personalized[1]	**H** adj., special; different from all others
9 .... edge	**I** n., the general opinion about something or somebody
10 .... reputation	**J** adj., made or done especially for a certain person

[1]BrE: personalised

Unit 7

PARAGRAPH 4

Words	Definitions
11 .... vital	**K** n., money earned after paying costs
12 .... potential	**L** adj., having enough money to pay what you owe
13 .... sound	**M** adj., very important; necessary for success
14 .... profit	**N** adj., possible
15 .... project	**O** adj., healthy; without financial risk
16 .... afloat	**P** v., to estimate; calculate a future amount

PARAGRAPHS 5–6

Words	Definitions
17 .... financial	**Q** adj., first; beginning
18 .... inevitably	**R** n., a piece of advice
19 .... tip	**S** adj., related to money
20 .... initial	**T** adv., certainly; to be expected

Reading

What Makes a Small Business Successful?

(1) The U.S. Small Business Administration (SBA) defines small businesses as those employing fewer than 500 employees, and many are much smaller than that. In the United States, about a third of small businesses employ fewer than twenty employees. Many thousands of new small businesses are started every year, but few survive. In fact, according to the SBA, one in three fails during the first two years, and only one in two survives beyond five years.

(2) People start small businesses for a variety of reasons, but whatever the **particular motivation**, certain **characteristics** make a small business more likely to succeed. Business advisers point to the importance of finding a **niche**. It is difficult for a small business to **compete** with the array of **products** or services a large business can offer. Instead, the small business that has defined what is

unique about the product or service it provides has a greater chance of success. A small business can offer customers **personalized** service and specialized products or knowledge that can be more difficult to find in a large chain store, for example.

(3) Related to the concept of finding a niche is the importance of maintaining a competitive **edge**. To be successful, a business has to look at what its competitors, whether large or small, are doing and find a way to stay ahead of the game. In addition to offering a specialized product or service, a business that has more efficient production or distribution systems, a better location, or a **reputation** for excellence in customer service can do well in a competitive market.

(4) Research and planning are **vital** steps in setting up a small business. It is essential to determine who the **potential** customers are and the best way to reach them. It is also necessary to develop a **sound** business plan that, among other things, shows how the business will make a **profit** and **projects** the cash flow that will help the business stay **afloat**.

(5) Naturally, a successful small business starts out with proper **financial** support. In addition to the costs of starting the business, there are also the costs of running it until it starts turning a profit. Typically, a small business takes one to two years to become profitable. During that time, there are still expenses that have to be met. Rent has to be paid, employees have to be paid their wages, and supplies have to be bought. If plans have not been made for supporting the costs of the business until it brings in a profit, **inevitably** it will fail.

(6) One important **tip** is to start small. This allows owners the opportunity to learn little by little without making huge costly mistakes. Working alone in one's basement during the **initial** phases of the business, for example, costs a great deal less than renting a space and hiring staff. If the business generates less income than expected or if the market needs to be redefined, the financial losses will be much less if expenses have been kept to a minimum.

(7) About half of private-sector employees in the United States work for small businesses. This number is even greater in other parts of the world. Successful small businesses make important contributions to the economy everywhere.

Unit 7

Answer the questions about **What Makes a Small Business Successful?**

Questions 1–3

Choose the correct letter, ***A, B, C,*** *or* ***D.***

1 How many small businesses fail during their initial two years in business?

A One-half
B One-third
C One-fourth
D One-fifth

2 What kind of edge can a small business have over a large business?

A Better business advisers
B A wider array of products
C Greater motivation to succeed
D More personalized service

3 How long does it usually take a small business to start earning a profit?

A Less than one year
B Between one and two years
C More than two years
D At least five years

Questions 4–7

Complete the summary below.
Choose ***NO MORE THAN ONE WORD*** *from the text for each answer.*

Vital Steps to Starting a Small Business

- Define what makes your product or service **4** .... or different from others in your sector.
- Identify your **5** .... customers.
- Write up a **6** .... business plan.
- Make sure you have the **7** .... support to keep the business running until you earn a profit.

Word Families

A

Complete each sentence with the correct word from the word family chart. Make nouns plural where necessary. Use the correct form of verbs.

noun	noun	verb	adjective	adverb
competition	competitor	compete	competitive	competitively

1 A small business can .... with large businesses by providing a specialized service.

2 Some small businesses are .... positioned to grab a market.

3 There is a lot of .... for the attention of customers.

4 A small business must stay .... in order to succeed.

5 Business owners need to pay attention to what their .... are doing.

noun	adjective	adverb
inevitability	inevitable	inevitably

6 The owner worried whether failure was an ....

7 If a businessman sells an inferior product, it will .... affect his reputation.

8 The failure of a small business is not .... if all the important pieces are in place.

noun	noun	verb	adjective	adverb
initiation	initiator	initiate	initial	initially

9 No one knew who the .... was, but the new approach changed the way companies did business.

10 Many small businesses fail during the .... stages.

11 It is a good idea to keep your business small ....

Unit 7

12 There is a lot of hard work and planning behind the .... of a new business.

13 In addition to good planning, financial support is necessary to .... a business.

noun	**verb**	**adjective**	**adjective**
motivation	motivate	motivated	motivating

14 There are many different situations that .... people to start small businesses.

15 The business owner gave a very .... speech about the importance of having a sound business plan.

16 A strong .... to succeed keeps many small businesses afloat.

17 A .... business owner will find a way to make her business succeed.

noun	**noun**	**noun**	**verb**	**adjective**	**adverb**
production	product	producer	produce	productive	productively

18 The .... of handmade items is very time consuming.

19 He hoped to be .... employed in his field.

20 The success of a small business depends in part on how many customers want the particular .... it sells.

21 Some small businesses also .... the items that they sell.

22 That company is a major .... of electronic equipment.

23 The business owner wants the employees to be ....

noun	**verb**	**adjective**	**adverb**
profit	profit	profitable	profitably

24 It is a good idea to look at what other similar businesses have done so that you can .... from their experience.

25 It usually takes several years for a small business to earn a ....

26 Some businesses never manage to function ....

27 If your business is not ...., you will have to figure out what changes can be made to improve the situation.

Word Families

B

Choose the correct word family member from the list below to complete each blank.

1 initiation	initiate	initial
2 motivation	motivate	motivated
3 competitor	compete	competitive
4 product	produce	productive
5 profit	profitably	profitable
6 inevitable	inevitably	inevitability

Many small businesses fail. You don't want yours to be one of them. How can you make sure your business succeeds? The answer lies in careful thought and planning. Before you **1**.......... your business, think about your reasons for doing so. What is your **2**..........? Being clear about this will help you keep going even when things get difficult. Then, do your research. What similar businesses are in your area? Will you be able to **3**.......... with them? How? Take the time to develop a sound plan. What will your business be about? Will you **4**.......... a unique item or provide a personalized service? Whatever you do, make sure it is different in some way from what other businesses are offering. As you make your plan, remember that it normally takes several years before a business becomes **5**.......... . Make sure you have enough money to keep going until then. If you follow all these tips, it is not **6**.......... that your business will fail.

Paraphrases

Read the sentence from the reading passage. Then, choose the sentence that has the same meaning.

1 *It is also necessary to develop a sound business plan that, among other things, shows how the business will make a profit and projects the cash flow that will help the business stay afloat.* (paragraph 4)

A A business plan should show how cash will be spent to improve the business.

B A small business needs a good plan for how it will make money and pay debts.

C A small business must have plans for asking for help when needed.

2 *Working alone in one's basement during the initial phases of the business, for example, costs a great deal less than renting a space and hiring staff.* (paragraph 6)

A Rent and staff salaries are among the greatest expenses a small business has.

B Spending nothing on rent and staff salaries is one way to save money when starting a business.

C Some business owners prefer working alone at home to working with others in an office.

Dictionary Skill

CHANGING STRESS

The meanings of some words change when different syllables are stressed. These words are spelled the same but are pronounced with different stress. Most are also different parts of speech.

Read the definitions below. Then read the sentences and write the letter of the correct definition for each sentence.

pro-ject [pro-JEKT]
A *verb.* to estimate, calculate a future amount

pro-ject [PRO-jekt]
B *noun.* a task, a defined program of work

.... **1** Our first *project* is to study the market and identify our potential customers.

.... **2** We *project* that we will start earning a profit by the end of next year.

Listening

Track 19 *Listen to the conversation. Choose **FOUR** letters, **A–G**.*

Which **FOUR** of the following characteristics of a successful small business describe the Sunshine Bakery?

A It does not have nearby competitors.

B It offers a unique product.

C It has a good reputation.

D The idea for it was based on research of potential customers.

E It was started with a sound business plan.

F It became profitable in the first year.

G It was started with the necessary financial support.

Writing
(Task 2)

In many places, large chain stores are taking over the market-place, making it impossible for small businesses to compete with them. What are the advantages and disadvantages of this situation?

Support your opinion with reasons and examples from your own knowledge or experience.

Write at least 250 words.

Speaking

Talk about the following topics:

Think of a store where you enjoy shopping. What characteristics draw you to it?

What kinds of products do you feel are worth spending a lot of money on?

What tips do you have for someone who is planning to buy an expensive product?

BRAND LOYALTY

Words

Write the letter of each definition with the word it defines. If you don't know the definition, use the context of the reading passage to help you. Look for the words in bold as you read the passage.

PARAGRAPHS 1–2

Words	Definitions
1 .... conglomerate	**A** n., large company that owns smaller companies
2 .... fleeting	**B** n., connection
3 .... brand	**C** n., company name for a product
4 .... bond	**D** adj., brief; ending quickly
5 .... reverse	**E** v., to turn around; change to its opposite

PARAGRAPHS 2–3

Words	Definitions
6 .... consistently	**F** n., a basic household item
7 .... passion	**G** v., to get somebody to do or believe something
8 .... convince	**H** n., a strong feeling or interest in
9 .... staple	**I** adv., regularly; always

PARAGRAPHS 4–5

Words	Definitions
10 .... endorsement	**J** v., to not pay attention to
11 .... status	**K** n., faithfulness, belief in something
12 .... ignore	**L** v., perform better than
13 .... outperform	**M** n., social position
14 .... loyalty	**N** n., public support for something

PARAGRAPHS 6–7

Words	Definitions
15 .... phenomenon	**O** adj., intentionally choosing some things and not others
16 .... prevail	**P** v., to be common among certain groups; be stronger
17 .... burgeoning	**Q** n., a strong desire for something
18 .... promote	**R** v., to advertise
19 .... thirst	**S** adj., growing
20 .... selective	**T** n., something unusual that happens; a fact

Reading

Brand Loyalty

(1) From the neighborhood[1] barber to the international **conglomerate**, most businesses have a common goal: repeat customers. Developing a committed clientele can be more valuable than attracting new customers, whose loyalty to a company's products may be **fleeting**.

(2) **Brand** loyalty is a psychological **bond** that, once established, is difficult to **reverse**—and it is more complicated than simply buying the same product time and again. True brand loyalty differs from what some marketing researchers refer to as spurious loyalty—a passive condition in which people **consistently** buy a brand for reasons, such as habit, convenience, price, and availability but not the result of any true loyalty or **passion** for the actual merchandise. It is usually not difficult to **convince** consumers with spurious loyalty to try another brand.

(3) Products that create true consumer loyalty tend to be nonessential day-to-day items such as tobacco, beverages, candy, and beauty products, as well as luxury purchases such as designer clothes and cars. Household **staples** such as milk, eggs, sugar, and paper products create little brand loyalty, with most consumers just as likely to purchase private labels or store brands or whatever is on sale.

---

[1]BrE: neighbourhood

(4) A product must have acceptable quality to establish true brand loyalty, but even top quality is not enough on its own to forge a strong connection with a consumer. Customers relate to products for emotional and symbolic reasons. People identify with the image associated with a brand, for example, as a result of a celebrity **endorsement** or because of the social values of the company. In addition, people consistently purchase pricey items because of the perceived **status** those items confer.

(5) Brand-loyal consumers are unlikely to defect to the competition because loyal consumers develop a preference for a product, **ignore** negative associations, and believe it **outperforms** others, even when there is little difference among brands. For example, beverage drinkers in blind taste tests regularly fail to select their favored brand—even though they mention taste as the primary reason for their **loyalty**.

(6) Brand loyalty is a worldwide **phenomenon**, but it is a luxury that **prevails** where people have more money to spend. In China's **burgeoning** economy, sales are soaring for certain top-of-the-line luxury cars after concerted efforts were made to **promote** them. At the same time, European fashion companies are taking advantage of Chinese consumers' **thirst** for designer labels, selling goods worth billions of U.S. dollars a year.

(7) Consumers become less **selective** about brands in economic downturns. During the recession of the early twenty-first century, more consumers in Europe and North America turned to brands that cost less instead of the ones they preferred, and more retailers packaged goods under their own private labels. Although private labels are also influencing shoppers in South Africa and Japan, they have had little effect in Hong Kong, where people have more disposable income and therefore remain loyal to the higher-priced brands.

(8) Brand loyalty is less prevalent in poorer countries where consumers have fewer choices and price is usually the priority.

Answer the questions about **Brand Loyalty**.

Questions 1–8

Do the following statements agree with the information in the reading passage?
Write

TRUE *if the statement agrees with the information.*
FALSE *if the statement contradicts the information.*
NOT GIVEN *if there is no information on this in the passage.*

.... **1** International conglomerates are more successful at creating brand loyalty than small businesses are.

.... **2** New customers may have only a fleeting interest in a particular brand.

.... **3** Brand loyalty occurs more often with household staples than with luxury items.

.... **4** Brand loyalty includes the belief that one brand outperforms other brands.

.... **5** Endorsement of a product by a famous person can help create brand loyalty.

.... **6** Companies can convince consumers to change their brand loyalty by lowering prices.

.... **7** The phenomenon of brand loyalty is seen in countries around the world.

.... **8** Consumers are drawn to certain brands because they believe these brands give them status.

Word Families

A

Complete each sentence with the correct word from the word family chart. Make nouns plural where necessary. Use the correct form of verbs.

noun	adjective	adverb
consistency	consistent	consistently

1 Brand loyalty is about the .... with which consumers buy a certain brand.

2 A company wants consumers to buy its brand ....

3 Not all consumers are .... when it comes to buying certain brands.

noun	**adjective**	**adverb**
loyalty	loyal	loyally

4 Customers may .... buy all the brands of a particular company.

5 A customer who feels .... to a certain brand will always buy that brand even when the price rises.

6 A company wants the .... of its customers.

noun	**adjective**	**adverb**
passion	passionate	passionately

7 A person who feels .... about a brand tends to ignore any problems that the product may have.

8 Customers may have a .... for a particular brand.

9 Loyal customers .... defend their favorite brands.

noun	**verb**	**adjective**
prevalence	prevail	prevalent

10 Brand loyalty is more .... in places where people have more money to spend.

11 The .... of certain brands is a result of the effort companies put into promoting them.

12 Brand loyalty usually .... over price.

noun	verb	adjective	adverb
selection	select	selective	selectively

13 Some people are very .... about the brands they buy.

14 People may .... a brand that they believe gives them status.

15 Some people shop ...., whereas others just buy whatever they see on the shelf.

16 Larger stores can offer a wide .... of brands.

noun	verb	adjective	adverb
thirst	thirst	thirsty	thirstily

17 The customers .... for the latest of everything.

18 As long as there is a .... for luxury items, companies will keep producing them.

19 In a burgeoning economy, consumers are .... for products that were not available to them in the past.

Word Families

B

Choose the correct word family member from the list below to complete each blank.

1 thirst	thirsty	thirsted
2 select	selective	selectively
3 passion	passionate	passionately
4 consistency	consistent	consistently
5 loyalty	loyal	loyally
6 prevalence	prevail	prevalent

In promoting their brands, companies try to create a **1**.......... for their products so that large numbers of people will want to buy them. Consumers who make purchases **2**.......... will choose the brands that they feel are the best ones. Therefore, companies try to create an image for their brands that is attractive to consumers. They want their brands to appear exciting. If consumers are **3**.......... about certain brands, then they are likely to be **4**.......... in buying them. When a company introduces new products to the market, **5**.......... customers will buy them because they already feel good about the company's brands and trust them. Companies that are successful in creating brand loyalty **6**.......... in the market.

Paraphrases

Read the sentence from the reading passage. Then, choose the sentence that has the same meaning.

1 *From the neighborhood barber to the international conglomerate, most businesses have a common goal: repeat customers.* (paragraph 1)
A Businesses of all sizes are interested in creating loyal customers.
B All kinds of businesses want to attract international customers.
C Customers shop more consistently at neighborhood businesses.

2 *True brand loyalty differs from what some marketing researchers refer to as spurious loyalty—a passive condition in which people consistently buy a brand for reasons such as habit, convenience, price, and availability but not because they have a passion for the actual merchandise.* (paragraph 2)
A If the products of a certain brand are regularly available and inexpensive, customers will start to feel loyalty toward that brand.
B Some shoppers are so loyal to a brand that they will buy products that they don't really need.
C Brand loyalty means having strong feelings about a brand, while spurious loyalty means choosing a brand for practical reasons.

Word Skill

PREFIX *OUT-*

The prefix *out-* can mean *better* or *greater.*

Read the sentences. Write a definition for each underlined word.

1 The company introduced a new car that outperforms other similar cars.

outperform: ....

2 This company is very good at promoting its brands, and its products always outsell the competitors.

outsell: ....

3 This company's products are very popular, and its loyal customers outnumber those of other companies.

outnumber: ....

Listening

Track 20

Listen to the talk. Complete the notes below.
*Write **NO MORE THAN ONE WORD** for each answer.*

Creating Brand Loyalty

Make your brand seem special.
Customers want to feel that your brand gives them **1**.......... .
Get **2**.......... from famous people.
Give the idea that the brand is bought by **3**.......... people.
Make customers feel **4**.......... about your brand.

Writing (Task 1)

The charts below show information about consumer decisions regarding mobile phone purchases in two different countries.

Summarize[1] the information by selecting and reporting the main information and making comparisons.

Write at least 150 words.

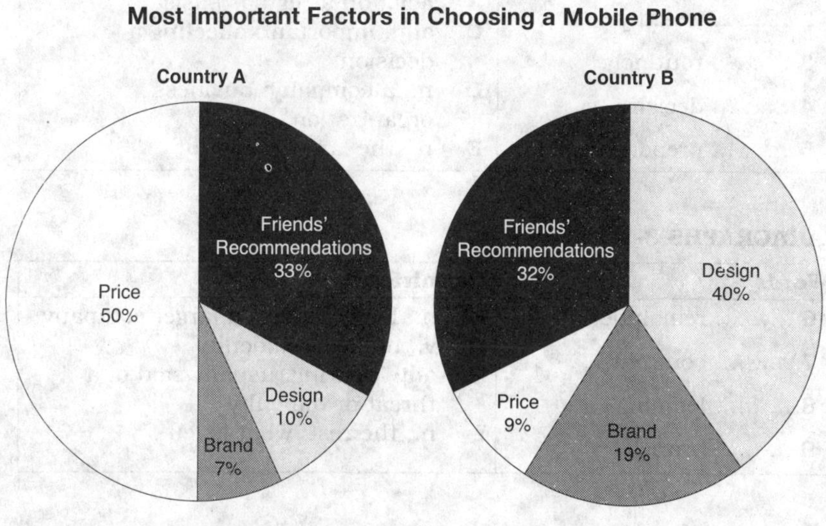

Speaking

Talk about the following topics.

Are you loyal to any particular brands? Why or why not?

Why do you think celebrity endorsements convince people to buy certain brands?

[1]BrE: summarise

GLOBAL OUTSOURCING

Words

Write the letter of each definition with the word it defines. If you don't know the definition, use the context of the reading passage to help you. Look for the words in bold as you read the passage.

PARAGRAPHS 1–3

Words	Definitions
1 .... firm	**A** adj., rich
2 .... wealthy	**B** adv., on a regular basis
3 .... routinely	**C** adj., important; affecting a decision
4 .... decisive	**D** n., a company; business organization[1]
5 .... preponderance	**E** n., the largest amount

PARAGRAPHS 3–5

Words	Definitions
6 .... remainder	**F** n., local office of a larger company
7 .... confront	**G** v., to face a difficulty
8 .... looming	**H** adj., nearing, usually said of a threat or difficulty
9 .... branch	**I** n., the rest; what is left

PARAGRAPH 6

Words	Definitions
10 .... controversy	**J** v., to call attention to
11 .... opponent	**K** n., supporter
12 .... point	**L** n., someone who disagrees and speaks out
13 .... proponent	**M** n., a lot of disagreement affecting many people
14 .... boon	**N** n., a benefit; advantage

[1]BrE: organisation

PARAGRAPHS 6–7

Words	Definitions
15 .... turnover	**O** n., central or most important place
16 .... shift	**P** v., to reach someone or something that is ahead
17 .... coincide	**Q** adj., attractive
18 .... epicenter[1]	**R** v., to happen at the same time
19 .... catch up	**S** n., period of work time
20 .... enticing	**T** n., the rate at which employees leave and are replaced

Reading

Global Outsourcing

(1) Outsourcing, subcontracting work to another company, has always been a part of doing business. Firms hire other **firms** to do work they cannot do themselves or can have done more cheaply elsewhere. With today's global economy, the practice is now so prevalent that even companies in the business of outsourcing are outsourcing work to others.

(2) **Wealthy** nations **routinely** send all types of work to countries where labor costs are cheaper, but currently the most frequently outsourced jobs are in information technology (IT), software, and customer service. Japan, Western European countries, and the United States outsource the most work, and India and China take in the most.

(3) Language skills are a **decisive** factor in where work is sent, with India and the Philippines serving English-speaking clients, Argentina working with Spain, Mexico serving Spanish speakers in the United States, and China handling Asian languages such as Mandarin, Cantonese, and Korean. As a **preponderance** of corporations conduct business in English, the bulk of outsourcing jobs in recent decades have gone to India, where its status as a former British colony resulted in millions of people speaking English as their first language. About half of India's outsourcing work comes from the United States, with about a quarter from European countries and the **remainder** from countries such as Japan and Australia.

[1]BrE: epicentre

(4) Some of the largest outsourcing firms in the world have headquarters in India. However, **confronted** with increasing demand, a **looming** shortage of skilled workers, and rising wages at home as the Indian economy grows, some of those outsourcing companies are now turning to other countries to help meet their own staffing needs. They outsource largely to China but also to dozens of other countries, including the Philippines, Mexico, Brazil, Saudi Arabia, and, in some cases, the country where the work originated. For example, a U.S.-based software company might outsource IT support to a company based in India, which then subcontracts part of the work to a company in the United States.

(5) Much of the IT support market is now moving to China, where a vast supply of highly trained people are willing to work for lower wages than people in India. With newer Chinese companies not yet well established in the outsourcing business, Indian firms are opening **branches** there, where their knowledge of English and well-developed managerial skills give them an advantage, at least for now, in dealing with international clients.

(6) Outsourcing has long been a source of **controversy**, with **opponents pointing** to the loss of jobs and damage to the economy in the home country, and **proponents** viewing the savings in labor costs as a **boon** to business. The receiving countries generally consider the well-paying jobs a benefit to their economy, but employees are not always happy with the work. Staff **turnover** can be high when employees have to work long night **shifts** to **coincide** with the business day in the outsourcing country.

(7) India remains the outsourcing **epicenter** for now, with China slowly **catching up**, but the situation will continue to change. Once wages rise high enough in India and China, foreign workers somewhere else will be as **enticing** to outsourcing countries as India and China now are to Europe, Japan, and the United States.

Answer the questions about **Global Outsourcing**.

Questions 1–7

Complete the summary using words from the list below.

boon	confront	firm	turnover
branch	enticing	looming	wealthy
catch up	epicenter	remainder	

Outsourcing is very common in today's global economy. A preponderance of companies in **1**.......... nations send work to countries where wages are lower. These countries are **2**.......... to large companies because labor costs are cheap. Because English is the language used by a large number of international corporations, a large percentage of outsourcing work has gone to India, and the **3**.......... has been sent to other countries. Now wages are rising in India, and more outsourcing work is being sent to other countries. Proponents of outsourcing point out that, as well as being beneficial to the outsourcing companies, it is also a major **4**.......... to the economies of receiving countries. Outsourcing companies may **5**.......... some difficulties, however. For example, there is sometimes a high **6**.......... of employees, who aren't always happy with nighttime work schedules. Labor costs are rising in India and China. When costs in these countries start to **7**.......... with costs in wealthier countries, companies will start sending their work to other places.

Word Families

A

Complete each sentence with the correct word from the word family chart. Make nouns plural where necessary. Use the correct form of verbs.

noun	adjective	adverb
controversy	controversial	controversially

1 Outsourcing labor is a .... issue.

2 Many major firms are .... sending more and more work to countries where labor is cheap.

3 There has been a good deal of .... around the issue of outsourcing labor.

noun	verb	adjective	adverb
decision	decide	decisive	decisively

4 The company responded .... by sending the work overseas.

5 Some firms .... not to outsource labor to other countries and hire local workers instead.

6 Many large firms have made the .... to outsource labor to other countries.

7 The cost of labor is a .... factor for outsourcing work.

noun	verb	adjective
enticement	entice	enticing

8 Low wages are often an .... for companies looking to cut costs.

9 Low labor costs .... outsourcing companies to open branches in certain parts of the world.

10 Outsourcing companies find low labor costs ....

noun	noun	verb	adjective
opposition	opponent	oppose	opposing

11 People hold .... views on the issue of outsourcing.

12 Many people who have lost their jobs .... outsourcing labor to other countries.

13 .... of the practice of outsourcing labor say that it is bad for the economy of the home country.

14 There has been a certain amount of .... to the practice of outsourcing labor.

noun	adjective	adverb
preponderance	preponderant	preponderantly

15 A .... of outsourcing work comes from the United States, Europe, and Japan.

16 .... large numbers of workers in this area are hired by foreign companies.

17 Jobs from international companies play a .... role in the economies of a number of countries.

noun	adjective	adverb
routine	routine	routinely

18 The work is .... and not very interesting.

19 The job is not difficult as all employees follow the same ....

20 Employees .... work night shifts.

Word Families

B

Choose the correct word family member from the list below to complete each blank.

1	decision	decide	decisive
2	opponent	opposition	oppose
3	controversy	controversial	controversially
4	preponderance	preponderant	preponderantly
5	routines	routine	routinely
6	enticement	entice	enticing

Many customer service companies outsource their work to other countries. The **1**.......... to use this practice is generally based on labor costs, because wages are lower in certain parts of the world. There are many people who **2**.......... this practice because it leads to loss of employment for workers in the company's home country. This is one reason why the outsourcing of labor has become **3**.......... . For the receiving countries, on the other hand, global outsourcing offers economic opportunities. Inconvenient night shifts are **4**.......... in customer service jobs and the work can be boring and **5**.........., but the **6**.......... is regular employment at a relatively decent wage.

Paraphrases

Read the sentence from the reading passage. Then, choose the sentence that has the same meaning.

1 *Outsourcing has long been a source of controversy, with opponents pointing to the loss of jobs and damage to the economy in the home country, and proponents viewing the savings in labor costs as a boon to business.* (paragraph 6)

A Outsourcing has been the source of many problems for businesses, including difficulties with hiring and financial loss.

B Some people are against outsourcing because of the harm it causes to workers and the local economy, while others support it because of its advantages for business.

C Many outsourcing companies have been losing money for a long time and are now cutting back on hiring new staff.

2 *Staff turnover can be high when people have to work long night shifts to coincide with the business day in the outsourcing country.* (paragraph 6)

A Employees often quit their jobs because they have to work all night.

B Employees need frequent breaks because they work for long periods of time.

C Employees have problems because the business day in outsourcing countries is generally long.

Dictionary Skill

DIFFERENT MEANINGS

Many words have more than one meaning.

Read the definitions below. Then read the sentences and write the letter of the correct definition for each sentence.

QUESTIONS 1–2

firm [FURM]

A *noun.* a company, business organization

B *adjective.* hard; steady; unchanging

.... **1** The prices on our products are *firm,* and we are not willing to change them.

.... **2** The directors of the *firm* are thinking about outsourcing some of the work to another company.

QUESTIONS 3–4

shift [SHIFT]
A *noun.* period of work time
B *verb.* move; change

.... **3** They decided to *shift* some of the work to another branch of the company.

.... **4** The *shifts* at this company are generally eight hours long.

Listening

Track 21

Listen to the talk. Complete the timeline below.
Write ***NO MORE THAN TWO WORDS AND/OR A NUMBER*** *for each answer.*

1......	The firm built the first factory.
1910	Owners decided to have a **2**......
3......	First branch factory built
1940	Original factory replaced
1998	The most **4**...... year for the company: no outsourcing of labor
Present:	Apex is a major employer in the region, with low **5**......

Writing
(Task 2)

There has been some controversy about the practice of companies in wealthy countries outsourcing labor to countries where wages are lower. What do you think are the advantages and disadvantages of this practice?

Support your opinion with reasons and examples from your own knowledge or experience.

Write at least 250 words.

Speaking

Talk about the following topics.

Describe a decisive moment in your life.

What are some difficulties you confront in your daily life as a professional (or student)?

Unit 8: Society

SOCIAL NETWORKING

Words

Write the letter of each definition with the word it defines. If you don't know the definition, use the context of the reading passage to help you. Look for the words in bold as you read the passage.

PARAGRAPHS 1–2

Words	Definitions
1 .... explode	**A** adv., seemingly
2 .... post	**B** n., information in the form of numbers; data
3 .... community	**C** n., movement in a certain direction; popular fashion
4 .... statistics	**D** n., a social group
5 .... apparently	**E** v., to display information in a public place
6 .... trend	**F** v., to grow suddenly and rapidly

PARAGRAPH 3

Words	Definitions
7 .... consequence	**G** n., result
8 .... immense	**H** n., communication; connection
9 .... contact	**I** adj., very big, huge
10 .... undergo	**J** v., to experience; suffer
11 .... carry out	**K** v., to remove completely
12 .... pursue	**L** v., to trade something
13 .... eradicate	**M** v., to do; perform
14 .... impose	**N** v., to force
15 .... exchange	**O** v., to hunt for; seek

Unit 8

PARAGRAPH 4

Words	Definitions
16 .... interact	**P** n., a friend you do not know well
17 .... adolescent	**Q** adj., easily affected
18 .... susceptible	**R** n., a person between the ages of thirteen and nineteen
19 .... acquaintance	**S** v., to develop; open up
20 .... unfold	**T** v., to communicate with

Reading

Social Networking

A

During the first decade of the twenty-first century, the phenomenon of social networking on the Internet **exploded** across the globe. Online social networking sites are websites that allow people to **post** personal information about themselves and to connect with people who have similar interests. It is a way of forming **community**, but a community that exists online rather than in physical space. Facebook, MySpace, LinkedIn, and Twitter are examples of some of the most commonly used social networking sites.

B

Recent **statistics** show that 75 percent[1] of Internet users around the world use social networking sites to some extent and that 22 percent of all time spent online is spent on these sites. Of all the countries in the world, Italy is **apparently** the place where social networking is most popular. Italians spend an average of six and a half hours per month per person on social networking sites, followed by Australians, with an average time of just over six hours a month. In comparison, the Japanese are much less interested in social networking, spending an average of just two and a half hours per person per month on these sites. The global average is close to five and a half hours per month. The social networking **trend** has increased among people of all ages.

C

The phenomenon of social networking sites may present unanticipated **consequences** for people's lives in the future. The **immense** popularity of these sites is evidence that they contribute to users'

[1]BrE: per cent

lives in positive ways, but there are drawbacks as well. Social networking sites allow people to broaden their social reach both personally and professionally. These sites allow users to stay in **contact** with friends and relatives and reconnect with old friends from the past. The sites also provide opportunities for people to connect with strangers in far-distant places who share similar interests or to seek support when **undergoing** difficulties such as a grave illness. In the business world, people use social networking sites to **carry out** business, **pursue** employment opportunities, or seek new business clients. Students of all ages discuss homework assignments and future educational and career plans. Social networking sites **eradicate** the limits **imposed** by the physical world and make it possible to communicate and **exchange** information with people everywhere.

D

On the other hand, concerns are growing about online social networking. As people spend more time **interacting** with each other online, they spend less time in face-to-face communication. Social networking can actually lead to separation as families and neighbors[2] spend less time together while they are busy using the Internet. There are also potential risks. Social networking involves making personal information available online, which means that, unless the user is careful, anyone can have access to that information. **Adolescents** may be particularly **susceptible** to this danger. It is also impossible to know anyone's true identity online. **Acquaintances** found on the Internet may not be who people think they are. The effects that social networking will have on our social relationships and sense of safety remain to be seen as the future **unfolds**.

Answer the questions about **Social Networking**.

Questions 1–4

The reading passage contains four paragraphs, ***A–D****.*
Which paragraphs discuss the following information?
Write the correct letter, ***A–D****.*

.... **1** The different reasons people pursue contacts on social networking sites

.... **2** Possible negative consequences of social networking

[2]BrE: neighbours

.... **3** The amount of time people spend interacting on social networking sites

.... **4** When the social networking trend became big

Questions 5–9

Complete the summary using words from the list below.

acquaintances	immense	statistics
exchanged	interact	susceptible
exploded	pursue	undergo

Recently, the popularity of social networking sites has **5**.......... . There are **6**.......... advantages to these sites. People use these sites to post information about themselves, seek new **7**.........., and **8**.......... professional opportunities. There are also drawbacks. Social networking online may mean that people **9**.......... less with the people around them. It also gives strangers access to personal information.

Word Families

A

Complete each sentence with the correct word from the word family chart. Make nouns plural where necessary. Use the correct form of verbs.

noun	noun	adjective
adolescence	adolescent	adolescent

1 Parents need to be aware of how their .... children spend their time on the Internet

2 These days, ... are used to making new acquaintances on the Internet.

3 As children enter ...., they start spending more time on the Internet, pursuing both educational and social activities.

noun	verb	adjective
eradication	eradicate	eradicable

4 The Internet .... the need for face-to-face communication.

5 Internet communication could lead to the .... of face-to-face communication in many aspects of our lives.

6 Internet communication has made the limits of the physical world ....

noun	verb	adjective
explosion	explode	explosive

7 Countries around the world are experiencing the .... of online social networking.

8 Interest in online social networking has .... everywhere.

9 The .... growth of online social networking has rapidly changed the way we communicate.

noun	adjective	adverb
immensity	immense	immensely

10 The .... of the effects that online social networking will have on our lives remains to be seen.

11 Online social networking will have .... effects on the way we communicate.

12 Adolescents are .... interested in online social networking.

noun	verb	adjective	adverb
interaction	interact	interactive	interactively

13 Some sites allow users to communicate ....

14 Online .... is very different from talking with someone face-to-face.

Unit 8

15 Some computer games are highly ....

16 The Internet makes it possible to .... with people in faraway places.

noun	noun	adjective	adverb
statistics	statistician	statistical	statistically

17 .... information is important, but it doesn't give us a complete picture.

18 We can learn a lot from ...., but we need to be careful about how we interpret them.

19 The differences in the data were not .... significant.

20 .... tell us that online social networking communities have grown explosively.

Word Families

B

Choose the correct word family member from the list below to complete each blank.

1	interactions	interacts	interactive
2	explosion	exploded	explosive
3	adolescence	adolescent	adolescents
4	Statistics	Statisticians	Statistical
5	eradication	eradicated	eradicable
6	immensity	immense	immensely

These days, many people are spending more time in online **1**.......... than they do in face-to-face communication with the people around them. The **2**.......... of interest in online social networking is especially prevalent among the **3**.......... age group. **4**.......... who study this trend report that a significant number of teenagers spend a large percentage of their free time online and that much of this time is spent on social networking sites. The Internet has apparently **5**.......... limits to communication. It is too soon to tell how **6**.......... this will affect teenagers' lives as they grow up. For now, experts recommend that parents impose restrictions on the amount of time their children spend on the Internet.

Paraphrases

Read the sentence from the reading passage. Then, choose the sentence that has the same meaning.

1 *The immense popularity of these sites is evidence that they contribute to users' lives in positive ways, but there are drawbacks as well.* (paragraph 3)

A The popularity of social networking will continue to grow as people learn about its great advantages.
B Many people are aware of the disadvantages of social networking but continue to use it in spite of this.
C Social networking is very popular because people enjoy its advantages, but there are also disadvantages.

2 *The effects that social networking will have on our social relationships and sense of safety remain to be seen as the future unfolds.* (paragraph 4)

A In the future, more and more people will feel the effects of social networking.
B We don't yet know what effects social networking will have on us in the future.
C People expect that social networking will become safer in the future.

Word Skill

PHRASAL VERBS WITH CARRY

Phrasal verbs are made up of two parts: a verb and one or two particles. The meaning of the phrasal verb is usually not related to the meanings of the individual parts.

Phrasal Verb		Meaning
carry verb	*out* particle	do or perform
carry verb	*through* particle	complete successfully
carry verb	*on* particle	continue

Choose the correct phrasal verb from the list above to complete each sentence.

1 We thought our friendship would end after we graduated from school, but we have been able to .... being friends through the Internet.

2 Some people .... all their business completely online.

3 They will .... with their plans to start a community center[1] for adolescents.

Listening

Track 22 *Listen to the conversation. Complete the notes below. Write* ***NO MORE THAN ONE WORD*** *for each answer.*

Online Social Networking

<u>Advantages</u>
1.......... with people all over the world
2.......... personal and professional opportunities

<u>Disadvantages</u>
loss of local **3**..........
don't know true identity of online **4**..........

[1]BrE: centre

Writing (Task 1)

The statistics below show basic information about users of three different online social networking sites.

Summarize[1] the information by selecting and reporting the main information and making comparisons.

Write at least 150 words.

Use of different social network sites by age group. Percentages are of total membership.

	Adolescents (13–17)	Younger adults (18–25)	Older adults (25+)
Site A	20%	47%	33%
Site B	7%	27%	66%
Site C	55%	35%	10%

Speaking

Talk about the following topics.

What kinds of information do you generally exchange with your friends online?

Do you feel that parents should impose any kinds of limits on their adolescent children's use of the Internet? Why or why not?

Do you believe that the online social networking trend will continue in the future? Why or why not?

[1]BrE: summarise

WHY ARE WOMEN LEAVING SCIENCE CAREERS?

Words

Write the letter of each definition with the word it defines. If you don't know the definition, use the context of the reading passage to help you. Look for the words in bold as you read the passage.

PARAGRAPH 1

Words	Definitions
1 .... struggle	**A** adj., very serious or extreme; very bad
2 .... persist	**B** adv., close but not exactly
3 .... dire	**C** v., to continue
4 .... approximately	**D** adj., related to school, especially the university
5 .... academic	**E** v., to fight

PARAGRAPHS 2–3

Words	Definitions
6 .... inordinate	**F** n., demands; responsibilities
7 .... equality	**G** n., not being present; time away
8 .... pressure	**H** n., being the same; having the same rights and opportunities
9 .... bear	**I** adj., more than is reasonable
10 .... absence	**J** v., to carry; have responsibility for

PARAGRAPHS 3–4

Words	Definitions
11 .... devote	**K** n., a person who gives help and advice
12 .... frustration	**L** v., give; commit
13 .... discrepancy	**M** n., difference between two things that should be the same
14 .... mentor	**N** n., lack of satisfaction; inability to reach goals
15 .... invaluable	**O** adj., very valuable; extremely useful

PARAGRAPH 4

Words	Definitions
16 .... guidance	**P** adj., similar in size or amount
17 .... validate	**Q** v., to move forward
18 .... funding	**R** v., to confirm; make a person feel valued
19 .... progress	**S** n., financial support
20 .... commensurate	**T** n., advice; assistance

Reading

Why Are Women Leaving Science Careers?

(1) Generations of women **struggled** for the right to pursue careers in science and technology, yet today nearly half the women scientists in Europe and the Americas leave their careers. The difference in numbers between men and women who advance and **persist** in their fields cannot be attributed to race, ethnic, or social group. The **dire** consequences of this loss may become more acute as the number of women entering science careers increases. Since the 1990s, more women than men have enrolled in college, earned higher grades, and majored in science or technology fields. If the trend continues and more than half these women leave their careers by their mid-forties, **approximately** one-third of all scientists will leave their careers in the next twenty years. So why are women leaving the science careers they worked so hard to attain? Studies by **academic** and professional associations show the causes for the loss of this valuable resource are threefold: time, family responsibilities, and lack of role models.

(2) High-level jobs in science, in both the corporate and the academic world, require **inordinate** amounts of time. With increased use of the Internet, cell phones, and other electronic forms of communication, scientists are not only required to be in the lab or office ten to twelve hours a day, but expected to be available the rest of the time, too. Professional time demands are the same for both men and women, but many more women opt out than men because of significant issues that men do not face.

Unit 8

(3) Although women are nearing **equality** in the professional world, the **pressures** of caring for family still rests largely with women. According to studies, professional women with children still **bear** the majority of the responsibilities at home. They spend more time with the children and on taking care of the home than men. Biology dictates that women require extended leaves of **absence** when they are pregnant and give birth, yet to advance in their careers, women cannot afford to take time off until their late thirties, when the optimal time for having healthy babies is ending. Women can **devote** the necessary attention to neither career nor home life, often creating intense **frustration**.

(4) **Discrepancies** in opportunities and salaries still exist between the sexes. Because there are fewer female role models in the upper levels of science and technology fields, women have fewer **mentors** who provide **invaluable** support. Without mentors, women in the sciences go without the support, **guidance**, and networking needed to lead them through the complications of corporate culture, to **validate** their ideas and secure **funding** for research, and to access those who can help them **progress** in their careers. Mentors also help scientists develop business expertise: Mentored scientists hold more patents, an important source of wealth. Women hold only 14 percent[1] of new patents awarded. Without mentors, women have to work harder to reach the same goals as men, and all the while, many women are still paid less than men for **commensurate** work.

(5) To keep women scientists in the workforce, some companies are instituting mentoring programs, on-site child care, flex-time, and other innovative accommodations. Unfortunately, many companies are content to outsource or to bring in men from other countries to fill positions that valuable but frustrated women scientists leave behind.

[1]BrE: per cent

Answer the questions about **Why Are Women Leaving Science Careers?**

Questions 1–3

Choose an ending from the list to complete each sentence. There are more endings than sentences, so you will not use them all.

A funding offered by the government.

B discrepancies in opportunities for men and women.

C pregnancy and childbirth.

D the type of guidance they receive in school.

E the need to divide their time between career and home life.

.... **1** Women may request permission for long periods of absence from work because of

.... **2** Women in science careers experience frustration because of

.... **3** Women often don't progress as far as men in science careers because of

Questions 4–7

Do the following statements agree with the information in the reading passage?

Write

TRUE	*if the statement agrees with the information.*
FALSE	*if the statement contradicts the information.*
NOT GIVEN	*if there is no information on this in the passage.*

.... **4** Women scientists are hired for academic jobs more often than for research jobs.

.... **5** Both men and women in science careers are expected to devote inordinate amounts of time to their jobs.

.... **6** Women in science careers tend to get less support from mentors than men do.

.... **7** Salaries for women in science careers are commensurate with men's salaries.

Word Families

A

Complete each sentence with the correct word from the word family chart. Make nouns plural where necessary. Use the correct form of verbs.

noun	verb	adjective	adverb
approximation	approximate	approximate	approximately

1 Researchers can only .... the number of women leaving science careers since not all departures are reported.

2 The studies tell us the .... numbers of women leaving science careers.

3 Researchers don't know the exact numbers of women leaving science careers; these statistics are only an ....

4 Scientists are required to spend .... sixty hours a week at their jobs.

noun	verb	verb	adjective	adverb
equality	equal	equalize[1]	equal	equally

5 The numbers of men and women in the sciences have .... over time.

6 Fifty percent .... one-half.

7 Men and women are not always treated .... in the workplace.

8 Women have struggled for decades for .... in the workplace.

9 Men and women do not always receive .... pay for equal work.

noun	verb	adjective	adjective
frustration	frustrate	frustrated	frustrating

10 Many women are .... by the combined pressures of family and career.

[1]BrE: equalise

11 The lack of equality in the workplace .... many women.

12 The lack of mentors for women in science careers is ....

13 The difficulties of balancing career and family responsibilities is a cause of .... for many women.

noun	noun	verb
guidance	guide	guide

14 It is helpful to have someone who can act as a .... when starting out in your career.

15 Mentors provide .... to their less experienced colleagues.

16 People new to the field need a more experienced person to .... them through the complications of corporate culture.

noun	verb	adjective	adverb
persistence	persist	persistent	persistently

17 A .... person will progress in her career.

18 .... is an important part of success in any profession.

19 Women have struggled .... to achieve equality in the workplace.

20 Some women .... in their careers despite the responsibilities they bear at home.

noun	noun	verb	adjective
validity	validation	validate	valid

21 People doubted the .... of the research.

22 Scientists need to be certain that their work is ....

23 It is important to have someone .... your ideas.

24 .... is important for any professional.

Word Families

B

Choose the correct word family member from the list below to complete each blank.

1	equality	equal	equally
2	persistence	persisted	persistently
3	frustration	frustrate	frustrated
4	guidance	guides	guide
5	validation	validate	valid
6	approximation	approximate	approximately

The lack of **1**.......... for women in the workplace is a dire problem that has **2**.......... over the years. Many well-educated women feel **3**.......... by the lack of opportunities to progress in their fields as far as men do. Women in male-dominated fields such as science and technology do not have role models to **4**.......... them. They cannot feel sure that they will get **5**.......... for their ideas. Although it is uncertain exactly what percentage of women scientists leave their careers every year, an **6**.......... figure is 50 percent.

Paraphrases

Read the sentence from the reading passage. Then, choose the sentence that has the same meaning.

1 *Women can devote the necessary attention to neither career nor home life, creating intense frustration.* (paragraph 3)

A Women may choose to have a career because they feel bored staying at home.

B Many women have to work to support their families even though they are unhappy with their jobs.

C Women feel dissatisfied because they have to divide their attention between home and work.

2 *Because there are fewer role models in the upper levels of science and technology fields, women have fewer mentors who provide invaluable support.* (paragraph 4)

A There aren't enough high-level women in science and technology to provide necessary guidance to women entering these fields.

B Women who hold high-level science and technology positions rely on the support of the women beneath them.

C Too few jobs have been created for women new to science and technology fields.

Dictionary Skill

PARTS OF SPEECH

Progress can be a noun or a verb. The stress changes with the part of speech.

Read the definitions below. Then read the sentences and write the letter of the correct definition for each sentence.

pro-gress [pro-GRESS]
A *verb.* to move forward

pro-gress [PRO-gress]
B *noun.* movement forward; advancement

.... **1** Scientists need to spend long hours at work to *progress* in their field.

.... **2** After many months of research, the scientists finally felt that they had made some *progress* in their work.

Listening

Track 23

*Listen to the talk. Choose the correct letter, **A**, **B**, or **C**.*

1 The Robertson Research Lab is devoted to .... research.

A governmental
B academic
C scientific

2 It took .... to get the funding to build the lab.

A exactly ten years
B more or less than ten years
C much more than ten years

3 .... bears the responsibility for running the lab.
A The university
B The government
C The Robertson family

4 Lab researchers provide science students with ....
A funding
B guidance
C validation

Writing
(Task 2)

Modern professional women confront a difficulty that men don't generally face: the struggle to balance the pressures of work and home. In your opinion, how can this difficulty best be solved?

Give reasons for your answer and include examples from your own knowledge or experience.

Write at least 250 words.

Speaking

Talk about the following topics.

What career advice have you received that you feel is invaluable?

What are some of the common pressures of your profession or of being a student?

WHEELCHAIR-ACCESSIBILITY ISSUES

Words

Write the letter of each definition with the word it defines. If you don't know the definition, use the context of the reading passage to help you. Look for the words in bold as you read the passage.

PARAGRAPH 1

Words	Definitions
1 .... disability	**A** n., the condition of being poor
2 .... incapacitated	**B** n., a condition that makes it difficult to do things other people do
3 .... poverty	**C** adj., unable to do things normally
4 .... account for	**D** v., to be responsible for; be the cause of

PARAGRAPH 2

Words	Definitions
5 .... unwieldy	**E** n., leisure activities
6 .... slippery	**F** v., to exist in large numbers
7 .... slope	**G** adj., causing things to slide or slip; difficult to hold or stand on
8 .... abound	**H** n., a surface at an angle, with the top higher than the bottom
9 .... recreation	**I** adj., difficult to manage

PARAGRAPHS 3–4

Words	Definitions
10 .... switch	**J** n., a smooth surface that allows access between levels
11 .... ramp	**K** n., the outside of something
12 .... exterior	**L** n., the raised edge of the street
13 .... curb[1]	**M** n., a button used to turn on lights or machines
14 .... interior	**N** n., the inside of something
15 .... corridor	**O** n., hallway

PARAGRAPHS 5–6

Words	Definitions
16 .... necessitate	**P** v., to make necessary
17 .... update	**Q** adj., small
18 .... capable	**R** adj., able to do something
19 .... terrain	**S** n., the surface of land
20 .... compact	**T** v., to modernize[2]; improve

[1]BrE: kerb
[2]BrE: modernise

Reading

Wheelchair-Accessibility Issues

(1) As many as 650 million people worldwide live with some form of physical **disability**, and about 100 million of the disabled need a wheelchair at least part of the time. Industrialized[1], higher-income nations in Asia, Europe, and North America are seeing an older population grow more **incapacitated** as they age, whereas in lower-income countries of Africa, Asia, and Latin America, **poverty**, conflict, injuries, and accidents **account for** most disabilities, many of them in children.

(2) Wheelchairs provide a more independent lifestyle, but they come with their own set of problems: They are wide, **unwieldy**, and difficult to maneuver[2] in tight spaces, on **slippery** surfaces, and on steep **slopes**—not to mention impassable stair steps. Accessibility issues **abound** at home, work, and school; in **recreation** activities; and in transportation[3].

(3) One of the most difficult places to use a wheelchair is the home. The average doorway width of about 76 centimeters[4] (30 inches) falls some 5 to 15 centimeters (2 to 6 inches) short of the space necessary to accommodate a wheelchair. To be accessible to a person in a wheelchair, bathrooms require grab bars in showers and tubs[5], built-in shower seats, lower sinks and mirrors, and higher toilet seats. Kitchens need lower counters and shelves as well as accessible **switches** for lights, garbage disposals, and exhaust fans. Also, because most homes have at least a few steps, a wheelchair **ramp** is a must.

(4) Many countries have laws requiring public buildings—workplaces, stores, restaurants, and entertainment and sports[6] facilities—to be wheelchair accessible. To accommodate wheelchairs, building **exteriors** need wide sidewalks[7] with **curb** cuts and ramps. Automatic doors, including those on elevators[8], must be broad and

Unit 8

---

[1]BrE: industrialised
[2]BrE: manouever
[3]BrE: transport
[4]BrE: centimetres
[5]BrE: baths
[6]BrE: sport
[7]BrE: pavements
[8]BrE: lifts

remain open long enough for a person in a wheelchair to come and go with ease. In a building **interior**, **corridors** must be wide enough for a person in a wheelchair and another person on foot to pass side by side, and carpeting should be firm enough for wheelchairs to roll over easily. Restrooms[9] must be wheelchair accessible, too. Although many countries have made these improvements, many more have yet to follow their example.

(5) Transportation needs must also be considered. With appropriate technology, some wheelchair users can drive cars, although getting in and out of a vehicle while in a wheelchair usually **necessitates** a portable ramp. Many cities have subway and bus systems that accommodate wheelchairs, and the list is growing. For example, Beijing **updated** its subway system for the 2008 Olympics, providing disabled riders there access to it for the first time.

(6) In most developing countries, a major concern is not so much wheelchair accessibility as access to a wheelchair. People may have limited finances and live in places without improved roads and sidewalks. Growing public awareness is contributing to less expensive types of wheelchairs being designed for specific environments—for example, chairs **capable** of maneuvering across dirt roads and rugged **terrain** but lightweight and **compact** so they can fold up to fit in crowded spaces, such as the aisle of a bus. These wheelchairs also must be affordable and constructed of locally available materials for easy repair.

(7) The number of people needing a wheelchair is expected to increase by 22 percent[10] over the next decade, with most of the increase coming in developing countries, where fewer than 1 percent of those in need now have access to one.

---

[9]BrE: toilets

[10]BrE: per cent

Answer the questions about **Wheelchair-Accessibility Issues.**

Questions 1–3

Choose the correct letter, ***A, B, C,*** *or* ***D.***

1 In industrialized nations, disabilities are found more often among
A older people.
B children.
C students.
D injured people.

2 To be accessible to wheelchairs, buildings need
A more compact curbs.
B wider doors and corridors.
C elevators on the exterior.
D carpets in the interior.

3 Compact wheelchairs are
A more unwieldy.
B easier to use on a bus.
C less affordable.
D much wider.

Questions 4–7

Complete the summary using words from the list below.

necessitated	ramps	slopes	terrain
poverty	recreation	switches	updated

For people in wheelchairs, accessibility is an issue in most areas of their lives, whether they are at home or at school, working, or enjoying **4**.......... during their free time. In homes, things need to be arranged so that they can be reached by a person in a wheelchair. Counters, shelves, and **5**.......... need to be placed lower than usual, and **6**.......... must be built in place of the usual front steps. Public buildings also need to be arranged to allow access to people in wheelchairs. Transportation is also an issue. Many cities have **7**.......... their buses and subways so that it is easier now than it was in the past for people in wheelchairs to get around.

Word Families

A

Complete each sentence with the correct word from the word family chart. Make nouns plural where necessary. Use the correct form of verbs.

noun	adjective	adverb
capability	capable	capably

1 Some wheelchairs are .... of being folded.

2 If a wheelchair has certain ...., it is easier to take on a crowded bus or subway.

3 People can get around quite .... with a wheelchair.

noun	noun	verb	adjective
disability	disabled	disable	disabled

4 The .... require many adjustments to a house.

5 An accident can .... a person for life.

6 Wheelchairs have helped many .... people get around.

7 A .... does not have to prevent a person from living a complete life.

noun	noun	verb	adjective
incapacity	incapacitation	incapacitate	incapacitated

8 His growing .... did not stop him from enjoying life.

9 People can become .... with age.

10 .... due to aging is one reason why people use wheelchairs.

11 Age, injury, and illness are all things that can .... people.

noun	verb	adjective	adverb
necessity	necessitate	necessary	necessarily

12 Wheelchairs .... the use of ramps and wide corridors.

13 Corridors in hospitals are .... wide to accommodate wheelchairs.

14 Ramps are .... to accommodate wheelchairs.

15 The aging population increases the .... for wheelchair accessible buildings.

noun	noun	verb	adjective
slip	slipperiness	slip	slippery

16 Ice can make a sidewalk too .... for a wheelchair.

17 The .... of the roads after an ice storm accounts for many accidents.

18 A wheelchair can .... on a wet or icy surface.

19 .... and falls are a major cause of injury in the elderly.

Word Families

B

Choose the correct word family member from the list below to complete each blank.

1 incapacity	incapacitate	incapacitated
2 necessitate	necessary	necessarily
3 disability	disable	disabled
4 capability	capable	capably
5 slipperiness	slip	slippery

Physical **1**.......... does not **2**.......... mean that one has to live a limited life. Wheelchairs, for example, help millions of **3**.......... people get around and live independent lives. Wheelchairs are **4**.......... of going just about everywhere. As with any form of transportation, the user has to be careful to avoid accidents. For example, after a snowstorm or rainstorm, the **5**.......... of sidewalks may make it difficult to maneuver a wheelchair safely.

Paraphrases

Read the sentence from the reading passage. Then, choose the sentence that has the same meaning.

1 *Industrialized, higher-income nations in Asia, Europe, and North America are seeing an older population grow more incapacitated as they age, whereas in lower-income countries of Africa, Asia, and Latin America, poverty, conflict, injuries, and accidents account for most disabilities, many of them in children.* (paragraph 1)

A In some countries, the occurrence of disabilities is more widespread than it is in other places.

B In some parts of the world, many disabilities occur because of old age, while in other areas, most disabilities happen because of accidents, war, or other reasons.

C In some parts of the world, most disabled people are elderly, but in other places, most disabled people are children.

2 *For example, Beijing updated its subway system for the 2008 Olympics, providing disabled riders there access to it for the first time.* (paragraph 5)

A When Beijing modernized its subway system in 2008, disabled people were finally able to use it.

B Many disabled people rode the Beijing subway during the 2008 Olympics.

C Disabled people did not have to pay to ride the Beijing subway during the 2008 Olympics.

Dictionary Skill

PARTS OF SPEECH

Exterior can be a noun or an adjective. *Interior* can also be a noun or an adjective.

Read the definitions below. Then read the sentences and write the letter of the correct definition for each sentence.

QUESTIONS 1–2

ex-te-ri-or [ex-TEE-ree-or]
A *noun.* the outside of something
B *adjective.* on or of the outside

.... **1** The *exterior* doors need to be wide enough to allow wheelchairs to enter the building.

.... **2** We need to make sure that the building's *exterior* can accommodate wheelchairs.

QUESTIONS 3–4

in-te-ri-or [in-TEE-ree-or]
A *noun.* the inside of something
B *adjective.* on or of the inside

.... **3** The *interior* has been altered to accommodate wheelchairs.

.... **4** The *interior* rooms need wider doors.

Listening

Track 24 *Listen to the conversation. Choose **FOUR** letters, **A–F**.*

Which **FOUR** accommodations for wheelchairs are already in place in the building?

A wide corridors

B wide doors

C ramp

D curb cuts

E elevator

F low switches

Writing (Task 1)

The graphs[1] below show basic information about employment among people with and without disabilities in a certain country.

Summarize[2] the information by selecting and reporting the main information and making comparisons.

Write at least 150 words.

Employment

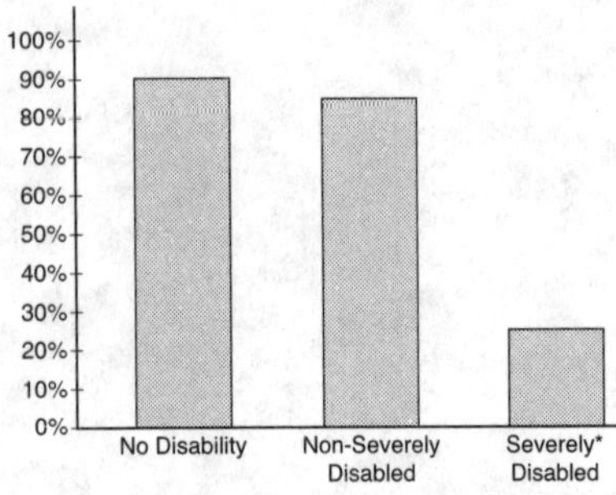

Average Monthly Salary

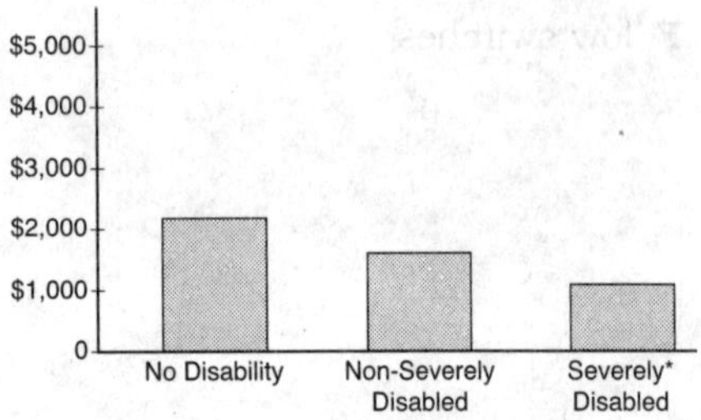

*Severely Disabled is defined as needing a wheelchair, crutches, or a cane and requiring assistance with personal activities.

Speaking

Talk about the following topics.

Are there laws in your country that require public buildings to be accessible to disabled people? Do you think such laws are a good idea?

Think about the building where you work or study. Is it accessible to people in wheelchairs? In what ways could accessibility be improved?

---

[1]BrE: charts
[2]BrE: summarise

Unit 9: Education

LEARNING STYLES

Words

Write the letter of each definition with the word it defines. If you don't know the definition, use the context of the reading passage to help you. Look for the words in bold as you read the passage.

PARAGRAPHS 1–2

Words	Definitions
1 .... approach	**A** n., method
2 .... circumstance	**B** adj., related to the face
3 .... obstruction	**C** n., situation
4 .... hinder	**D** n., something that blocks or stands in the way
5 .... facial	**E** v., to prevent; get in the way

PARAGRAPHS 2–3

Words	Definitions
6 .... blend	**F** adj., related to words
7 .... diagram	**G** v., to say or repeat out loud
8 .... confidence	**H** n., a simple drawing to explain how something works
9 .... auditory	**I** adj., related to hearing
10 .... verbal	**J** n., a mixture; combination
11 .... recite	**K** n., belief in one's abilities

Unit 9

PARAGRAPH 4

Words	Definitions
12 .... kinesthetic[1]	**L** v., to move constantly in a nervous manner
13 .... conventional	**M** adj., normal; traditional
14 .... fidget	**N** adj., related to body motion
15 .... manipulate	**O** v., to move things around with the hands

PARAGRAPHS 4–6

Words	Definitions
16 .... incorporate	**P** n., praise; support to keep going
17 .... encouragement	**Q** adj., more important, stronger
18 .... solitary	**R** v., to add in; bring together
19 .... expose	**S** v., to give an opportunity to experience or learn new things
20 .... dominant	**T** adj., done alone; independent

Reading

Learning Styles

(1) There are three basic types of classroom learning styles: visual, auditory, and kinesthetic[1]. These learning styles describe the most common ways that people learn. Individuals tend to instinctively prefer one style over the others; thus each person has a learning style that is dominant even though he or she may also rely somewhat on the other **approaches** at different times and in different **circumstances**.

(2) Visual learners prefer to sit somewhere in the classroom where no **obstructions hinder** their view of the lesson. They rely on the teacher's **facial** expressions and body language to aid their learning. They learn best from a **blend** of visual displays and presentations

[1]BrE: kinaesthetic

such as colorful[1] videos, **diagrams**, and flip-charts. Often, these learners think in pictures and may even close their eyes to visualize[2] or remember something. When they are bored, they look around for something to watch. Many visual learners lack **confidence** in their **auditory** memory skills and so may take detailed notes during classroom discussions and lectures.

(3) Auditory learners sit where they can hear well. They enjoy listening and talking, so discussions and **verbal** lectures stimulate them. Listening to what others have to say and then talking the subject through helps them process new information. These learners may be heard reading to themselves out loud because they can absorb written information better in this way. Sounding out spelling words, **reciting** mathematical theories, or talking their way across a map are examples of the types of activities that improve their understanding.

(4) **Kinesthetic** learners may find it difficult to sit still in a **conventional** classroom. They need to be physically active and take frequent breaks. When they are bored, they **fidget** in their seats. They prefer to sit someplace where there is room to move about. They benefit from **manipulating** materials and learn best when classroom subjects such as math, science, and reading are processed through hands-on experiences. **Incorporating** arts-and-crafts activities, building projects, and sports into lessons helps kinesthetic learners process new information. Physical expressions of **encouragement**, such as a pat on the back, are often appreciated.

(5) In addition to these traditional ways of describing learning styles, educators have identified other ways some students prefer to learn. Verbal learners, for example, enjoy using words, both written and spoken. Logical learners are strong in the areas of logic and reasoning. Social learners do best when working in groups, whereas **solitary** learners prefer to work alone. Research shows that each of these learning styles, as well as the visual, auditory, and kinesthetic styles, uses different parts of the brain. Students may prefer to focus on just one style, but practicing[3] other styles involves more of the brain's potential and therefore helps students remember more of what they learn.

(6) Teachers who present their lessons using varied techniques that stimulate all learning styles **expose** students to both their **dominant** and less preferred methods of learning, aiding them to more fully reach their potential as learners.

Unit 9

[1]BrE: colourful
[2]BrE: visualise
[3]BrE: practising

Answer the questions about **Learning Styles**.

Questions 1–6

Look at the following descriptions of different styles of learners.
Match each type of learner with the correct description.
Write the correct letter, **A**, **B**, *or* **C**, *next to numbers 1–6.*

A Visual learners

B Auditory learners

C Kinesthetic learners

.... **1** They are stimulated by lessons that incorporate discussions and verbal lectures.

.... **2** Facial expressions are important to them.

.... **3** They learn best in circumstances where they can manipulate objects.

.... **4** Taking notes is one approach they use for processing information.

.... **5** They often fidget in a conventional classroom setting.

.... **6** Reciting information helps them absorb it better.

Questions 7–9

*Choose the correct letter, **A**, **B**, **C**, or **D**.*

7 Verbal learners are
- **A** better at writing than speaking.
- **B** good with words.
- **C** solitary people.
- **D** skilled at reasoning.

8 Social learners need
- **A** other people around them.
- **B** very little encouragement.
- **C** both spoken and written instructions.
- **D** information presented through diagrams.

9 When teachers expose students to all learning styles, the students
- **A** change their dominant style.
- **B** lose their confidence.
- **C** get confused.
- **D** learn more.

Word Families

A

Complete each sentence with the correct word from the word family chart. Make nouns plural where necessary. Use the correct form of verbs.

noun	adjective	adverb
confidence	confident	confidently

1 Students learn .... when they are allowed to use learning styles that they feel comfortable with.

2 Developing .... in one's abilities is an important part of learning.

3 Students who feel .... do better in school.

noun	adjective	adverb
convention	conventional	conventionally

4 Classroom .... sometimes need to be adapted to fit the learning styles of all the students.

5 .... teaching methods are changing as educators understand the need to address all styles of learning.

6 A .... taught lesson may not incorporate approaches suited to all the students' learning styles.

noun	verb	adjective
dominance	dominate	dominant

7 In each individual, one learning style tends to .... over the others.

8 Students can learn to use other styles in addition to the one that is ....

9 The .... of one learning style over others does not mean that the learner relies on that one style alone.

noun	verb
exposure	expose

10 It is a good idea for teachers to .... students to a variety of learning experiences.

11 Students benefit a great deal from .... to different styles of learning.

noun	verb	adjective
face	face	facial

12 Visual learners like to .... the teacher during a lesson.

13 .... expressions are an important part of communication.

14 Visual learners like to be able to see the teacher's .... during a lesson.

noun	adjective	adverb
solitude	solitary	solitarily

15 .... learners would rather work alone than in a group.

16 Some students do better when they can work ....

17 Some students prefer to work in ....

Word Families

B

Choose the correct word family member from the list below to complete each blank.

1	Conventions	Conventional	Conventionally
2	dominance	dominates	dominant
3	Exposure	Exposes	Exposed
4	solitude	solitary	solitarily
5	confidence	confident	confidently
6	faces	facial	faced

1.......... approaches to learning have students sitting at their desks listening to the teacher or working in their textbooks. These days, however, teachers have changed their methods, and modern classrooms no longer look like this, at least not all the time. Teachers now incorporate activities into their lessons that address the learning needs of all the students. Although students each have a particular learning style that **2**.........., it is important to give them the opportunity to practice other learning styles as well. **3**.......... to a variety of activities encourages students to use different parts of their brains, thus increasing their learning potential. Students who have a tendency to work in **4**.........., for example, will benefit from working in small groups some of the time. Students who get used to different ways of working in the classroom will become more **5**.......... learners. The results will be seen in the quality of the work they do, and on their proud and happy **6**.......... as well.

Paraphrases

Read the sentence from the reading passage. Then, choose the sentence that has the same meaning.

1 *Visual learners prefer to sit somewhere in the classroom where no obstructions hinder their view of the lesson.* (paragraph 2)
A Visual learners can easily remember things they see during a lesson.
B Visual learners like to sit where they can easily see the lesson.
C Visual leaners are more comfortable when no one is watching them during a lesson.

2 *They benefit from manipulating materials and learn best when classroom subjects, such as math, science, and reading, are processed through hands-on experiences.* (paragraph 4)
A They tend to be good at math and science and enjoy reading materials about these subjects.
B They like to share their learning experiences with others in the classroom.
C They learn best when they can touch things and use their hands.

Dictionary Skill

PARTS OF SPEECH

Blend can be a noun or a verb.

Read the definitions below. Then read the sentences and write the letter of the correct definition for each sentence.

blend [BLEND]
A *noun.* a mixture, combination
B *verb.* to mix, combine

.... **1** There is a *blend* of learning styles in every classroom.

.... **2** When forming learning groups in the classroom, it is a good idea to *blend* students with different learning styles.

Listening

Track 25

Listen to the lecture. Complete the notes below.
Write ***NO MORE THAN ONE WORD*** *for each answer.*

Needs of Different Students

Visual Learners:
They need to see the teacher's face.
They need lessons with **1**.......... and pictures.

Auditory Learners:
They need to hear words.
They need to read aloud and **2**.......... rules.

Kinesthetic Learners
They need to do things.
They need to move around and **3**.......... items.

All students need **4**.......... .

Writing (Task 2)

Confidence in oneself is an important part of learning. What factors in a classroom can contribute to a student's feeling of confidence?

Give reasons for your answer and include examples from your own knowledge or experience.

Write at least 250 words.

Speaking

Talk about the following topics.

Think about the three learning styles—visual, auditory, and kinesthetic. Which do you think is your dominant style? Why?

Would you describe yourself as a solitary learner or a social learner?

What things hinder your learning?

THE HOMESCHOOL OPTION

Words

Write the letter of each definition with the word it defines. If you don't know the definition, use the context of the reading passage to help you. Look for the words in bold as you read the passage.

PARAGRAPHS 1–2

Words	Definitions
1 .... alternative	A adj., near the end
2 .... novel	B n., a choice
3 .... relatively	C adj., required
4 .... latter	D adv., in comparison to something else
5 .... compulsory	E adj., new and unusual

PARAGRAPH 2

Words	Definitions
6 .... prior	F n., teaching
7 .... widespread	G n., a private teacher
8 .... tutor	H adj., before, previous
9 .... instruction	I adj., common

PARAGRAPH 3

Words	Definitions
10 .... vast	J adj., special, above average
11 .... majority	K n., the larger part; most
12 .... exceptional	L adj., not pleased
13 .... dissatisfied	M adj., very big

PARAGRAPHS 3–4

Words	Definitions
14 .... philosophy	**N** adj., required
15 .... concerned	**O** adj., worried
16 .... adequately	**P** n., set of beliefs and values
17 .... address	**Q** adv., well enough
18 .... mandate	**R** v., to deal with a problem or issue
19 .... periodic	**S** adj., repeated regularly
20 .... obligatory	**T** v., to order officially; require

Reading

The Homeschool Option

(1) Educating children at home as an **alternative** to formal education is an option chosen by families in many parts of the world. The homeschooling movement is popular in the United States, where close to one million children are educated at home. In Canada, 1 percent[1] of school-age children are homeschooled, and the idea also enjoys growing popularity in Australia, where 20,000 families homeschool their children. The movement is not limited to these countries. Homeschooling families can be found all over the world, from Japan to Taiwan to Argentina to South Africa.

(2) Homeschooling is not a **novel** idea. In fact, the idea of sending children to spend most of their day away from home at a formal school is a **relatively** new custom. In the United States, for example, it was not until the **latter** part of the nineteenth century that state governments began making school attendance **compulsory**. **Prior** to that, the concept of a formal education was not so **widespread**. Children learned the skills they would need for adult life at home from **tutors** or their parents, through formal **instruction** or by working side by side with the adults of the family.

[1]BrE: per cent

(3) In the modern developed world, where the **vast majority** of children attend school, families choose homeschooling for a variety of reasons. For people who live in remote areas, such as the Australian outback or the Alaskan wilderness, homeschooling may be their only option. Children who have **exceptional** talents in the arts or other areas may be homeschooled so that they have more time to devote to their special interests. Much of the homeschooling movement is made up of families who, for various reasons, are **dissatisfied** with the schools available to them. They may have a differing educational **philosophy**, they may be **concerned** about the safety of the school environment, or they may feel that the local schools cannot **adequately address** their children's educational needs.

(4) The legal environment surrounding homeschooling varies. In some places, a government-approved course of study is **mandated**, whereas in others, homeschoolers may be required only to follow general guidelines, or even none at all. Sometimes **periodic** progress reports, tests, or professional evaluations are **obligatory**. There are different approaches to homeschooling that individual families can take. Some follow a particular educational philosophy, such as the Montessori method or Waldorf education. Others use a mixed approach, borrowing from a variety of methods and materials. A large selection of prepared educational products is available to specifically address the needs of homeschooling families, and correspondence courses can also be purchased. In addition, homeschooling magazines and websites give families the opportunity to read about others' experiences and get ideas for different kinds of educational activities to try. As the homeschooling movement grows around the world, so, too, do the opportunities for homeschooling families to share experiences and ideas at conferences and on the Internet. Although most families continue to choose a traditional classroom education for their children, homeschooling as an alternative educational option is becoming more popular.

Answer the questions about **The Homeschool Option**.

Questions 1–3

Which of the following reasons that families choose homeschooling are mentioned in the passage?
Choose ***three*** *answers from the list below.*

A The large size of local schools

B The exceptional talents of their children

C The lack of variety of instruction in the majority of schools

D Disagreement with the educational philosophy of local schools

E Belief that local schools cannot adequately meet their children's needs

F Opposition to the periodic testing of their children

Questions 4–8

Do the following statements agree with the information in the reading passage?
Write

TRUE	*if the statement agrees with the information.*
FALSE	*if the statement contradicts the information.*
NOT GIVEN	*if there is no information on this in the passage.*

.... **4** School attendance was mandated in the United States near the beginning of the nineteenth century.

.... **5** Before the late 1800s, the majority of children did not attend school.

.... **6** Many nineteenth-century tutors were not adequately trained for the job.

.... **7** The majority of homeschooling families follow a similar educational philosophy.

.... **8** Although there is growing interest in homeschooling, relatively few families practice[1] it.

---

[1]BrE: practise

Word Families

A

Complete each sentence with the correct word from the word family chart. Make nouns plural where necessary. Use the correct form of verbs.

noun	adjective	adverb
alternative	alternative	alternatively

1 Some homeschooling families follow an educational program similar to that found in formal schools, while others choose .... methods.

2 Parents can choose to teach their children themselves; ...., they can join homeschooling groups and share teaching responsibilities with other families.

3 Some families choose private school as an .... to public school.

noun	verb	adjective
concern	concern	concerned

4 Parents feel .... when their children don't do well in school.

5 The quality of public schools .... a growing number of families.

6 The safety of the school environment is a .... for many modern parents.

noun	noun	verb	adjective	adverb
instruction	instructor	instruct	instructional	instructionally

7 Some homeschooling parents .... their children for a set number of hours everyday, while others follow a less structured schedule.

8 Materials used for homeschooling must be .... sound.

9 Some parents aren't happy with the .... their children get at school.

10 Some people feel that parents are the best .... for their children.

11 Homeschooling parents try to provide their children with good .... materials.

noun	verb	adjective
obligation	obligate	obligatory

12 Parents have the .... to protect their children and provide for their needs.

13 School is .... for young children in most parts of the world.

14 A teacher might .... his students to spend several hours a day doing homework.

noun	adjective	adverb
period	periodic	periodically

15 Teachers give their students tests ....

16 In some places, homeschooling families are required to receive .... visits from professional educators.

17 Children should be given several rest .... during the school day.

Word Families

B

Choose the correct word family member from the list below to complete each blank.

1	alternative	alternatives	alternatively
2	instructor	instruct	instruction
3	concern	concerns	concerned
4	period	periodic	periodically
5	obligation	obligate	obligatory

Many families are interested in **1**.......... forms of education. Some send their children to private schools that follow certain educational methods, and others choose to **2**.......... their children themselves at home. Providing children with a thorough education in all subject areas can be a **3**.......... for homeschooling families. However, there are many places they can turn to for support. There are several homeschooling organizations[1] that can give them guidance with this. Communicating with other homeschooling families **4**.......... to exchange ideas and discuss problems is an important source of support for many homeschoolers. Whether they choose formal schooling or homeschooling, parents have the **5**.......... to make sure that their children get a good education.

[1]BrE: organisations

Paraphrases

Read the sentence from the reading passage. Then, choose the sentence that has the same meaning.

1 *In the United States, for example, it was not until the latter part of the nineteenth century that state governments began making school attendance compulsory.* (paragraph 2)
A Going to school became a requirement in the United States near the end of the 1800s.
B During the 1800s, free education in state-run schools became common throughout the United States.
C The United States government began making records of school attendance in the 1800s.

2 *In some places, a government-approved course of study is* ***mandated****, whereas in others, homeschoolers may be required only to follow general guidelines, or even none at all.* (paragraph 4)
A Some homeschoolers choose to follow government guidelines, while others prefer to design their own course of study.
B In some places, the government provides study materials to homeschoolers who want them.
C Requirements for homeschoolers are stricter in some places than in others.

Word Skill

PREFIX *DIS–*
The prefix *dis–* makes the meaning of the word negative.

Read the sentences. Write a definition for each underlined word.

1 Many families are <u>satisfied</u> with the results they get from homeschooling and would never send their children back to a traditional school.

satisfied: ....

2 Parents who are <u>dissatisfied</u> with traditional education look for alternative schools for their children.

dissatisfied: ....

Listening

Track 26

*Listen to the talk. Choose **FOUR** letters, **A–G**.*

Which **FOUR** of the following are compulsory for parents who homeschool their children in the speaker's city?

A Informing the city of their plans to homeschool

B Hiring professional tutors

C Having prior experience teaching

D Addressing all subjects taught in the local school

E Using books provided by the city

F Giving periodic tests

G Submitting a yearly report

Writing (Task 2)

Interest in homeschooling is becoming more widespread around the world. In your opinion, should school be compulsory for all children, or should families be allowed the right to choose to educate their children at home?

Support your opinion with reasons and examples from your own knowledge and experience.

Write at least 250 words.

Speaking

Talk about the following topics.

For what ages should education be compulsory, in your opinion?

Which subjects do you think should be obligatory in high schools?

What concerns do you have about education in your country?

EDUCATING THE GIFTED

Words

Write the letter of each definition with the word it defines. If you don't know the definition, use the context of the reading passage to help you. Look for the words in bold as you read the passage.

PARAGRAPHS 1–2

Words	Definitions
1 .... gifted **2** .... inquisitiveness **3** .... assess **4** .... profoundly **5** .... recognize[1] **6** .... moderately	**A** v., to identify **B** v., to measure; to evaluate **C** adj., having special talents or abilities **D** adv., greatly; extremely **E** n., desire for knowledge **F** adv., somewhat

PARAGRAPH 2

Words	Definitions
7 .... transfer **8** .... turn into **9** .... discipline **10** .... constructive **11** .... extraordinary	**G** n., the ability to maintain correct behavior[2] **H** v., to become **I** v., to move from one place to another **J** adj., positive; beneficial **K** adj., special; exceptional

[1]BrE: recognise
[2]BrE: behaviour

PARAGRAPH 3

Words	Definitions
12 .... enriched	**L** adj., improved; describing something of higher quality
13 .... curriculum	**M** n., understanding
14 .... peer	**N** n., the set of subjects taught at a school
15 .... sophisticated	**O** adj., advanced, complex
16 .... interpretation	**P** n., a person at an equal level with another

PARAGRAPHS 3–4

Words	Definitions
17 .... simultaneous	**Q** adj., describing educational programs designed to address some area of difficulty
18 .... withdrawal	**R** v., to give; devote
19 .... dedicate	**S** n., not wanting to participate
20 .... remedial	**T** adj., happening at the same time

Unit 9

Reading

Educating the Gifted

(1) What is a **gifted** child? There are different ways to define this term. It may refer to special talents in the arts or to a high level of academic abilities. A child may be gifted in one specific area, such as music, or have talents in many areas. According to the U.S. National Association for Gifted Children, a gifted child shows an "exceptional level of performance" in one or more areas. In general usage, giftedness includes high levels of cognitive ability, motivation, **inquisitiveness**, creativity, and leadership. Gifted children represent approximately 3 to 5 percent[1] of the school-aged population.

(2) Although giftedness cannot be **assessed** by an intelligence test alone, these tests are often used to indicate giftedness. By and large, giftedness begins at an IQ of 115, or about one in six children. Highly gifted children have IQs over 145, or about one in a thousand children. **Profoundly** gifted children have IQs over 180, or about one in a million children. Because very few education programs include any courses on teaching the gifted, teachers are often not able to **recognize** the profoundly gifted. Teachers are more likely to recognize **moderately** gifted children because they are ahead of the other children, but not so far ahead as to be unrecognizable. For instance, children who can read older children's books in first and second grade are often **transferred** into gifted classes, but children who are reading adult books are told to stop reading them. Those profoundly gifted students who are not recognized often **turn into discipline** problems when they are not offered **constructive** ways to focus their **extraordinary** creativity.

(3) The practice of creating a separate, **enriched curriculum** for gifted students began in the early twentieth century. At that time, social scientists noted that gifted children often speak, read, and move at an earlier age than their **peers**. At a younger age they are able to work at a higher conceptual level, develop more **sophisticated** methods to solve problems, and show more creativity in their methods and **interpretation** of assignments. After the first schools for the gifted were established, these students were followed for many years to see if enriched education made a difference. It did. Gifted students who were grouped together and taught a special curriculum earned fifty times more doctoral degrees than gifted students who were not given an enriched curriculum. When gifted programs[2] have been cut, the parents of the participants have

[1]BrE: per cent

[2]BrE: programmes

reported decreased inquisitiveness, motivation, and energy levels in their children, and a **simultaneous withdrawal** from the classroom experience. Identified gifted students who attend schools without any program for the gifted show a steady decrease in motivation and test scores between first and sixth grade.

(4) There are still very few opportunities for educating the gifted in the lowest socioeconomic levels. The schools that service the poorest areas often **dedicate** their efforts toward **remedial** teaching rather than accelerated curriculum, and students with extraordinary talents are often not recognized. About 25 percent of the world's gifted population are too poor to be noticed.

Answer the questions about **Educating the Gifted**.

Questions 1–9

Complete the summary using words from the list below.

assessed	discipline	moderately	remedial
constructive	extraordinary	peers	transferred
curriculum	inquisitiveness	profoundly	
dedicate	interpretation	recognize	

Gifted children are children with **1**.......... talents. Their talents may be artistic or academic. There are different levels of giftedness. The most gifted children are called **2**.......... gifted, but very few children are so gifted. It is more common to see **3**.......... gifted children, and it is easier for teachers to **4**.......... them. These are the children who are ahead of their **5**.......... but not too far ahead. These children are more likely to be **6**.......... from regular classes to classes where a special **7**.......... for the gifted is taught. When schools **8**.......... programs to gifted education, the participants do well in school. When these programs are cut, the children appear to lose interest in school learning and their levels of **9**.......... decline.

Unit 9

Word Families

A

Complete each sentence with the correct word from the word family chart. Make nouns plural where necessary. Use the correct form of verbs.

noun	noun	verb
assessment	assessor	assess

1 Different methods are used to .... gifted children.

2 It is not always easy to find the proper .... for gifted children.

3 The school used one of the teachers as an .... for the program.

noun	verb	adjective	adjective
enrichment	enrich	enriched	enriching

4 Participants found the whole experience quite ....

5 Special programs for gifted children .... their school experience.

6 Parents hope that programs for the gifted will provide their children with an .... school experience.

7 A school system's approach to educating gifted children usually includes .... of the regular curriculum.

noun	verb	adjective	adjective
recognition	recognize	recognizable	unrecognizable

8 When transferred to a program for highly gifted children, the previously undisciplined child was ....; he became an attentive and focused student.

9 Children with .... talents may be transferred to a gifted education program.

10 Gifted children don't always get .... for their extraordinary talents.

11 Teachers need to be trained to .... gifted children in their classrooms.

adjective	adverb
simultaneous	simultaneously

12 When gifted children are transferred to special programs, their scores rise ....

13 We usually see a .... improvement in test scores when a gifted child enters a program with an enriched curriculum.

noun	adjective
sophistication	sophisticated

14 Gifted children can solve problems with great ....

15 Gifted children take .... approaches to problem solving.

noun	verb	adjective
withdrawal	withdraw	withdrawn

16 A gifted child who is bored in a regular classroom may .... from all classroom activities.

17 .... from classroom activities is a sign that a child needs special attention.

18 A gifted child who is kept in a regular classroom may either become .... or turn into a discipline problem.

Word Families

B

Choose the correct word family member from the list below to complete each blank.

1 recognition	recognizes	recognizable
2 sophistication	sophisticated	
3 assessments	assesses	assessing
4 enrichment	enrich	enriched
5 simultaneous	simultaneously	
6 withdrawal	withdraw	withdrawn

Education of the gifted starts with **1**.......... . Gifted children may show certain characteristics. For example, they may solve problems more quickly and with greater **2**.......... than their peers do. Once a teacher identifies a potentially gifted student, then **3**......... are used to determine the giftedness of the child. Identified gifted children are placed in special classes for educational **4**.......... . It has been observed that gifted students' level of interest in school usually increases **5**.......... . Gifted children who are not identified and not placed in special programs may lose interest in school and **6**......... from classroom participation.

Paraphrases

Read the sentence from the reading passage. Then, choose the sentence that has the same meaning.

1 *Although giftedness cannot be assessed by an intelligence test alone, these tests are often used to indicate giftedness.* (paragraph 2)

A Children with special talents usually enjoy answering questions on intelligence tests.

B Some intelligence tests have been specially designed to measure the talents of gifted children.

C Intelligence tests cannot provide a complete evaluation of a child's special talents, but they are still used.

2 *Teachers are more likely to recognize* ***moderately*** *gifted children because they are ahead of the other children, but not so far ahead as to be unrecognizable.* (paragraph 2)

A Some teachers like to have a gifted child in the classroom to motivate the other students.

B It is easier for teachers to identify children who are somewhat gifted because they are not too far ahead of their classmates.

C Teachers tend to pay more attention to gifted children than to the other children in the classroom.

Word Skill

PHRASAL VERBS WITH *TURN*

Phrasal verbs are made up of two parts: a verb and one or two particles. The meaning of the phrasal verb is usually not related to the meanings of the individual parts.

Phrasal Verb		Meaning
turn verb	*into* particle	become
turn verb	*up* particle	appear, arrive
turn verb	*out* particle	result

Choose the correct phrasal verb from the list above to complete each sentence.

1 We expect at least 100 people to .... at the school meeting about gifted education.

2 Our school's gifted education program serves only a few children now, but we hope it will .... a large program some day.

3 The children enjoyed the trip to the museum with their teachers, so the day .... well.

Listening

Track 27

Listen to the discussion. Complete the notes below.
*Write **NO MORE THAN ONE WORD** for each answer.*

How to **1**.......... gifted children

- They read books for older children or adults.
- They have **2**.......... approaches to problem solving.
- They may need help with **3**.......... .

How to support:

- Give them **4**.......... activities.
- Provide a special **5**.......... .

Writing (Task 1)

The charts[1] below show information about the percentage of first-year students enrolled in remedial education courses at two different universities.

Summarize[2] the information by selecting and reporting the main information and making comparisons.

Write at least 150 words.

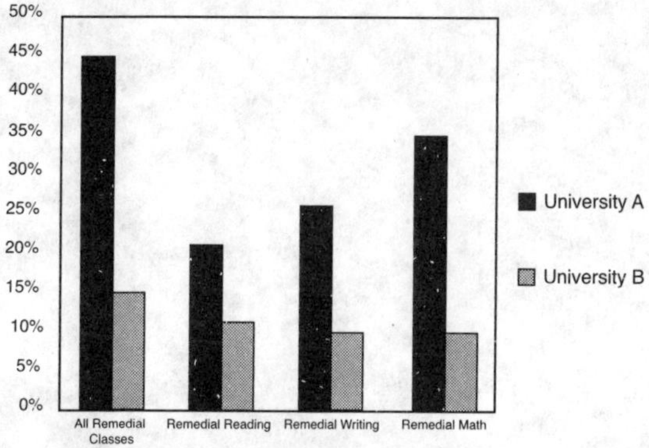

Speaking

Talk about the following topics.

If you could choose to have any extraordinary talent, what would you choose?

What programs for gifted children are there in your country?

How do you think education for gifted children will be different in the future?

[1]BrE: tables
[2]BrE: summarise

Unit 10: Technology/Inventions

THE DEVELOPMENT OF THE LIGHTBULB

Words

Write the letter of each definition with the word it defines. If you don't know the definition, use the context of the reading passage to help you. Look for the words in bold as you read the passage.

PARAGRAPHS 1–2

Words	Definitions
1 .... inventor	**A** n., a flow of electricity, water, or air
2 .... inspiration	**B** n., a person who creates new things
3 .... derive	**C** n., improvement
4 .... current	**D** v., to get from something; from something else; originate
5 .... refinement	**E** n., a sudden good idea; a role model for creativity

PARAGRAPHS 2–3

Words	Definitions
6 .... unveil	**F** v., to officially record something
7 .... critical	**G** adv., exactly; for a particular reason
8 .... device	**H** n., a right to an invention granted by the government
9 .... file	**I** n., a machine or tool
10 .... patent	**J** adj., very important
11 .... specifically	**K** v., to make public; to uncover

PARAGRAPHS 3–4

Words	Definitions
12 .... entrepreneur	**L** adj., appropriate; acceptable for something
13 .... back	**M** v., to search thoroughly, often violently or carelessly
14 .... investor	**N** v., to support, especially financially
15 .... ransack	**O** n., somebody who starts a business
16 .... suitable	**P** n., a person who puts money into a business

PARAGRAPHS 4–5

Words	Definitions
17 .... clamp	**Q** n., an action that breaks a rule or law
18 .... infringement	**R** v., to fasten or hold tightly
19 .... invalid	**S** n., a legal decision
20 .... ruling	**T** adj., not legally correct or acceptable

Reading

The Development of the Lightbulb

(1) Thomas Edison is generally credited with the invention of the lightbulb. In fact, he was just one **inventor** among many involved in the process of moving the concept of incandescent light from **inspiration** to marketable reality. What he actually invented in 1879 was a carbon filament that lasted for forty hours. In 1880, he improved his idea, producing a filament **derived** from bamboo that burned for 1,200 hours.

(2) The first person to successfully produce light with an electric **current** was Humphry Davy, who connected a carbon filament to a battery in 1809. Other inventors worked on **refinements** of this idea. In 1835, James Lindsay **unveiled** an electric lamp, which cast enough light to read a book one and a half feet away. In 1854, Henrich Globel created the first actual lightbulb—a glass bulb containing a filament that glowed when electrical current passed through it. However, it burned out too quickly to have any commercial value.

The next **critical** idea was an invention by the Gemran chemist, Hermann Sprengel. This was the Sprengel Pump, a **device** that used mercury to create a vacuum. Reducing the oxygen in the bulb allowed the filament to glow longer before burning out.

(3) In 1874, Henry Woodward and Matthew Evans **filed** a **patent** for a light **specifically** described as "a shaped piece of carbon held between two electrodes enclosed in a glass vessel." Woodward and Evans attempted to raise the necessary money to improve and market their invention; however, as **entrepreneurs**, they had little success finding anyone to **back** them financially. Eventually they sold the rights to their patents to Thomas Edison.

(4) Edison had already been working on the same idea, but for him money was not a critical issue. He was no longer a solitary inventor working in his basement, but the head of a laboratory with the support of **investors**. He worked to refine the Woodward and Evans light because its filament burned out too quickly. Edison set about testing every material possible for use as a filament. "Before I got through," Edison recalled, "I tested no fewer than 6,000 vegetable growths, and **ransacked** the world for the most **suitable** filament material." He even considered using tungsten, which is the material currently used. Eventually, Edison tried a carbonized cotton thread filament **clamped** to platinum wires. When tested, it lasted forty hours. In 1880, he received a patent for this invention. By the end of the year, Edison had perfected a sixteen-watt bulb that lasted for 1,500 hours.

(5) At the same time, Sir Joseph Swan was working on similar ideas in England. In 1860, he obtained a patent for a carbon filament incandescent lamp, and in 1878, another for an improved version of his lightbulb. He presented it in a public lecture in 1879. In 1882, Swan sued Edison for patent **infringement**. As part of the settlement, Edison had to take Swan as a partner in his British electric works. Also, in 1877 and 1878, William Edward Sawyer and Albon Man were granted patents for electric lamps. Based on these patents, the U.S. Patent Office ruled in 1883 that Edison's patents were **invalid**. Edison fought to appeal that **ruling**, and in 1889, the court determined that his patents were indeed valid.

(6) Edison is famous for having said, "Genius is one percent inspiration and ninety-nine percent perspiration." It is an understandable statement coming from someone whose laboratory tested more than 6,000 filament possibilities. Nevertheless, one might also consider the adage "History is written by the winners." Edison may not have been the actual inventor of the lightbulb, but he was the man who had the genius, the business sense, and the financial backing to invent the first one that was commercially viable.

Answer the questions about **The Development of the Lightbulb**.

Questions 1–5

Complete the summary using the list of words below.

backers	current	filed	refinement
clamped	device	inventors	unveiled

In the 1800s, many **1**............ experimented with using electrical **2**.......... to produce light. James Lindsay **3**........... his version of an electric light in 1835. It was bright enough for reading a book. Henrich Globel developed the first lightbulb in 1854. His **4**............, unfortunately, did not have commercial value. It needed **5**........... because it burned out very quickly.

Questions 6–9

Choose an ending from the list to complete each sentence. There are more endings than sentences, so you will not use them all.

A a cotton thread filament that he clamped to wires.

B a filament derived from bamboo.

C a tungsten filament like those used today.

D a long-lasting lightbulb filament.

E a filament that burned out very quickly.

F the most suitable material for a lightbulb filament.

.... **6** Edison did not invent the lightbulb in 1879; he invented

.... **7** Edison ransacked the world searching for

.... **8** Edison's first lightbulb consisted of

.... **9** Edison refined his idea in 1880 with the development of

Word Families

A

Complete each sentence with the correct word from the word family chart. Make nouns plural where necessary. Use the correct form of verbs.

noun	noun	verb
invention	inventor	invent

1 People .... new things every day.

2 Thomas Edison is probably the most well-known American ....

3 The computer is an .... that has completely changed our way of life.

noun	noun	verb
investor	investment	invest

4 Keeping all your money in the bank is not a good ....

5 If you .... wisely, you can make a good deal of money.

6 Every .... hopes to get a good return on his or her money.

noun	verb	adjective	adverb
inspiration	inspire	inspiring	inspired

7 The work of previous inventors .... Edison.

8 Edison's achievements have been an .... to many people.

9 I felt .... after my visit to the museum.

10 The work of great artists is ....

Unit 10

noun	verb	adjective
refinement	refine	refined

11 Any piece of work can always use ....

12 Edison worked very hard to .... his inventions.

13 In 1880, Edison developed a lightbulb, which was a .... version of his earlier lightbulb.

noun	verb	adjective	adverb
specification	specify	specific	specifically

14 According to the ...., you cannot put a bulb stronger than 60 watts in this lamp.

15 The professor gave .... directions about how she wanted the assignment to be completed.

16 The customer ordered some lightbulbs, but he didn't .... which kind he wanted.

17 Edison made an important contribution to the development of the lightbulb, ..., a long-lasting filament.

noun	verb	adjective	adverb
suitability	suit	suitable	suitably

18 They decided to rent the laboratory space because it was .... located.

19 She is a solitary person, so it .... her to work alone.

20 Many materials were not .... for a lightbulb filament because they did not burn long enough.

21 Edison tested many materials for their .... as a lightbulb filament.

Word Families

B

Choose the correct word family member from the list below to complete each blank.

1	inspiration	inspire	inspiring
2	inventor	invention	invent
3	refinement	refine	refined
4	investor	investment	invest
5	Suit	Suitable	Suitably
6	specify	specific	specifically

It takes a creative person to come up with ideas for new products. However, **1**.......... is not enough. It takes more than good ideas to develop an **2**.......... into a product that is practical and useful and can be successfully marketed. It takes hard work and determination. Teams must test new products and then **3**.......... the design, again and again, until there are no improvements to be made. Once the design is perfected, the new product is ready for mass production. This takes money. It takes finding people who believe in the product enough to **4**.......... money in it. **5**.......... people should be found, that is, people who not only can provide the financing, but are interested in the product and in the business. In addition, market research needs to be done to target the **6**.......... groups of people who might be interested in buying the product. Marketing to certain types of people rather than to a general audience can be a very successful approach.

Paraphrases

Read the sentence from the reading passage. Then, choose the sentence that has the same meaning.

1 *Other inventors worked on refinements of this idea.* (paragraph 2)
A Other people improved on Davy's invention.
B Other inventors copied Davy's idea.
C Other scientists helped Davy make his electric light.

2 *Edison may not have been the actual inventor of the light bulb, but he was the man who had the genius, the business sense, and the financial backing to invent the first one that was commercially practical.* (paragraph 6)
A If Edison had had more money, he would have been able to make a better light bulb.
B Edison did not create the first light bulb, but he had the skills and money to make one that could be sold.
C Edison was finally able to market his light bulb when he reduced the price.

Dictionary Skill

DIFFERENT MEANINGS

Many words have more than one meaning.

Read the definitions below. Then read the sentences and write the letter of the correct definition for each sentence.

cur-rent [KUR-uhnt]
A *noun.* a flow of electricity, water, or air
B *adjective.* of the present time

.... **1** Don't touch a wire that has an electric *current* running through it.

.... **2** We are able to do many things now that were difficult just a few years ago because of the *current* state of technology.

Listening

Track 28

Listen to the talk. Complete the notes below.
Write ***NO MORE THAN THREE WORDS*** *for each answer.*

Getting Ready to Market Your Invention

First, do a **1**........... .

Next, file **2**........... .

At the same time, you will have to **3**........... .

Look for financial **4**........... .

Writing (Task 2)

In your opinion, what has been the most important invention of the past 100 years?

Support your opinion with reasons and examples from your own knowledge or experience.

Write at least 250 words.

Speaking

Talk about the following topics.

Who was an inspiration to you when you were growing up?

Who is an inspiration to you now?

Do you find any type of music or art inspiring? How does it inspire you?

THE INVENTION OF VARIABLE-PITCH PROPELLERS

Words

Write the letter of each definition with the word it defines. If you don't know the definition, use the context of the reading passage to help you. Look for the words in bold as you read the passage.

PARAGRAPH 1

Words	Definitions
1 .... propeller	**A** n., a device that causes an airplane or boat to move
2 .... sustained	**B** adj., rough; not smooth
3 .... coarse	**C** n., inability to change
4 .... prolonged	**D** adj., continuing for a long time, often in a negative sense
5 .... inflexibility	**E** adj., having the ability to continue for a long time

PARAGRAPH 2

Words	Definitions
6 .... variable	**F** v., to travel at a steady speed
7 .... pitch	**G** adj., able to change
8 .... blade	**H** n., a thin, flat part of a machine
9 .... rotation	**I** n., turning motion
10 .... cruise	**J** n., the angle or slope of something

PARAGRAPHS 2–4

Words	Definitions
11 .... reliably	**K** n., the development, design, and use of aircraft
12 .... handle	**L** n., a plan for making something
13 .... turbulence	**M** v., to manage; work well with
14 .... aviation	**N** n., strong, sudden movements in air
15 .... design	**O** adv., dependably

PARAGRAPH 5

Words	Definitions
16 .... confer	**P** n., a person who is very interested in something
17 .... enthusiast	**Q** n., interest; need to know
18 .... isolation	**R** v., to discuss; consult with somebody
19 .... curiosity	**S** n., the condition of being alone or separated from others
20 .... revolutionize[1]	**T** v., to change completely

[1]BrE: revolutionise

Reading

The Invention of Variable-Pitch Propellers

(1) Until the late 1920s, airplane **propellers** were made of a single piece of wood attached at the center[1] to the driveshaft of the engine. The tilt of the propeller, that is, how flatly it faced the wind, was fixed, which meant planes flew as if they had only one gear. If the plane had a fine propeller, it traveled the entire time as if in first gear, working well on takeoff and landing but working inefficiently during **sustained** flight. If the plane had a thick, **coarse** propeller, it traveled the entire time as if in high gear, working efficiently during sustained flight, but making takeoffs and landings dangerous and **prolonged**. This **inflexibility** meant that commercial uses of such aircraft were limited because the planes could not carry heavy loads either safely or efficiently.

(2) In 1922, Wallace Rupert Turnbull patented his latest invention, the **Variable-Pitch** propeller. His propeller in effect gave airplanes gears. The propeller's **blades** were separate from each other, attached at the driveshaft in the center, and could be moved independently or together to chop the air at different angles. The propellers could be tilted at takeoff and landing to act as if in first gear, chopping less air with each **rotation**, and could be tilted when **cruising** to act as if in high gear, chopping more air with each rotation. With this Variable-Pitch propeller, planes could now take off and land more safely and **reliably**, carry varying weights, and **handle** greater variations in wind speed and **turbulence**.

(3) Turnbull was born in New Brunswick in eastern Canada in 1876. He studied mechanical engineering at Cornell, then continued his post-graduate studies in Europe, and returned to work at the Edison labs in New Jersey. In 1902, just one year before the Wright brothers made their historic flight, Turnbull went back home, set up his own lab in a barn, and started running his own **aviation** experiments.

(4) To begin, Turnbull needed a wind tunnel. He built a wind tunnel, the first in the world, out of packing materials. In it, he tested different **designs** for propellers and wings; his research is the basis for many of the successful designs still in use today. Alone in his barn, Turnbull designed and tested his Variable-Pitch propeller. It was tested successfully in flight in Borden, Ontario, on June 6, 1927.

---

[1]BrE: centre

(5) Turnbull spent his life experimenting and designing for the new science of aviation in his barn in Rothesay. He sometimes **conferred** with fellow aviation **enthusiast** Alexander Graham Bell in Nova Scotia, but for the most part, he worked in **isolation**. Unlike most engineers, he chose not to work in a university laboratory or in a lab such as Edison's, where he would have been supported by like-minded engineers and physicists. Instead, he spent his adult life in a barn he equipped himself. Depending only on his intelligence, **curiosity**, and work ethic, he **revolutionized** flight. He is honored[2] in Canada as a pioneer in aviation and a genius in the study of aerodynamics.

Answer the questions about **The Invention of Variable-Pitch Propellers**.

Questions 1–5

Do the following statements agree with the information in the reading passage?
Write

TRUE	*if the statement agrees with the information.*
FALSE	*if the statement contradicts the information.*
NOT GIVEN	*if there is no information on this in the passage.*

.... **1** A coarse propeller worked better during sustained flight than during landing.

.... **2** Variable-Pitch propellers caused problems because of their inflexibility.

.... **3** The blades of a Variable-Pitch propeller could be moved to different angles.

.... **4** A plane with a Variable-Pitch propeller was easier to handle in turbulence.

.... **5** Variable-Pitch propellers were expensive to manufacture.

Unit 10

[2]BrE: honoured

Questions 6–7

*Choose the correct letter, **A**, **B**, **C**, or **D**.*

6 Wallace Rupert Turnbull designed his Variable-Pitch propeller
- **A** at Cornell University.
- **B** in Canada.
- **C** at the home of Alexander Graham Bell.
- **D** in Edison's lab.

7 Turnbull preferred to work
- **A** with other inventors.
- **B** in a university lab.
- **C** with like-minded engineers.
- **D** in isolation.

Word Families

A

Complete each sentence with the correct word from the word family chart. Make nouns plural where necessary. Use the correct form of verbs.

noun	noun	adjective	adverb
enthusiasm	enthusiast	enthusiastic	enthusiastically

1 Aviation .... are very interested in flying.

2 The inventor worked .... to turn his idea into reality.

3 Turnbull's .... for aviation kept him searching for a better propeller design.

4 Turnbull was .... about aviation.

noun	adjective	adverb
inflexibility	inflexible	inflexibly

5 An inventor should not work ....

6 The successful inventor cannot be ....

7 The .... of early propellers made planes difficult to fly.

noun	verb	adjective
isolation	isolate	isolated

8 Inventors often prefer to work in ....

9 An inventor may need to .... herself in order to do her best work.

10 Turnbull set up his lab in an .... location.

noun	verb	adjective	adverb
reliance	rely	reliable	reliably

11 The Variable-Pitch propeller made planes more ....

12 A plane with a Variable-Pitch propeller flew more .... than earlier planes.

13 Early pilots could not .... on their planes to carry heavy loads.

14 His .... on the work of others caused some to question his research.

noun	verb	adjective
revolution	revolutionize	revolutionary

15 Turnbull's propeller was a .... invention.

16 New inventions .... the way we do things.

17 The invention of the Variable-Pitch propeller led to a .... in flight.

noun	verb	adjective	adverb
variable	vary	variable	variably

18 It might be more difficult to fly if the winds are ....

19 Planes carry different kinds of loads, and the size of the load ....

20 Planes carry .... heavy loads.

21 Researchers look at different .... in their studies.

Word Families

B

Choose the correct word family member from the list below to complete each blank.

1	enthusiast	enthusiastic	enthusiastically
2	inflexibility	inflexible	inflexibly
3	rely	reliable	reliably
4	isolation	isolate	isolated
5	vary	variable	variably
6	revolution	revolutionize	revolutionary

Like most inventors, Wallace Rupert Turnbull was filled with curiosity about many things. He became **1**.......... about designing a propeller that would fly more efficiently, during takeoff and landing as well as while cruising. Propellers on early planes were **2**.......... , that is, the angle could not be changed, so they did not fly efficiently under certain conditions. Because of this, pilots could not always **3**.......... on their planes to perform well. Turnbull worked in an **4**.......... barn in New Brunswick to develop a new kind of propeller. He could **5**.......... the angle, or pitch, of this propeller, which made it efficient under different conditions. Turnbull's invention led to a **6**.......... in flight.

Paraphrases

Read the sentence from the reading passage. Then, choose the sentence that has the same meaning.

1 *Although he sometimes conferred with fellow aviation enthusiast Alexander Graham Bell in Nova Scotia, for the most part, he worked in isolation.* (paragraph 5)

A Turnbull relied on the support of Bell to keep working on his inventions.

B Turnbull invited Bell to work with him in his barn because he didn't like to work alone.

C Turnbull occasionally discussed his work with Bell, but mostly he worked alone.

2 *Depending only on his intelligence, curiosity, and work ethic, he revolutionized flight.* (paragraph 5)

A Turnbull worked hard to learn all he could about flying.

B Turnbull was not able to get the support of other inventors working in aviation.

C Turnbull's hard work and deep interest in flying led him to completely change aviation.

Word Skill

PREFIX *IN*–

The prefix *in*– can make the meaning of a word negative.

Read the sentences. Write a definition for each underlined word.

1 Inventing involves trying out different ways of doing things, so it is important for an inventor to be flexible.

flexible: ....

2 Because the position of the propeller on early airplanes was inflexible, it was always set at the same angle.

inflexible: ....

Unit 10

Listening

Track 29

Listen to the conversation. Choose **FOUR** *letters,* ***A–G.***

Which **FOUR** facts about the flight demonstration will the students include in their report?

A the name of the plane's designer

B the names of the passengers

C the number of passengers

D the size of the propeller

E the speed of rotation

F the length of the flight

G the weather conditions

Writing (Task 1)

The charts[1] below show basic information about different models of light sport aircraft and very light jets for aviation enthusiasts.

Summarize[2] the information by selecting and reporting the main information and making comparisons.

Write at least 150 words.

Light Sport Aircraft

Manufacturer	Cruise Speed	Passenger Capacity	Price
Airways	75 mph	0	$39,000
Tiger, Inc.	115 mph	1	$134,000
McGregor	130 mph	1	$194,000

Very Light Jets

Manufacturer	Cruise Speed	Passenger Capacity	Price
Airways	300 mph	2	$900,000
Tiger, Inc.	350 mph	4	$2,250,000
McGregor	425 mph	6	$3,650,000

Speaking

Talk about the following topics.

Do you prefer to work (study) with a group or in isolation? Why?

When you run into a problem with work (studies), do you confer with others or do you prefer to find your own solution?

What makes you feel enthusiastic about your work (studies)?

[1]BrE: tables
[2]BrE: summarise

Unit 10

THE TRANSATLANTIC CABLE

Words

Write the letter of each definition with the word it defines. If you don't know the definition, use the context of the reading passage to help you. Look for the words in bold as you read the passage.

PARAGRAPHS 1–2

Words	Definitions
1 .... cable	**A** adj., extremely bad
2 .... disparate	**B** n., an official investigation
3 .... utterly	**C** v., to gather support
4 .... rally	**D** adj., different
5 .... catastrophic	**E** adv., totally
6 .... inquiry	**F** n., wire used for sending electric signals

PARAGRAPHS 3–4

Words	Definitions
7 .... insulation	**G** v., to start an activity
8 .... requisite	**H** n., need; requirement
9 .... set out	**I** v., to pull behind
10 .... tow	**J** n., material used to prevent the passage of electricity, heat, or sound

PARAGRAPH 4

Words	Definitions
11 .... transmit	**K** v., to make up for; balance out
12 .... snap	**L** v., to send
13 .... inexplicably	**M** n., measure of electric power
14 .... compensate	**N** adv., without explanation
15 .... voltage	**O** adj., having one's reputation ruined; being spoken about in a bad way
16 .... vilified	**P** v., to break suddenly

PARAGRAPH 5

Words	Definitions
17 .... indispensable	**Q** n., a mistake or weakness, especially in design
18 .... flaw	**R** n., continuation with a task despite difficulties
19 .... perseverance	**S** v., to succeed; win
20 .... triumph	**T** adj., completely necessary

Reading

The Transatlantic Cable

(1) Laying the transatlantic **cable** was the culmination of the unflagging perseverance of one man leading like-minded men, of **disparate** technical and scientific advances, and of the need for faster communication. The first attempts at laying the cable in the 1850s, each of which cost an enormous amount of money, failed **utterly**. Yet as technology and science improved, and the need for faster communication increased, perseverance finally paid off.

(2) The man who **rallied** support and raised money for the transatlantic cable venture was Cyrus Field, a New York businessman, who started the New York, Newfoundland, and London Telegraph Company in 1854. For the next twelve years, Field raised money and expectations in North America and England for repeated attempts at laying a cable, despite **catastrophic** cable breaks and a formal **inquiry** when the first cable stopped working within days.

(3) The scientific and technological advances began with electricity, the study of which was attracting the greatest minds of the age. Samuel Morse invented a code that made it possible to send information over electric wires, and he made the first successful transmission in 1842. The next year, d'Alameida, a Portuguese engineer, announced the use of gutta-percha, a rubberlike sap from the gutta tree, as an **insulation** for wires. Thus, two of the **requisites** for an underwater cable were met. In the next several years, telegraph cables were laid in Atlantic Canada, across the English Channel and around Europe, and across the United States.

(4) In 1857, the company Field founded **set out** to lay the cable that had taken months and almost a million dollars to make. The cable was made of 340,000 miles of copper and iron wire and three tons of gutta-percha insulation, too much for one ship to carry. The cable was divided between two ships, each **towed** by another, all four provided by the British and American navies. After only 255 miles of cable had been laid, the cable stopped **transmitting** and then **snapped**, sinking to the depths of the ocean. The second attempt was made in 1858, beginning at the midpoint of the Atlantic, from which each ship lay cable as she sailed to her home shores. Again, the cable **inexplicably** stopped working. They tried again a month later, beginning again from the middle and sailing in opposite directions. This time, success! Queen Victoria sent a message to President Buchanan, and both countries celebrated. Within hours, however, the signal began failing. To **compensate** for the fading transmissions, Whitehouse, the American engineer, transmitted messages at higher **voltages**, eventually burning out the cable. Once a hero, Field was now **vilified**.

(5) Work on the transatlantic cable was halted because of the American Civil War. During the war, the telegraph became **indispensable**, and enthusiasm for a transatlantic cable mounted. In Scotland, William Thomson, who would later be knighted Lord Kelvin for his work, corrected the design **flaws** in Whitehouse's cable. Kelvin also designed a mirror-galvanometer that could detect weak currents, thus allowing lower voltages and weaker currents to transmit information. In 1866, the world's largest steamship laid Kelvin's new cable, an unqualified success. Field's **perseverance** had **triumphed** in the end.

Answer the questions about **The Transatlantic Cable.**

Questions 1–4

Look at the following inventors and the list of descriptions below. Match each inventor with the correct description, ***A–F***.

A burned out the first transatlantic cable by using high voltages

B was the first to be utterly successful in getting the transatlantic cable laid

C invented a type of insulation from the sap of a tree

D sent a telegraph message to President Buchanan

E was the first to attempt to have a transatlantic cable laid

F developed a code for transmitting messages by electric cable

.... **1** Morse

.... **2** d'Alameida

.... **3** Field

.... **4** Kelvin

Unit 10

Questions 5–9

Complete the summary using words from the list below.

compensated	rallied	towed	triumph
insulation	snapped	transmitted	voltage

In the 1850s, several unsuccessful attempts were made to lay a telegraph cable across the Atlantic Ocean. For the first attempt, a cable was manufactured of copper and iron wire with gutta-percha **5**.......... . It was so heavy that the ships that carried it had to be **6**.......... by other ships. This cable failed because it **7**.......... and sank beneath the sea. The second attempt also failed. The third attempt appeared to be successful, and a message was **8**.......... from England to the United States. However, the telegraph company did not **9**.......... this time either. This attempt also turned out to be a failure when the cable stopped working, and the reputations of the project leaders were vilified.

Word Families

A

Complete each sentence with the correct word from the word family chart. Make nouns plural where necessary. Use the correct form of verbs.

noun	adjective	adverb
catastrophe	catastrophic	catastrophically

1 The failure of the initial attempts to lay the transatlantic cable resulted in a .... loss of money.

2 Field failed .... in his attempts to lay a transatlantic cable.

3 The initial attempts to lay a transatlantic cable ended in .... for Field.

noun	verb	adjective
compensation	compensate	compensatory

4 There is no .... for hard work and perseverance.

5 When the signals began to fade, they took .... measures to keep the cable working.

6 Hard work can sometimes .... for bad luck.

noun	noun	verb	adjective
insulation	insulator	insulate	insulated

7 Rubber is a good ....

8 The transatlantic cable was .... with gutta-percha.

9 It was important to find a practical way to .... the cable.

10 Rubber makes good .... for an electric wire.

noun	verb	adjective
perseverance	persevere	persevering

11 A .... person can find a way to achieve her dreams.

12 An inventor must .... to turn his ideas into reality.

13 Because of Field's ...., a telegraph cable was eventually laid under the Atlantic Ocean.

noun	verb	adjective	adverb
triumph	triumph	triumphant	triumphantly

14 It was a .... day when the English queen sent a telegraph message to the American president.

15 The laying of the cable in 1866 was a .... for Kelvin.

16 Many people worked hard to make the idea of a transatlantic cable into a reality, and they finally ....

17 They .... announced the completion of the project.

Word Families

B

Choose the correct word family member from the list below to complete each blank.

1	catastrophes	catastrophic	catastrophically
2	perseverance	persevere	persevering
3	triumph	triumphs	triumphant
4	insulation	insulate	insulated
5	compensation	compensate	compensatory

Invention is all about hard work. An inventor may have a brilliant idea, but he has to test it many times. The process may be filled with **1**.......... . It is the **2**......... inventor who will eventually be **3**......... . For example, there were many failed attempts before the transatlantic telegraph cable was successfully manufactured and laid. After a material was found that could suitably **4**.......... the cable, they thought the major difficulties had been solved. However, they met with many more difficulties when they actually tried to put the cable in place. They tried to **5**.......... for the flaws in their method but were unsuccessful. It wasn't until almost ten years later that another group of people succeeded in laying the cable.

Paraphrases

Read the sentence from the reading passage. Then, choose the sentence that has the same meaning.

1 *After only 255 miles of cable had been laid, the cable stopped transmitting and then snapped, sinking to the depths of the ocean.* (paragraph 4)

A The ships traveled 255 miles and then stopped, so the cable sank.
B Before long, the cable stopped sending signals and broke.
C The cable was too short, so the ships just let it sink to the bottom of the sea.

2 *During the war, the telegraph became indispensable, and the enthusiasm for a transatlantic cable mounted.* (paragraph 5)

A The telegraph was very necessary during the war, so interest in a transatlantic cable grew.
B Telegraph technology improved during the war and more cables were laid.
C Telegraph systems were damaged during the war, so people turned their attention to the transatlantic cable.

Word Skill

PHRASAL VERBS WITH *SET*.

Phrasal verbs are made up of two parts: a verb and one or two particles. The meaning of the phrasal verb is usually not related to the meanings of the individual parts.

Phrasal Verb		Meaning
set verb	*out* particle	begin a project
set verb	*back* particle	delay
set verb	*up* particle	arrange

Choose the correct phrasal verb from the list above to complete each sentence.

Unit 10

1 The two inventors .... to design a new kind of cable.

2 They .... a meeting to talk about their project.

3 The meeting was .... several days because of bad weather.

Listening

Track 30

Listen to the talk. Complete the timeline below.
Write ***NO MORE THAN TWO WORDS AND/OR A NUMBER*** *for each answer.*

1.....	The mayor got the idea for a museum.
1976	The mayor **2**....... to get the requisite money.
1977	A large gift of money was lost.
3.....	Construction of the museum began.
4.....	museum opened
1998	opening of exhibit on **5**.....

Writing
(Task 2)

In your opinion, which is more important for success, perseverance or good luck?

Support your opinion with reasons and examples from your own knowledge or experience.

Write at least 250 words.

Speaking

Talk about the following topics.

What profession do you work in or do you plan to work in? What are the usual requisites for entering this profession?

In your opinion, what personal qualities are indispensable for success in your profession?

APPENDIX

Word List

A
abound (221)
abroad (119)
absence (212)
absorb (138)
abstract (109)
academic (212)
accelerate (83)
accessible (148)
accommodations (157)
accompany (100)
account for (221)
accumulate (27)
acknowledge (55)
acquaintance (204)
acquire (166)
adapt (26)
address (244)
adequately (244)
administer (119)
adolescent (204)
adopt (91)
adventurous (147)
aerobic (127)
afloat (176)
agricultural (91)
alleviate (139)
altar (100)
alternative (243)
ancient (45)
anticipate (37)
apparently (203)
appeal (82)
approach (233)
approximately (212)
aquatic (9)
archeologist (147)
architecture (74)
array (9)
ascertain (139)
aspect (17)
assess (252)
athlete (37)
atmosphere (110)
attribute (91)
auditory (233)
authority (55)
aviation (273)
avoid (156)

B
backers (266)
band (45)
barrier (157)
bear (212)
benefit (100)
blade (272)
blend (233)
blur (37)
bond (185)
boon (194)
boundary (38)
branch (194)
brand (185)
breed (17)
breeze (166)
broad (167)
budget (167)
bulk (119)
burgeoning (186)

C
cable (282)
capable (222)
capacity (127)
carry out (203)

Answer Key

UNIT 1: NATURAL WORLD

Environmental Impacts of Logging

WORDS (page 9)

1. C	6. K	11. F	16. N
2. D	7. J	12. M	17. Q
3. A	8. G	13. L	18. S
4. E	9. I	14. P	19. T
5. B	10. H	15. O	20. R

READING (page 12)

1. E	3. D	5. fells	7. habitats
2. B	4. C	6. myriad	8. defense

WORD FAMILIES

A (page 13)

1. defense	6. environment	11. extent
2. defend	7. erodes	12. extensively
3. defender	8. erosion	13. pollutants
4. environmentally	9. extends	14. pollutes
5. environmental	10. extensive	15. pollution

B (page 14)

1. environment	3. extensive	5. erode
2. pollutants	4. stability	6. Defenders

PARAPHRASES (page 15)

1. B 2. A

WORD SKILL (page 15)

1. remove the forest
2. remove the bones
3. remove the ice

LISTENING (page 16)

1. B 2. A 3. C 4. B

WRITING (page 16)

(sample response)

Deforestation is a serious problem, and finding a solution to it will not be simple. It involves a lot of different countries and many political and economic factors. However, as individuals we can each make our contribution to the solution. It involves being more responsible about our use of products that come from logging.

Logging companies fell trees so that we can have wood to make a lot of useful products: houses, bags and boxes, writing paper, furniture. We all use these things in our daily lives and would not want to give them up. We can, however, be less wasteful in the way we use these things. Paper products, in particular, offer many opportunities for reusing, recycling, and reducing our use of them.

Many paper products can be reused. We tend to go shopping, carry our purchases home in a paper bag, and then throw the bag away. That means the bag is used only once, when it really has enough life in it to be used several times. We can take the bag with us on our next shopping trip or find other uses for it around the house. This is just one example of a paper product that can be reused.

Recycling is another important part of being less wasteful. Most kinds of household and office paper can be recycled, and these days most cities have recycling centers. Recycling paper is so easy that there is really no excuse not to do it.

Reducing our use of paper might be the most effective action of all. Electronic technology makes a lot of uses of paper unnecessary. We can create documents and read news articles on a computer without using paper. There are many other things we can do in our daily lives, such as using cloth napkins and towels instead of paper ones, to reduce our use of paper.

These actions may seem small compared with the terrible impacts of deforestation. However, they are things that we can each do and that, when added up, really can make a difference.

SPEAKING (page 16)

(sample response)

I don't get a lot of time to spend in nature, but when I do, I like being in the mountains. When you're in the mountains, you're really far away from everything, from cities, I mean, and civilization. You can really feel like you're in nature. Also, mountains are different from other environments. They're higher up, so you see different kinds of vegetation, and if you go up high enough, there aren't even any trees, just plants low down to the ground. I really enjoy hiking. That's the main reason I like mountains. I like to hike to the top of a mountain, breathe the fresh, cool air, and enjoy the view.

There are a lot of different causes of environmental pollution, so there are a lot of different solutions. One of my favorites is transportation. Cars really pollute the air a lot. They really have an impact on the environment. Think about how it would be if no one drove cars. The air would be really clean! Of course, that won't happen. However, people would drive less if better public transportation was available. If we had good bus and train and subway systems, we would need fewer cars. I think that would be a really important part of any solution.

Bird Migration

WORDS (page 17)

1. A	6. F	11. M	16. Q
2. D	7. G	12. L	17. S
3. B	8. I	13. K	18. R
4. E	9. H	14. O	19. P
5. C	10. J	15. N	20. T

READING (page 18)

1. True	4. Not Given	7. B
2. False	5. A	8. A
3. True	6. B	

WORD FAMILIES

A (page 22)

1. evolved	7. migration	13. navigation
2. evolutions	8. migratory	14. navigate
3. evolutionary	9. migrate	15. observe
4. fascinating	10. migrants	16. observer
5. fascinates	11. navigational	17. observation
6. fascination	12. navigators	18. observant

B (page 22)

1. fascinating	3. migratory	5. navigate
2. observer	4. evolved	

PARAPHRASES (page 23)

1. C 2. B

DICTIONARY SKILL (page 24)

1. B 2. A

LISTENING (page 24)

1. B	3. E	5. C
2. A	4. D	

WRITING (page 25)

(sample response)

The chart shows a list of some of the species of birds that can be seen in Woodchuck County in two different seasons: winter and summer. Information is given about eight different species of birds. Three of the species listed cardinals, crows, and woodpeckers are observed in both summer and winter. That means that they are probably not migratory birds but live in the region all year. They can tolerate the winter weather in that area. Four of the species listed bluebirds, mockingbirds, orioles, and vireos are observed only in the summer. They must be migratory birds that travel to Woodchuck County for their breeding season and spend the winter in another place where the weather is warmer. One species of bird juncos is seen in Woodchuck County in the winter but not in the summer. Perhaps it migrates farther north in the summer for its breeding season.

SPEAKING (page 25)

(sample response)

I think people are fascinated by birds because they seem so free. They can fly, so it seems like they can go anywhere. People can't fly and are stuck on the ground. So birds are very different from us in that way. Some birds are also very beautiful. Some are very colorful. Swans are very graceful. So I think people are also fascinated by birds because of their beauty.

I'm not particularly fascinated by birds. I live in the city, so I don't see any interesting birds around me in my everyday life. I just see those brown and gray city birds. They aren't pretty, and they're a bit dirty, so I don't like them. If I lived somewhere where there were more interesting birds, probably I would be interested in them.

I'm not fascinated by animals in general, but I am a little bit interested in pet cats. I think they have very nice lives. They nap all day on a soft chair or in the sun, and then in the evening they get fed. They just nap and eat. They can chase mice if they feel like it. They can do whatever they like. What a life!

Plant Life in the Taklimakan Desert

WORDS (page 26)

1. D	6. G	11. K	16. M
2. A	7. I	12. O	17. T
3. E	8. J	13. L	18. S
4. B	9. H	14. P	19. Q
5. C	10. F	15. N	20. R

READING (page 29)

1. C
2. B
3. C
4. B
5. D
6. E
7. F

WORD FAMILIES

A (page 30)

1. adapt
2. adaptations
3. adaptable
4. diverse
5. diversification
6. diversity
7. diversify
8. extreme
9. extremely
10. extreme
11. resilient
12. resiliently
13. resilience
14. stress
15. stress
16. stressor
17. stressful
18. violence
19. violent
20. violently

B (page 32)

1. adaptations
2. extremely
3. stress
4. resilience
5. Violent
6. diversity

PARAPHRASES (page 33)

1. A
2. B

DICTIONARY SKILL (page 34)

1. C
2. A
3. B

LISTENING (page 34)

1. transitional
2. extreme
3. evaporation
4. accumulate

WRITING (page 35)

(sample response)

The charts show information about the size, rainfall, and temperatures of three deserts on three different continents. At 9,000,000 square kilometers in area, the Sahara Desert in Africa is much larger than the other two deserts shown. The Taklimakan, at 337,600 square kilometers, and the Great Basin, at 305,775 square kilometers, are similar to each other in size. The Taklimakan has the sparsest rainfall, with an average of 1 to 3.8 centimeters per year. The three deserts have similar summer temperatures: 30°C in the Sahara and Great Basin deserts and 25°C in the Taklimakan Desert. However, winters in the Sahara, with an average temperature of 13°C, are much warmer than in the other two deserts, where the average winter temperatures are -8°C and -9°C. The highest temperatures recorded in the Sahara and Great Basin are almost the same: 57°C and 58°C. The other extreme, the lowest recorded temperature, is not shown for those two deserts, but it is shown for the Taklimakan: -26.1°C.

SPEAKING (page 36)

(sample response)

I don't think I would like to go to the top of a high mountain because I don't like to be cold. And I think climbing high mountains like Mount Everest is dangerous. It might be interesting to visit a desert because I would like to see the different kinds of plants that grow there. I think they would be very unusual and interesting to look at. But I don't like to be too hot, either, so I wouldn't want to stay in the desert for a long time. I don't really like extreme environments. I prefer to be comfortable.

I think people like extreme environments for two reasons. One is adventure. Some people like doing unusual or dangerous things. They want to see if they can climb to the top of high mountains or endure extreme hot or cold. They want to prove how strong they are and how much they can endure. The other reason is interest. Some people are interested in studying unusual plants or animals or rocks, different kinds of things, so they have to go to unusual places to find these things.

I can adapt easily to new climates as long as they aren't extreme! In the wintertime, it's very cold in my city. If I have the opportunity, I like to take a vacation at that time and go to a warm place with a nice beach. I certainly can adapt easily to a warm beach climate, especially when I think about the cold weather I have left behind at home! However, I don't like to go anywhere that's too hot, or too cold either. I can't adapt to that.

UNIT 2: LEISURE TIME

Peripheral Vision in Sports

WORDS (page 37)

1. B	6. I	11. M	16. Q
2. E	7. J	12. O	17. P
3. D	8. F	13. L	18. T
4. A	9. G	14. K	19. S
5. C	10. H	15. N	20. R

READING (page 39)

1. True	4. Not Given	7. True
2. False	5. False	
3. True	6. True	

WORD FAMILIES

A (page 40)

1. complications
2. complicated
3. complicates
4. coordinated
5. coordinate
6. coordination
7. demonstration
8. demonstrate
9. demonstrative
10. performed
11. performance
12. performers
13. tolerant
14. tolerate
15. tolerance
16. visual
17. visually
18. vision

B (page 42)

1. perform
2. demonstrate
3. coordination
4. visual
5. tolerant
6. Complications

PARAPHRASES (page 42)

1. A
2. C

DICTIONARY SKILL (page 43)

1. B
2. A
3. A
4. B

LISTENING (page 44)

1. focus
2. anticipate
3. scan
4. unconsciously

WRITING (page 44)

(sample response)

People everywhere like watching sports. Many top athletes are admired throughout their countries, and some even have fans all around the world. These athletes are good role models for young people in many ways, although in some ways they can also be a bad example.

Top athletes get the attention of young people. Most children and teenagers like to follow professional sports. Professional athletes become heroes to them, and children want to be like their heroes. This means they will want to play sports, which is good for their health. Playing sports also teaches important lessons such as teamwork and learning how to lose (and win) gracefully. Professional athletes also demonstrate the importance of working hard for your goals, of practicing regularly to become good at something. This is a good example for children to follow.

However, professional athletes are not always good role models. For one thing, the most famous athletes get paid very high salaries, much higher than most normal people can expect to earn. They also get a lot of attention, not only when they play their sports, but in other parts of their lives as well. This can lead children to believe that money and fame are an important part of sports. Children might focus more on these aspects than on the fun of the game or on the challenge of learning how to play well. Then there are those athletes who behave badly. For example, some take drugs to improve their performance in their game. This kind of behavior sends the wrong message to children.

Professional athletes can be very good role models for children, as long as they focus on the positive aspects of playing sports.

SPEAKING (page 44)

(sample response)

I know that some people find noise distracting, but I actually prefer to study in a noisy environment. I don't know why. When things are quiet, somehow I seem to notice that. It distracts me in a way. But when there is some noise around me—I don't mean loud noise like a rock concert or anything like that, but when I hear people talking in the next room, or people walking down the hall, just people going about their normal activities around me—I feel comfortable. I guess then I know I'm not alone. That feeling of having people around me actually helps me focus on my studies.

Like I said, being in a noisy environment isn't distracting to me, but sudden loud noises, such as the telephone ringing or a car horn honking, really bother me. Then it takes me a few minutes to get my focus back and go on studying. Also, as I mentioned before, quiet can be distracting to me. If there are no noises around me, no people talking or no cars rushing by, I notice the lack of noise. I just don't like it. That's why I don't really like to study at the library. It's too quiet!

I anticipate a big, big change in my study situation. For one thing, I will graduate in a few months. That's a major change. Then, I'm hoping to be able to go to graduate school. I'm working on the applications now, so it will be a while before I find out whether I'm accepted at any of the schools. All the schools I'm applying to are in other countries, so maybe a year from now I'll be living in a foreign country. That would be a huge change. If I don't get accepted at any of the schools, then I'll have to find a job and work for a while and apply to graduate school again. Whatever happens, by next year my life will be very different from what it is now.

History of the Circus

WORDS (page 45)

1. D	6. I	11. K	16. O
2. A	7. G	12. N	17. S
3. B	8. F	13. P	18. R
4. E	9. J	14. L	19. Q
5. C	10. H	15. M	20. T

READING (page 47)

1. C	3. B	5. C	7. A
2. A	4. A	6. B	

WORD FAMILIES

A (page 48)

1. developed
2. developer
3. development
4. entertain
5. entertaining
6. entertainer
7. entertainment
8. permanent
9. permanence
10. permanently
11. popular
12. popularly
13. popularize
14. popularity
15. survival
16. survived
17. survivor
18. trained
19. train
20. trainer

B (page 50)

1. development
2. entertained
3. trained
4. popular
5. survived
6. permanent

PARAPHRASES (page 51)

1. B
2. A

DICTIONARY SKILL (page 51)

1. B
2. A
3. A
4. B

LISTENING (page 52)

1. C
2. A
3. A
4. B

WRITING (page 53)

(sample response)

These days, technology has made it possible for us to be entertained without even leaving our homes. TV, DVDs, and computers can provide us with endless hours of entertainment. It may seem strange that people still like to go out to see live performances such as a circus. The circus, however, can provide things that electronic entertainment cannot.

I think the most attractive aspect of the circus is that, compared with the electronics we are used to, it seems exotic. Seeing a circus is very different from the things we are used to seeing and experiencing in our daily lives. We do not normally get to see live animals, especially trained ones that perform, or real people who dress in funny clothes and do difficult tricks. In ancient times, circus audiences may have been awed to see things they had never even heard of. In modern times, we have heard of these things and have probably even seen them on TV, but we rarely get to see these interesting things in real life.

Going to the circus is a special experience because it is different from the things we normally do. We get to leave the house and go to a special stadium or circus tent. We get to hear all the sounds and smell all the smells and eat all the special circus junk food that is sold before the performance. It takes us out of our daily experience and transports us for a short while to a different world in a way that electronic games or TV shows cannot. It is something that is not available to us every day, and that makes it even more special.

Even though we live in a world filled with modern technology, the circus can still offer us a special and exciting experience.

SPEAKING (page 53)

(sample response)

In my city, there are a lot of different forms of entertainment. There are movies, theaters, concerts, and nightclubs. It's a big city, so you can find almost anything to do that you want. I suppose a special form of entertainment we have is the summer theater festival. During the summer, there are live theater performances in the park. Some of the shows are free, and others you have to buy tickets for. When festival time comes around, almost everybody goes to at least one of the performances. That's one kind of entertainment we have that's very popular, and everyone talks about it. During the winter holidays, we also have a series of concerts that a lot of people enjoy. Other than those special events, people in my city mostly just enjoy the usual kinds of entertainment that people everywhere like.

I definitely prefer to see live entertainment. I really enjoy going to concerts, and nothing beats seeing a live concert performance. It really makes a difference to be in the same room with the musicians and to be able to watch them as they perform. It's a totally different experience from listening to recorded music. For music, seeing a live performance is really important. For other kinds of entertainment, it doesn't matter to me as much. Going to a play in a theater or watching a movie on TV is all the same to me.

I like to play the guitar, but I don't think I can say that I'm very talented at it. I wish I were, but I enjoy it anyway because I love music. I don't have any other performing arts talents. I have some artistic talents, though. I like to paint and draw, and I'm trying to develop those talents more. I take art classes occasionally. That's about all the talents I have.

Uses of Leisure Time

WORDS (page 54)

1. C	6. H	11. J	16. M
2. D	7. F	12. K	17. T
3. A	8. E	13. P	18. Q
4. B	9. L	14. O	19. S
5. G	10. I	15. N	20. R

READING (page 57)

1. C
2. B
3. E
4. A
5. B
6. D

WORD FAMILIES

A (page 58)

1. authoritatively
2. authorized
3. authoritative
4. authorities
5. deliberated
6. deliberately
7. deliberation
8. deliberate
9. emotions
10. emotionally
11. emotional
12. industrious
13. industriously
14. industry
15. intellectuals
16. intellectually
17. intellectual
18. intellect
19. reluctantly
20. reluctant
21. Reluctance

B (page 60)

1. emotional
2. industriously
3. intellectual
4. deliberate
5. reluctant
6. authorities

PARAPHRASES (page 60)

1. A
2. C

DICTIONARY SKILL (page 61)

1. B
2. A
3. B
4. A

LISTENING (page 62)

1. passive
2. physical
3. intellectual
4. obesity (*or* depression)
5. depression (*or* obesity)

WRITING (page 63)

(sample response)

The chart shows how much time people of different ages spend engaged in various pastimes. It shows two intellectual activities—reading and computer use. There is also a column for physical activities—sports and exercise. The information is about how people spend their leisure time on weekends.

According to the chart, teenagers spend the least amount of time reading, much less than adults do. They spend just five minutes a day reading, whereas adults aged twenty to sixty-five years old spend thirty minutes a day and adults aged sixty-six and older spend an hour a day in this pastime. Teenagers spend more time on the computer than people in the other two age groups—seventy-five minutes a day. The age group that spends the most time engaged in physical activities is adults aged twenty to sixty-five, and the age group that spends the most time reading is adults sixty-six and older. Adults aged sixty-six and older are the ones who spend the least amount of time engaged in physical activities—just twenty minutes a day.

SPEAKING (page 64)

(sample response)

One of my favorite pastimes is going to the movies. I really enjoy movies of all kinds. I like drama and comedy and action movies. I like going to the movies with my friends and then talking about the movie afterward. We often go to a restaurant or a café and talk about the movie: whether or not we liked it and why, what we thought about the actors, how it compares with other movies, things like that. It's really interesting. So I think I could say that's my favorite pastime. I also like to read, I enjoy watching sports, and sometimes I play a little tennis.

I enjoy both physical and intellectual activities, but I guess I prefer intellectual activities a little more. As I said, I love discussing movies. I also like talking about books I read or articles I read in the newspaper. It's great to spend an evening at a café with my friends talking about these kinds of things. But physical activities are important, too. Maybe I don't do them every day, but I like to get some exercise a few times a week. I like to play tennis or sometimes just take a walk.

UNIT 3: TRANSPORTATION

First Headlamps

WORDS (page 65)

1. D	6. F	11. N	16. Q
2. A	7. H	12. M	17. P
3. E	8. G	13. K	18. S
4. B	9. J	14. L	19. T
5. C	10. I	15. O	20. R

READING (page 68)

1. B	3. D	5. C	7. C
2. E	4. A	6. D	8. B

WORD FAMILIES

A (page 68)

1. Efficiency
2. efficiently
3. Efficient
4. generate
5. generation
6. generator
7. illumination
8. illuminate
9. illuminator
10. innovation
11. innovative
12. innovators
13. intensify
14. intensely
15. intensity
16. intense
17. reflect
18. reflection
19. reflector
20. reflective

B (page 70)

1. efficiently
2. innovations
3. illuminated
4. reflective
5. intensify
6. generate

PARAPHRASES (page 71)

1. C
2. B

DICTIONARY SKILL (page 71)

1. A
2. B
3. A
4. B

LISTENING (page 72)

1. A
2. B
3. D
4. F

WRITING (page 72)

(sample response)

Trains, planes, and automobiles have all become common modes of travel within the past 200 years, and they have all had significant effects on the way we live. If I had to choose which one of these three was the most significant, I would choose automobiles. Automobiles affect the way we live and work, and they affect the way the world around us looks.

Automobiles have given us easy access to many things in our daily lives, so we have more choices about a lot of different things. We can shop at a variety of stores, for example, because we can get to them by car. We do not have to shop only at the stores that are nearby. We have more choices about which doctors we want to have treat us or which lawyer we want to hire or which hairstylist we want to use because automobiles have increased the distances that we can easily travel. We have more choices about places to study or work because we can get to more places by car.

Automobiles have also affected the way the world around us looks. Because so many people depend on automobiles, there are paved roads and parking lots everywhere. This was not true in the days before automobiles. Houses, shopping malls, and apartment buildings are all built with garages attached to accommodate cars. Gas stations are everywhere. The world today looks very different than it did 100 years ago, and much of this is because of the automobile.

Automobiles have made a lot of changes in the way people go about their daily lives. This is why I think the automobile is the most significant transportation innovation of recent times.

SPEAKING (page 72)

(sample response)

In my city, people generally use buses, bicycles, and cars to get around. In my opinion, bicycles are the most efficient mode of transportation. I say this because there's a lot of traffic on our streets, especially during rush hour. Sometimes the cars and buses don't seem to move at all because there are so many of them. We have terrible traffic jams. For me, however, this isn't a problem because I almost always use my bike to get around. When all the cars and buses are sitting there waiting to move, I speed right by them on my bike. I never get stuck in traffic jams. I get everywhere quickly and efficiently on my bike. I really love it. The only time I don't like riding my bike is when it rains.

I think trains are great for long-distance travel. They're a lot more comfortable than buses because they have more space. You can get up and walk around on a train, but you can't do that on a bus. Trains are more relaxing than cars because you don't have to do the driving yourself and you don't have to deal with traffic jams or worry about getting lost. Trains usually have comfortable seats. They have large windows so you can enjoy the scenery. I love traveling by train.

In my opinion, there are very few drawbacks to train travel. Sometimes the tickets are expensive, but that depends on where you're going . Sometimes the schedule isn't completely convenient, but I don't mind changing my plans a little to fit a train schedule. A lot of people don't like trains because they don't give you the same independence that traveling by car does, but I don't mind that.

Major Subways of Europe

WORDS (page 73)

1. C	6. F	11. L	16. O
2. E	7. H	12. K	17. R
3. A	8. I	13. M	18. S
4. D	9. G	14. Q	19. P
5. B	10. J	15. N	20. T

READING (page 75)

1. C	3. A	5. B	7. A
2. C	4. B	6. C	

WORD FAMILIES

A (page 76)

1. architecturally
2. architecture
3. architect
4. architectural
5. decorations
6. decorative
7. decorator
8. decorate
9. destroy
10. destruction
11. destructive
12. disruptive
13. disruptions
14. disrupt
15. expansion
16. expand
17. expandable
18. operate
19. operation
20. operator

B (page 78)

1. Architects
2. decorative
3. destruction
4. disruption
5. expansion
6. operate

PARAPHRASES (page 79)

1. B
2. A

WORD SKILL (page 80)

1. below the surface of the water
2. a coat of paint below the surface coat of paint
3. a road that passes below another road or structure

LISTENING (page 80)

1. surface
2. vents
3. shield
4. destroy

WRITING (page 81)

(sample response)

The chart shows the size of three different subway systems using different measures: track length, number of stations, and number of passengers.

Each one of the subway systems shown could be said to be the largest one, depending on which measure you use. The London Underground has the most track, the Paris Metro has the most stations, and the Moscow Metro carries the most passengers. The London Underground has almost twice as much track as the Paris Metro but twenty-five fewer stations, so the stations on the Paris Metro must be much closer together. In fact, of the three systems shown, Paris has the most stations but the least total track length. The Moscow Metro carries twice as many passengers as the London Underground, although it is only about three-quarters the size of the London system. Its trains might be very crowded. Although the Moscow Metro carries the most passengers of the three systems, it has the fewest stations.

SPEAKING (page 81)

(sample response)

The subway stations in my city do not have interesting architecture, in my opinion. They are very modern, and I don't like that style. It just isn't warm and inviting. It isn't comfortable. It's all straight lines and no pretty decorations. Our train station, on the other hand, has very beautiful architecture. It's an old building and was built in the classical Greek style, which I like very much. It has columns and statues of mythological figures. It's a very interesting building to look at.

Our city library usually has exhibits of paintings and other kinds of art by local artists. It's interesting because they change the exhibits several times a year, so there's often something new to see. I think this is a great way to use space in the library, because a lot of people go there. They get to see what artists in our community are doing. I think there's also work by local artists in our city hall, but the problem with that is that most people don't go there very often. They don't have a reason to go there, so that art doesn't get seen by as many people. The library is a better place. Subway stations would be a good place, too, because most people use the subway. However, in my city, there isn't any artwork in the subway stations, unfortunately.

Electric Cars Around the Globe

WORDS (page 82)

1. D	6. F	11. O	16. T
2. E	7. I	12. N	17. P
3. A	8. G	13. M	18. R
4. C	9. J	14. K	19. Q
5. B	10. H	15. L	20. S

READING (page 84)

1. suburban	3. fumes	5. standard	7. commuters
2. consumed	4. plodding	6. embraced	

WORD FAMILIES

A (page 85)

1. appeal	8. commute	15. marked
2. appealing	9. commute	16. mark
3. appeal	10. consume	17. monetary
4. class	11. consumption	18. monetarily
5. classify	12. Consumers	19. money
6. classification	13. markedly	
7. Commuters	14. marked	

B (page 87)

1. class	3. consume	5. money
2. commuters	4. appealing	6. marked

PARAPHRASES (page 87)

1. C 2. A

DICTIONARY SKILL (page 88)

1. B 2. A 3. B 4. A

LISTENING (page 89)

1. Urban 2. Commuter 3. Suburban 4. Restaurant

WRITING (page 90)

(sample response)

If more people drove electric cars, that would help solve some of the problems created by gasoline-powered cars. I believe that money, convenience, and education are the three major factors that would persuade more people to drive electric cars.

Money is a powerful incentive. If electric cars are cheaper to buy than gasoline-powered cars, then people will become interested in them. If electricity is cheaper to use than gasoline, then people will want to own electric cars. Clearly, gasoline is becoming more expensive every day. If car manufacturers can produce electric cars cheaply, then the monetary incentives will be in place and more and more people will start buying electric cars.

Convenience is almost as important as money. Electric cars need to be easy to use for them to be appealing. If putting a charge in a car battery is as easy or easier than filling up the tank with gasoline, then people will find electric cars attractive. If electric cars are small and easier to park than larger gasoline-powered cars, that would be another attraction. If people see electric cars as easy to own and easy to use, they will be more interested in buying them.

The third factor is education. People will become more interested in driving electric cars when they understand the problems with gasoline-powered cars. Educating the public about issues of pollution and decreasing oil reserves may persuade more people to consider electric cars.

If people believe that electric cars are cheap and easy to use and if they understand the reasons why we need to move away from gasoline, they will be more likely to embrace them.

SPEAKING (page 90)

(sample response)

I'm not very interested in cars. I just want something that will take me places. I don't care if a car has flair. I don't care if it can go really fast or what color it is or anything. I just want a car that is easy to take care of and that doesn't need repairs all the time. I know some people are very interested in cars and know all about the different models and the different things that different cars can do, but that's not me. I just need transportation.

I prefer to live in an urban area. I grew up in the city, and I still live there. I can't imagine living anywhere else. A city has everything. It has all kinds of stores so you can buy anything you need. It has movies and theaters and museums and restaurants. All my friends live in the city, and most of my relatives do, too, so I feel like I have everybody nearby. I don't like rural areas. They are so quiet, it makes me feel afraid. And there's nothing to do. There are no stores or museums or anything. And the suburbs just seem so boring. I don't know why anybody would live anywhere that wasn't a city.

UNIT 4: CULTURE

Origins of Writing

WORDS (page 91)

1. B	6. D	11. I	16. O
2. A	7. H	12. G	17. Q
3. C	8. J	13. M	18. S
4. E	9. L	14. P	19. R
5. F	10. K	15. N	20. T

READING (page 94)

1. B	4. A	7. A	10. False
2. C	5. C	8. True	
3. A	6. B	9. Not Given	

WORD FAMILIES

A (page 95)

1. agricultural	9. Excavators	17. myths
2. agriculture	10. excavated	18. Mythology
3. agriculturally	11. excavations	19. specializations
4. creatively	12. Literacy	20. specialty
5. creative	13. literate	21. specialized
6. creation	14. illiterate	22. specialize
7. creators	15. Illiteracy	
8. created	16. mythological	

B (page 97)

1. Excavators
2. agriculture
3. created
4. specialized
5. literate
6. myths

PARAPHRASES (page 97)

1. B
2. C

DICTIONARY SKILL (page 98)

1. A
2. B

LISTENING (page 98)

1. D
2. A
3. C
4. B
5. E

WRITING (page 99)

(sample response)

The chart shows literacy rates for the adult population in four different countries, as well as literacy rates for the entire world. It also shows the differences in male and female literacy rates.

Two countries have literacy rates higher than the world rate of 82 percent. Country D has almost 100 percent literacy, and the rate is the same for both the male and female populations. Country C has a literacy rate just over 90 percent, but there is a significant difference between the male and female rates. In fact, in all the countries except for Country D, there is a difference between the male and female literacy rates. This reflects the world literacy rates, which show a 10 percent difference between male and female rates. In Countries A and B, the difference between male and female literacy is very large. In Country A there is a 30 percent difference, and in Country B there is a 40 percent difference. Around the world, there are more literate men than literate women.

SPEAKING (page 99)

(sample response)

Of course it would be best to have a teacher who specializes in the subject being taught and is also very skilled at teaching, but if I had to make a choice, I think I would choose the one who is skilled at teaching. Of course, I assume this teacher would have a certain amount of knowledge about the subject. I think the best teachers are the ones who make their students want to learn and can show them how to learn. If you know how to learn, you can find any information you need. And if you want to learn, you will look for that information. So a teacher might not know every last piece of information about something, but a good teacher can help the students figure out how to find that information. I have had teachers who knew a lot about their subjects but who were so boring that I learned very little from them. To me it didn't matter what they knew. They still didn't help me learn about it.

Clearly, the most basic skills children need to learn to function in modern society are computer skills. Computers in today's world are like books have been, or were. Nowadays, computer literacy is as important as reading and writing. Children have to learn how to use different kinds of software and how to find information on the Internet and things like that. But I also think there is a skill even more basic than that that we need to function in modern society. That skill is the ability to change rapidly. Technology changes rapidly, and we have to keep up with it. Today, we use computers in a certain way, but a few years from now everything might be different and we'll have to adopt new methods of work and communication. What we teach children in school today might not be completely useful by the time they graduate. Learning the skill of changing is as important as anything else.

Hula Dancing in Hawaiian Culture

WORDS (page 100)

1. B	6. F	11. L	16. P
2. C	7. H	12. N	17. S
3. E	8. G	13. M	18. O
4. A	9. J	14. K	19. Q
5. D	10. I	15. T	20. R

READING (page 102)

1. D	3. A	5. graceful	7. evidence
2. B	4. B	6. elaborate	

WORD FAMILIES

A (page 104)

1. accompany	7. celebrations	13. influence
2. accompaniment	8. Celebratory	14. influenced
3. beneficial	9. energetically	15. influential
4. benefits	10. energy	16. traditionally
5. benefit	11. Energetic	17. tradition
6. celebrate	12. energized	18. traditional

B (page 106)

1. traditional	3. accompaniment	5. celebrations
2. energetically	4. influenced	6. beneficial

PARAPHRASES (page 106)

1. A 2. A

DICTIONARY SKILL (page 107)

1. A 2. B

LISTENING (page 107)

1. A 2. D 3. E 4. G

WRITING (page 108)

(sample response)

Celebrations are very important for any society. They bring families together, give people a sense of identity, and provide a break from the usual routines of life.

An important benefit of traditional celebrations is that they give family members opportunities to spend time together. This is especially important in the modern world, where families are becoming more separated. Family members often do not live in the same city, or even the same country, like they did in the past. When there is an important celebration, family members usually want to spend it together. Often they have special family traditions such as preparing special food together or gathering at a certain place. Families look forward to the special days in the year when they can do these things together.

Traditional celebrations give people a sense of identity. Celebrations that are traditional in a certain place or for a certain culture help people feel more connected to their place or their culture. They help people feel that they are part of something that is meaningful.

Celebrations give people a break from their normal routines. Whether it is something that takes place every year or a one-time special event, a celebration is a chance to relax and have fun with friends and relatives. It is something that adds a little bit of excitement to life. Annual celebrations are especially important because they give people something to look forward to throughout the year.

Humans have been enjoying celebrations since ancient times. Celebrations are important to individuals, families, and society as a whole.

SPEAKING (page 108)

(sample response)

At the beginning of the year, New Year's Day celebrations are important. Everybody enjoys this celebration because we stay up and have a party until very late. We want to be awake at midnight when the new year begins, and the party usually continues past that hour. Another very important day in my country is Independence Day. Everybody in the whole country is excited when that day is approaching. It's a day with a lot of meaning for us. We have many other traditional celebrations throughout the year. We really like to celebrate in my country!

In my country, Mexico, we celebrate the Day of the Dead at the beginning of November. It's the day when we remember our loved ones who have died. The traditional ritual is to make an altar in the house. We put special food on the altar and things that remind us of our dead loved ones. We decorate it with yellow flowers and other traditional decorations. Some people make very beautiful altars. It's a very old tradition.

The Art of Mime

WORDS (page 109)

1. B
2. C
3. D
4. A
5. E
6. H
7. F
8. G
9. J
10. L
11. I
12. K
13. P
14. O
15. M
16. N
17. T
18. R
19. Q
20. S

READING (page 112)

1. gestures
2. literal
3. humorous
4. abstract
5. emerged
6. renowned
7. merged

WORD FAMILIES

A (page 113)

1. considerable
2. considerably
3. effect
4. effective
5. effect
6. effectively
7. exaggerated
8. exaggeration
9. exaggerate
10. frail
11. frailty
12. portrayers
13. portrayal
14. portray
15. reminiscent
16. reminisce
17. Reminiscences

B (page 114)

1. exaggerate
2. effectively
3. considerable
4. portray
5. frailties
6. reminisce

PARAPHRASES (page 115)

1. C
2. B

DICTIONARY SKILL (page 116)

1. B
2. A
3. A
4. B

LISTENING (page 117)

1. props
2. illusions
3. gestures
4. portray
5. conflict

WRITING (page 118)

(sample response)

The chart shows ticket sales at the National Theater for the six-month period from January through June.

The most popular group of performers during that time was the National Mime Troupe. Five thousand tickets were sold for their performance titled "Humorous Situations." Only half as many tickets were sold for the performance of Carmen, put on by the City Opera. That was the least popular of all the performances listed on the chart. The second least popular performance was "Works of Beethoven" by the National Symphony Orchestra, with 3,000 tickets sold. The "Rock Stars Live!" concert and the Swan Lake ballet were both almost as popular as the "Humorous Situations" mime performance. There were 4,750 tickets sold for each of those performances.

Overall, opera and classical music do not appear to be very popular forms of entertainment at the National Theater. People appear to prefer less serious forms of entertainment such as humorous mime and rock music.

SPEAKING (page 118)

(sample response)

I usually prefer to see humorous performances. I like to see funny things and hear jokes. If I spend the money and time to go to the theater to see a live performance, then I want to have a good time. I want to laugh. I want to relax and forget about my worries. I actually enjoy serious performances, too. The most important thing, really, is to have the chance to watch skilled performers. But I choose to see humorous performances more often than serious ones.

My country is small. We have some renowned actors and musicians whom we really love, but they're known only to people in our country. They aren't famous in other places. We also enjoy performers from other countries. We like the famous Hollywood actors and musicians from different places. We like all the international stars, just like people everywhere.

I like both kinds of movies. I like real stories and made-up ones, but I particularly enjoy movies that portray real events and people from history. I enjoy seeing what life was like during a different period in history. I like to see what the houses looked like, the clothes, the towns and cities, all the details of daily life. I especially enjoy movies that show those details and show them correctly, that make the effort to really show what life was like. Historical events are interesting to learn about, but to me learning about the details of daily life in the past is even more interesting.

UNIT 5: HEALTH

Nurse Migration

WORDS (page 119)

1. C
2. D
3. A
4. B
5. E
6. J
7. H
8. I
9. F
10. G
11. L
12. N
13. M
14. O
15. K
16. S
17. T
18. P
19. Q
20. R

READING (page 121)

1. shortage
2. abroad
3. lure
4. qualified
5. administered
6. rudimentary
7. True
8. False
9. Not Given

WORD FAMILIES

A (page 122)

1. complexity
2. complex
3. qualifications
4. Qualified
5. qualify
6. rampant
7. rampantly
8. shorten
9. short
10. shortage
11. vacant
12. vacancy
13. vacate

B (page 124)

1. short
2. complexities
3. rampant
4. vacate
5. qualified

PARAPHRASES (page 124)

1. B
2. A

WORD SKILL (page 125)

1. a situation where something stops or stands still
2. a person or thing that is much better than all others

LISTENING (page 125)

1. 4
2. 25
3. 5
4. 114,000

WRITING (page 126)

(sample response)

The salaries paid to nurses and doctors vary widely, according to the information in the chart. The two countries with the lowest salaries, Country A and Country B, are source countries. They provide a supply of health care workers to the destination countries. The salaries paid to doctors and nurses in these source countries are much lower than the salaries paid in Country C and Country D, which are destination countries. The salaries in Country A are much lower even than the salaries in Country B. In Country B, nurses earn ten times as much as in Country A. The difference in doctors' salaries is even greater.

The difference in salaries between the source countries and the destination countries is greater still. Nurses in Country D, for example, earn almost ten times as much as nurses in Country B. Doctors in Country D earn almost fifteen times as much as doctors in Country B. It is easy to see why source countries have a hard time retaining health care professionals. From the standpoint of the doctors and nurses, working abroad is a much better deal.

SPEAKING (page 126)

(sample response)

I am a journalist. I chose this profession for several reasons. First, I like to write and always have, ever since I was a small child. I'm also interested in politics and current events. I like to keep up with what's happening and analyze different political situations, and I love telling people my opinion about things. As a journalist, I get to do all these things that I really love: write, follow the news, and tell people my opinion. It's great!

Because I am just starting out in my profession, I hope things will change a lot for me over the next decade. Right now I have a job as a reporter for a small newspaper in my city. I hope that in ten years I will be working for a much larger newspaper. I also hope by then to be working as a foreign correspondent, reporting the news from abroad. That's really my biggest goal. I think I can make it in ten years.

My profession offers a lot of opportunities for working abroad. A lot of people are lured to journalism because they are interested in traveling to other countries. As I mentioned, that's a primary goal for me, too. Some journalists live abroad and report the news regularly back to the newspaper in their own country. Other journalists don't live abroad but travel regularly, depending on where the news is happening. There is always important news happening all over the world, so journalists get to travel a lot if that's what they want to do.

Aerobic Exercise and Brain Health

WORDS (page 127)

1. A	6. G	11. N	16. S
2. D	7. H	12. M	17. O
3. B	8. E	13. K	18. T
4. C	9. F	14. L	19. R
5. J	10. I	15. Q	20. P

READING (page 130)

1. mood
2. regulates
3. concentrations
4. gravity
5. capacity
6. deterioration
7. diagnosed
8. counteract

WORD FAMILIES

A (page 131)

1. diagnostician
2. diagnostic
3. diagnosis
4. diagnose
5. gravely
6. grave
7. gravity
8. indication
9. indicate
10. indicative
11. indicators
12. impairments
13. impair
14. Impaired
15. moodily
16. moodiness
17. mood
18. moody

B (page 133)

1. mood
2. indicate
3. diagnosis
4. grave
5. impairment

PARAPHRASES (page 133)

1. A
2. B

DICTIONARY SKILL (page 134)

1. B
2. A
3. B
4. A

LISTENING (page 135)

1. Clark
2. aerobic
3. yoga
4. mood
5. weight

WRITING (page 136)

(sample response)

The chart shows information about two groups of patients who were suffering from mild cognitive impairment. Each group followed a program of one hour of daily exercise for six months, but they did different kinds of exercise. Group A did aerobic exercise, and Group B did nonaerobic exercise. The charts show changes in mental capacity in each group after six months of exercise. Group A showed improvement in two areas: thinking speed and word fluency. Capacity in memory did not change. Group B had a much worse experience, because there was deterioration in all three areas. This information shows that aerobic exercise can have positive effects on mental capacity for patients suffering from cognitive impairment. Although it did not help patients improve their memory, it appeared to at least stave off deterioration in this area. Nonaerobic exercise had no positive effects, and the patients' mental capacity continued to deteriorate during the study.

SPEAKING (page 137)

(sample response)

I think that exercise improves my mood. I play soccer often with my friends, and I always feel really good afterward. Of course, there are other factors. It's great to spend the time with my friends, and if we win a game, that makes me feel really good. But I think the exercise affects my mood, too. Even if I go for a run by myself, it puts me in a better mood. Other things that help improve my mood are listening to music, if it's happy music, of course, or energetic music. Sad music would only make me feel worse. Watching funny movies usually helps me feel better, too.

I'm not sure if improving brain capacity will make exercising more popular. Exercise won't make you smarter, at least I don't think it will; it just slows the deterioration of the brain as you get older. That's probably important for older people, but younger people are more interested in other things. Some people like to exercise, but a lot of people don't, or they don't have time for it. I don't think this research will change that. I think people will just keep doing whatever they did previously. Some will exercise and others won't, depending on whether or not they enjoy it.

Personally, I think exercising is important and I try to get regular exercise. However, I also think it's up to each individual to choose whether or not to exercise. All the information is there. Everybody knows the benefits of exercise or can easily find them out. If some people choose not to exercise, they're the ones who have to live with the results of that. They might have poor health or be more depressed or something like that, but it's their choice. I think information should always be made available, but after that, each person has to decide what he or she will do with that information.

How Drugs Are Studied

WORDS (page 138)

1. D	6. H	11. L	16. T
2. C	7. I	12. M	17. Q
3. A	8. E	13. N	18. R
4. B	9. G	14. K	19. O
5. F	10. J	15. P	20. S

READING (page 141)

1. B	3. F	5. A	7. B
2. C	4. G	6. D	

WORD FAMILIES

A (PAGE 142)

1. absorbent
2. absorption
3. absorbs
4. desired
5. desire
6. desire
7. investigative
8. investigate
9. investigation
10. investigator
11. theorize
12. theoretically
13. theoretical
14. theory
15. toxicity
16. toxic
17. toxically
18. toxins

B (PAGE 144)

1. investigate
2. theory
3. absorption
4. toxins
5. desire

PARAPHRASES (page 145)

1. A
2. C

DICTIONARY SKILL (page 145)

1. B
2. A
3. C

LISTENING (page 146)

1. culture
2. Monitor
3. Ascertain
4. outcome

WRITING (page 146)

(sample response)

Modern medicine has made it possible for people to live longer lives. Drugs have been developed to cure many common diseases and alleviate many chronic conditions. This has obvious benefits for individuals, but the benefits for society are a bit less certain.

Because of modern medicine, people nowadays not only live longer but live healthier lives, too. Fewer people die young of communicable diseases because there are drugs to cure or prevent such diseases. The lives of many older people are enhanced by medicine that prevents or controls many of the conditions that can cause illness in the elderly. Modern medicine has enabled many people to have many more years to enjoy their lives. Most individuals would agree that this is a desirable outcome.

On the other hand, more people living longer means that a larger fraction of society is made up of older people. If many of these people are past retirement age, that means they are no longer making an economic contribution to society. However, they still require support for themselves. Many people living longer also means that the population is larger. The longer people live, the more resources they use, and society must find a way to provide for their needs.

Modern medical science aims to help people live longer lives and healthier lives, too. This is a good thing in many ways, but it is a situation that also has many complications.

SPEAKING (page 146)

(sample response)

I think it is important to spend money on investigating new drugs, of course. After all, drugs can cure many diseases and alleviate many conditions. But we also need to think about prevention. It would be a good idea to spend more money on educating the public about things that can be harmful to the health, such as smoking, or drinking too much, or eating junk food. There is education about those things, but people still smoke and drink and do other things that are unhealthy. People need to really understand the effects of bad habits. Too many people have chronic diseases because they drink too much or eat the wrong kind of food. I really think education is an important part of health care.

I think when people live healthy lifestyles, they get sick less frequently. I think targeting dietary and exercise habits is really important. Lack of exercise and a poor diet can have different kinds of negative outcomes. For example, they can lead to obesity, being overweight, which can cause heart disease. Poor diet can also lead to diabetes, which is a serious health problem. I think encouraging people to eat well and exercise frequently are important areas to focus on.

Doctors can give injections that prevent influenza, so everyone should get these injections. That's the easiest way to combat this disease, and many other diseases, too. There are injections to prevent many of the most common diseases. People also need to be educated about good habits to prevent spreading disease, such as washing their hands, or staying home if they are sick. There are some common diseases, such as the common cold, that can't be cured or prevented with an injection. Scientists need to keep investigating these diseases until they discover a way to cure them.

UNIT 6: TOURISM

Hiking the Inca Trail

WORDS (page 147)

1. F	6. B	11. J	16. S
2. G	7. E	12. K	17. T
3. C	8. L	13. H	18. N
4. D	9. M	14. R	19. O
5. A	10. I	15. Q	20. P

READING (page 150)

1. ceremonial/sacred/Incan
2. archeologist
3. functions
4. draw
5. network
6. adventurous
7. marvels
8. preserve/protect
9. luxury

WORD FAMILIES

A (page 150)

1. accessible
2. inaccessible
3. access
4. accessibility
5. access
6. adventure
7. Adventurous
8. adventurers
9. adventurously
10. archeology
11. archeological
12. archeologist
13. luxurious
14. luxuriated
15. luxuriously
16. luxury
17. Restrictions
18. restricts
19. restrictive
20. precise
21. precisely
22. precision

B (page 152)

1. access
2. restricted
3. luxurious
4. archeological
5. precisely
6. adventure

PARAPHRASES (page 153)

1. B
2. C

DICTIONARY SKILL (page 154)

1. B
2. A
3. B
4. A

LISTENING (page 155)

1. network
2. Access
3. ceremonial
4. Native

WRITING (page 155)

(sample response)

The preservation of archeological sites is extremely important. The reason is quite simple: Once they are gone, they are gone forever. Those who hope to preserve such sites need to provide education so that the public understands their importance.

Archeological sites contain buildings and objects that have been around for a long time, for thousands of years in some cases. They provide us with a connection to past civilizations, to the people who came before us. They contain valuable information about our ancestors and where we came from. If we lose this information, we lose the possibility of learning many things about our history. It is terrible to think that something that has lasted for thousands of years can be destroyed in a relatively short period of time by the idle curiosity of modern tourists.

Often people are interested in visiting these sites because it is a popular thing to do. They are not drawn to a place out of respect or appreciation for what it represents. They go because everyone else goes or because they want an interesting adventure. Therefore, education is very important. People need to understand the meaning and value of these ancient sites and the impact that tourism has on them. This is an important part of preserving these sites. Then, if access to the sites is restricted, perhaps people will understand the reasons why and will not protest so much. Whether or not the general public agrees, however, everything possible must be done to preserve archeological sites.

SPEAKING (page 155)

(sample response)

I'm not really interested in outdoor adventures like hiking or rafting. I don't like physical danger. For me a really interesting adventure is to visit a new city where I've never been before. I like trying to find my way around a new place. I enjoy trying to figure out the people and what life is like in that city and where the interesting places are to go. It's not a dangerous kind of adventure at all, but it's interesting, and it's even more interesting and exciting when you're visiting a city in a foreign country.

When I travel, I like to stay in really comfortable hotels. I like the hotels that have really comfortable rooms with high-quality sheets and blankets on the bed. I like hotels that have really good personal service, and most of all I like hotels with good food. It's a special luxury to order breakfast from room service. I don't mind paying more for a luxury hotel. Staying in a hotel like that is half the fun of traveling.

It's not really important to me to have luxuries in my daily life. Most of the time I'm very practical. I just live a normal life with normal things, and that's okay with me. But I do like to have luxuries on special occasions, like staying in a luxury hotel when I'm traveling, or going to an expensive restaurant on my birthday. When you save luxuries for special occasions, then they're more appreciated. When you have them every day, like driving around in an expensive car, for example, then they don't seem so special any more. You don't even notice them, and they stop feeling luxurious.

What Is Ecotourism?

WORDS (page 156)

1. D	6. E	11. L	16. Q
2. C	7. J	12. N	17. R
3. F	8. I	13. M	18. T
4. A	9. G	14. K	19. P
5. B	10. H	15. O	20. S

READING (page 159)

1. False	4. True	7. True
2. True	5. True	8. True
3. Not Given	6. False	9. Not Given

WORD FAMILIES

A (page 160)

1. accommodations
2. accommodating
3. accommodate
4. avoid
5. avoidable
6. Avoidance
7. conceive
8. conceptually
9. concept
10. conceptual
11. injurious
12. injure
13. injury
14. publicize
15. publicly
16. publicity
17. public
18. wild
19. wild
20. wilderness
21. wildly

B (page 162)

1. avoidance
2. concept
3. accommodations
4. wild
5. injury
6. publicize

PARAPHRASES (page 163)

1. B
2. A

DICTIONARY SKILL (page 163)

1. C
2. A
3. B

LISTENING (page 164)

1. Wilderness
2. January
3. accommodations
4. publicity

WRITING (page 164)

(sample response)

The charts show whether or not three different cruise companies follow certain environmentally friendly practices, and they compare this information in two different years: 2000 and 2010.

In 2000, two of the companies were already recycling most of their waste and avoiding dumping wastewater into the sea. These companies were Sun Cruises and Water World Tours. The Sea Adventure company did not follow these practices. None of the three companies had systems to reduce air pollution in 2000, and none of them avoided traveling to places with delicate underwater ecosystems.

By 2010, all three companies had made changes to become more environmentally friendly. In fact, in that year, two of the companies, Sun Cruises and Water World Tours, were following all the practices shown on the chart. Sea Adventure was recycling waste and avoiding dumping wastewater into the sea, but they still did not have a system to reduce air pollution and still traveled to destinations with delicate underwater ecosystems. Sun Cruises and Water World Tours are probably more attractive to people who are interested in ecotourism than Sea Adventure is.

SPEAKING (page 165)

(sample response)

I always choose to spend my vacations somewhere in the wilderness. I live in a big city, and I'm surrounded by crowds and noise all the time, so when I'm on vacation, I want to be in a really quiet place. I try to find as remote a place as possible. I like hiking and camping in the mountains. Once I went on a rafting trip on a river. Really, I'm happy spending my vacation anywhere out in the woods.

When I travel, I avoid any place with crowds. That doesn't mean just cities. Some national parks can get very crowded, too, and then you don't feel like you're in the wilderness. I try to avoid taking my vacation in the summer because that's when everyone else travels and every place is crowded. I like to travel in the fall. It's a beautiful time of year, and it's much easier to avoid crowds then.

Luxury accommodations aren't important to me. In fact, they make me feel a little uncomfortable because I'm not used to them. I like everything plain and simple and especially inexpensive. My favorite place to stay when I'm traveling is in my tent. For one thing, it's inexpensive. For another, it allows me to be in the middle of nature. I go to sleep at night to the sound of the wind blowing through the trees above me. I wake up in the morning surrounded by birdsong. What could be better than that?

Learning Vacations

WORDS (page 166)

1. C
2. B
3. A
4. D
5. I
6. F
7. H
8. G
9. E
10. N
11. J
12. M
13. L
14. K
15. Q
16. O
17. T
18. R
19. P
20. S

READING (page 168)

1. A
2. B
3. E
4. False
5. True
6. Not Given
7. True

WORD FAMILIES

A (page 169)

1. acquire
2. acquisition
3. cost
4. costly
5. cost
6. economical
7. economize
8. economically
9. economy
10. Enrollees
11. enrollment
12. enroll
13. Residential
14. residence
15. residents
16. reside
17. supervision
18. supervisory
19. supervise
20. supervisor

B (page 171)

1. acquire
2. cost
3. economize
4. Enrollment
5. supervision
6. residence

PARAPHRASES (page 172)

1. C
2. A

DICTIONARY SKILL (page 173)

1. A
2. B

LISTENING (page 173)

1. resort
2. Residential
3. Sponsor
4. Enrollment

WRITING (page 174)

(sample response)

The table shows the percentage of the total number of students who enrolled in courses in the Art and Academic Departments at Barkford College during the summers of 2012 and 2013. In the summer of 2012, more students enrolled in art classes than in academic classes. Sixty-five percent of all students took classes in the Art Department while thirty-five percent took classes in the Academic Department. Painting was the most popular of all the classes offered. Forty percent of all students took that class. History was the most popular academic class, with twenty percent of students enrolled in it. Science was the least popular, with just five percent enrollment. In 2013, enrollment was divided equally between the Art and Academic Departments. A lower percentage of students took painting, but it was still the most popular class, with thirty percent enrollment. Enrollment in history remained steady at twenty percent, but both philosophy and science were more popular than they had been the previous year.

SPEAKING (page 174)

(sample response)

I'm from the coast, so the cuisine of my city is all about seafood. We have a lot of different fish dishes. We are famous for a special kind of seafood stew that we make. We enjoy this dish on all our national holidays. There are also some different kinds of baked fish dishes that are famous in my city. We have a variety of seafood dishes, and tourists always eat them when they come to our city.

Different kinds of fish, of course, are the most common ingredients in our cuisine. Almost all our traditional fish dishes contain garlic, so that's another common ingredient. Also, we eat almost everything with rice. Besides that, because it's a tropical area, we have a lot of tropical fruits that we use in our cooking—mangoes, coconuts, things like that. They're common ingredients in stews and soups as well as in desserts.

We still enjoy the traditional fish dishes that our city has always been famous for, but we use more modern cooking methods now. Instead of cooking over a fire, people usually cook on a gas stove or in a microwave oven. People now have more access to ingredients from other places, for example, different kinds of spices that are common in other countries—people in my country are used to them now, too. They aren't traditional flavors for us, but they're becoming more common in our cooking. I think in the past, people ate the traditional dishes more often, maybe even every day. Now we're so busy, we don't have time to cook as often, so we eat those traditional dishes less often, maybe once a week or even once a month. In the future, I think this will be even more true. People will eat more fast food and more frozen food from the grocery store. They'll have less and less time to cook the traditional dishes, and maybe they'll even forget how to cook them. I hope not, but it could happen.

UNIT 7: BUSINESS

What Makes a Small Business Successful?

WORDS (page 175)

1. C	6. E	11. M	16. L
2. B	7. H	12. N	17. S
3. F	8. J	13. O	18. T
4. D	9. G	14. K	19. R
5. A	10. I	15. P	20. Q

READING (page 178)

1. B	3. B	5. potential	7. financial
2. D	4. unique	6. sound	

WORD FAMILIES

A (page 179)

1. compete	10. initial	19. productively
2. competitively	11. initially	20. product
3. competition	12. initiation	21. produce
4. competitive	13. initiate	22. producer
5. competitors	14. motivate	23. productive
6. inevitability	15. motivating	24. profit
7. inevitably	16. motivation	25. profit
8. inevitable	17. motivated	26. profitably
9. initiator	18. production	27. profitable

B (page 181)

1. initiate
2. motivation
3. compete
4. produce
5. profitable
6. inevitable

PARAPHRASES (page 182)

1. B
2. B

DICTIONARY SKILL (page 183)

1. B
2. A

LISTENING (page 183)

1. A
2. C
3. E
4. G

WRITING (page 184)

(sample response)

Many people enjoy shopping in large chain stores, whereas many others have a great dislike for them. Large chain stores offer a number of advantages to shoppers. However, they also have several drawbacks.

One of the advantages of large chain stores is that they generally offer a wider selection of products than smaller, locally owned businesses do. Because a chain store is owned by a large company, it has access to many more sources of products than its smaller competitors do. This allows it to offer a greater variety of products on the store shelves. Chain stores can also sell products in their stores at lower prices. One reason is that, being part of a large company, it is easier for them to seek out the manufacturers that charge less. Another reason is that they get discounts for buying in very large quantities.

Chain stores also have disadvantages. They cannot offer the personalized services that small stores can. People who run small stores are very familiar with the products they sell. They can make knowledgeable recommendations to their customers, they can answer questions about the products, and they can special-order items. Employees in chain stores, on the other hand, usually know very little about the items they sell. They often cannot help customers beyond telling them in which part of the store something is located.

Chain stores make things more convenient for shoppers, but they also have the effect of making things less personal. A place that has a balanced mix of large and small stores, if it exists, would offer shoppers the best of both worlds.

SPEAKING (page 184)

(sample response)

A store where I enjoy shopping is a large bookstore near my house. One characteristic that draws me to it is that it is a welcoming place. Anyone can go there and spend as long as he or she wants. No one bothers you if you sit down with a book and spend a long time reading it. You might buy it or you might not. No one bothers you about it. It's a place where you can feel comfortable just relaxing. Another thing I like is that it has all kinds of books as well as magazines and CDs. Whatever mood I'm in, I'm sure to find something I feel like looking at or buying. The best thing of all is the coffee shop. They sell great coffee and pastries. It's a nice place to spend a Sunday afternoon, reading and sipping coffee, no pressure, just relaxation.

I think it's important to spend money on clothes. I mean professional clothes. The clothes you wear are an important part of your professional image. Your clothes aren't, of course, as important as your professional skills and experience, but they really add to it. I mean, if you look like a professional, people will believe you are one. They will pay more attention to what you can do than if you dress like a slob. I always spend a lot of money on business suits. I buy suits with a good cut and high-quality material. It's really worth the money.

If you're going to spend a lot of money on something, you have to be sure you know what you're buying. It doesn't matter if it's clothes or a car or a house. You want to make sure you're getting what you want. So, you have to do research. Find out what the clothes are made of or which car goes the fastest or if the house is in good condition. Think about why it's worth it to you to spend money on this product, and then make sure that the one you buy has these characteristics. One thing I do before I spend a lot of money on something is find a friend or relative who knows about the thing I want to buy. Before I bought a car, for example, I talked to my uncle because he owns a car similar to the one I wanted. I asked him about his experience with it and how he bought it. That helped me a lot when I finally bought my car. Doing research and asking advice from experienced people are, I think, the most important tips.

Brand Loyalty

WORDS (page 185)

1. A	6. I	11. M	16. P
2. D	7. H	12. J	17. S
3. C	8. G	13. L	18. R
4. B	9. F	14. K	19. Q
5. E	10. N	15. T	20. O

READING (page 188)

1. Not Given	4. True	7. True
2. True	5. True	8. True
3. False	6. Not Given	

WORD FAMILIES

A (page 188)

1. consistency
2. consistently
3. consistent
4. loyally
5. loyal
6. loyalty
7. passionate
8. passion
9. passionately
10. prevalent
11. prevalence
12. prevails
13. selective
14. select
15. selectively
16. selection
17. thirst
18. thirst
19. thirsty

B (Page 190)

1. thirst
2. selectively
3. passionate
4. consistent
5. loyal
6. prevail

PARAPHRASES (page 191)

1. A
2. C

WORD SKILL (page 192)

1. perform better
2. sell better
3. greater in number

LISTENING (page 192)

1. status
2. endorsements
3. selective
4. passionate

WRITING (page 193)

(sample response)

The charts show reasons for consumers' decisions when choosing a mobile phone. The information is given for two different countries.

In Country A, price is the top reason, with 50 percent of consumers mentioning it as the most important factor in buying a phone. Brand is the least popular reason, with only 7 percent of consumers mentioning it as the most important factor. Brand loyalty is also low in Country B, although a bit higher than in Country A. In Country B, 19 percent of consumers mention brand as the most important factor in choosing a mobile phone. The top reason in Country B is design, which is the most important factor for 40 percent of consumers. Price, the top reason in Country A, is the least important reason in Country B. Only 9 percent of consumers in that country mentioned price as the most important factor in choosing a mobile phone.

SPEAKING (page 193)

(sample response)

I like to run. I run almost every day for exercise, so the shoes I wear for running are really important. If my running shoes don't fit me right, I could have a lot of problems. It's not just about comfort, but I could have a lot of physical problems if I don't wear the right shoes, because I run every day. That's why I'm loyal to a certain brand of running shoes. I've found a company that makes shoes that fit me just right. I really like them. I always buy that brand of shoes because I know they're exactly what I want. I think that's the only case where I have brand loyalty. Other things aren't as important to me. I might choose something because the price is right or I like the way it looks or something like that, but not usually because of the brand. I'm really selective only about running shoes.

Celebrity endorsements are used a lot in promoting products, so they must persuade a lot of people to buy certain brands. Some people pay a lot of attention to celebrities; they really admire them and want everything their favorite celebrities have. Some people think that a celebrity endorsement means that the product is better or more popular. But it doesn't convince me. It makes no difference to me what a movie star or athlete buys. Anyhow, I don't think celebrities really buy those things. They make an endorsement, but that doesn't mean they really use the product.

Global Outsourcing

WORDS (page 194)

1. D	6. I	11. L	16. S
2. A	7. G	12. J	17. R
3. B	8. H	13. K	18. O
4. C	9. F	14. N	19. P
5. E	10. M	15. T	20. Q

READING (page 196)

1. wealthy	4. boon	7. catch up
2. enticing	5. confront	
3. remainder	6. turnover	

WORD FAMILIES

A (page 197)

1. controversial	8. enticement	15. preponderance
2. controversially	9. entice	16. preponderantly
3. controversy	10. enticing	17. preponderant
4. decisively	11. opposing	18. routine
5. decide	12. oppose	19. routine
6. decision	13. Opponents	20. routinely
7. decisive	14. opposition	

B (page 199)

1. decision
2. oppose
3. controversial
4. preponderant
5. routine
6. enticement

PARAPHRASES (page 200)

1. B
2. A

DICTIONARY SKILL (page 200)

1. B
2. A
3. B
4. A

LISTENING (page 201)

1. 1900
2. night shift
3. 1915
4. decisive
5. employee turnover

WRITING (page 202)

(sample response)

Outsourcing of labor to other countries has become a common practice. The advantages and disadvantages of this practice depend on your point of view. The effects on a customer or worker in the company's home country are different from the effects on the people in other countries that do the outsourced labor.

There are both advantages and disadvantages for people in the company's home country. For the company's customers, there may be the advantage of lower prices. If the company saves money on labor, then it can offer lower prices to its customers. On the other hand, there are some disadvantages when a company outsources customer services to a foreign country. There can be difficulties with communication when the customer service provider does not understand the customer's language or culture very well. In addition to disadvantages for customers, there is the serious disadvantage for workers, who become unemployed when their jobs are sent to workers abroad.

For workers doing the outsourced labor, the significant advantage, of course, is that outsourced labor provides them with opportunities for employment. But there are some disadvantages to this sort of work. Especially for customer service work, employees might have to work night shifts to provide service to customers in a different time zone. In addition, difficulties with understanding a foreign language and culture affect the workers as well as the customers.

The reason that companies outsource labor is that they gain a big advantage—lower costs. The needs of customers and employees are probably not considered. However, customers and employees both feel the effects of this practice.

SPEAKING (page 202)

(sample response)

A decisive moment in my life was when I chose my career. This really was the most difficult decision of my life. My father always wanted me to be a doctor. Ever since I was a child, I knew that this was his plan for me. I always accepted it because it was what my father wanted. However, in high school I realized that I didn't want to be a doctor. There was nothing about it that interested me. I decided that I wanted to study architecture and learn how to design buildings. I was afraid to tell my father this because I knew he really wanted me to be a doctor. But I really wanted to study architecture, and I actually applied to be an architecture student. When I was accepted into the program, I knew I had to tell my father. So, I finally dared to tell him. He wasn't very happy about it, but he accepted my decision because he saw how much I wanted to do it. It was a difficult thing for me to do, to ruin my father's dream, but I knew I had to follow my own dream. Now I'm glad I did, and I think my father is, too.

There are a number of little difficulties I confront every day in my life as a university student. The first one is getting to my morning classes on time, because I like to sleep late. Some days I have class at 8:00 in the morning. I really don't like that. Another difficulty is trying to get all my assignments done. I always have so much studying to do—reading articles and writing research papers and preparing presentations. They give us a lot of work to do, and it isn't always easy to find time to do it all. That's the biggest difficulty, I think. I don't have much difficulty with the content of my classes. I think they're really interesting. And I get along with most of my classmates and my professors. Mostly I enjoy university life—just the workload is sometimes too much.

UNIT 8: SOCIETY

Social Networking

WORDS (page 203)

1. F
2. E
3. D
4. B
5. A
6. C
7. G
8. I
9. H
10. J
11. M
12. O
13. K
14. N
15. L
16. T
17. R
18. Q
19. P
20. S

READING (page 205)

1. C
2. D
3. B
4. A
5. exploded
6. immense
7. acquaintances
8. pursue
9. interact

WORD FAMILIES

A (page 206)

1. adolescent
2. adolescents
3. adolescence
4. eradicates
5. eradication
6. eradicable
7. explosion
8. exploded
9. explosive
10. immensity
11. immense
12. immensely
13. interactively
14. interaction
15. interactive
16. interact
17. Statistical
18. statistics
19. statistically
20. Statisticians

B (page 208)

1. interactions
2. explosion
3. adolescent
4. Statisticians
5. eradicated
6. immensely

PARAPHRASES (page 209)

1. C
2. B

WORD SKILL (page 209)

1. carry on
2. carry out
3. carry through

LISTENING (page 210)

1. contact
2. pursue
3. community
4. acquaintances

WRITING (page 211)

(sample response)

The chart shows the percentage of each site's total membership in three different age groups: adolescent, younger adult, and older adult. The statistics show that each site attracts more members of a particular age group. Site A is apparently more popular with younger adults than with adolescents or older adults. Close to half of the members of that site fall into the younger adult age group. Site B is much more popular with older adults than with people of other ages, since two-thirds of its members belong to that age group. At the same time, the site has very few adolescent members—only 7 percent of its total membership. Site C seems to be the site that draws the most adolescent members. More than half of its members are adolescents. A little more than one-third are younger adults. However, very few are older adults—only 10 percent of its total membership.

SPEAKING (page 211)

(sample response)

The kind of information I exchange with my friends online is usually just everyday information. I tell them what I did today or what my plans for the weekend are. If I go someplace interesting or do something fun, then I take photos and post them online. My friends and I post a lot of photos online. It's fun to see what everyone has been doing. Sometimes if I need some special kind of information, like I want to buy something expensive or if I'm looking for a job, then I post that online and ask my friends for help or advice.

I think it's really important for parents to pay attention to what their kids do online. Adolescents, especially, like to use the Internet a lot. It's the main way they communicate with their friends, but there are a lot of dangers for them online and they're too young to understand that. Parents should know what their kids do online, what sites they like to visit, what acquaintances they make. Maybe they should impose limits about how much time their kids spend online. Knowing how to use the Internet is important, but it's also important to spend time doing other things.

I'm sure the trend will continue, but I can't say exactly how it will unfold. Things change so rapidly. But I believe that online social networking has already become a really important form of communication. Perhaps in the near future it will become the way that most of us find jobs. Maybe it will be the way that we find our husbands and wives. There are a lot of possibilities.

Why Are Women Leaving Science Careers?

WORDS (page 212)

1. E	6. I	11. L	16. T
2. C	7. H	12. N	17. R
3. A	8. F	13. M	18. S
4. B	9. J	14. K	19. Q
5. D	10. G	15. O	20. P

READING (page 215)

1. C	4. Not Given	7. False
2. E	5. True	
3. B	6. True	

WORD FAMILIES

A (page 216)

1. approximate	9. equal	17. persistent
2. approximate	10. frustrated	18. Persistence
3. approximation	11. frustrates	19. persistently
4. approximately	12. frustrating	20. persist
5. equalized	13. frustration	21. validity
6. equals	14. guide	22. valid
7. equally	15. guidance	23. validate
8. equality	16. guide	24. Validation

B (page 218)

1. equality
2. persisted
3. frustrated
4. guide
5. validation
6. approximate

PARAPHRASES (page 218)

1. C
2. A

DICTIONARY SKILL (page 219)

1. A
2. B

LISTENING (page 219)

1. C
2. B
3. A
4. B

WRITING (page 220)

(sample response)

Women are an invaluable part of the workforce. We need the contributions that they make. Women should be allowed to devote some of their time and attention to their families without losing opportunities or status at work. The best way to do this, in my opinion, is for governments to pass laws requiring companies to support the needs of women.

Although attitudes have changed a little in some places, modern women continue to bear more responsibilities at home than men do. That is a fact of life in most parts of the world. I think the best thing we can do is acknowledge this situation and provide women with the support they need to meet these responsibilities. That is the only fair way because women's home responsibilities are as important to society as their professional jobs are.

Companies could be required by law to support women's needs. For example, they could be required to allow women time off when they have babies. They could be required to provide child care at the company so women could be close to their babies but still do their work. They could be required to allow mothers (and fathers, too) flexible schedules so that they can meet their children's needs: visit their schools, take them to doctor's appointments, and things like that.

Passing laws that require companies to support women's needs would show that society values women's contributions, both at home and at work. Because everybody benefits from women's work, it seems to be the fairest thing to do.

SPEAKING (page 220)

(sample response)

The most important career advice I received was given to me when I was quite young. I was still in high school. I will always remember it. I was thinking about the university and trying to decide what I would want to study. My uncle told me to choose a career that was interesting to me and not to worry about what other people might say. He said a lot of people might try to influence me to choose certain careers for a lot of different reasons but to always remember that it would be my career. I would have to devote the years to studying for it, and then I would devote the rest of my life to working in it. I should choose something that I wanted to do, that I thought I would like, and I shouldn't choose something based on other people's reasons. That advice seems simple, but it's very important, and I can say it's helped me because I really enjoy my job now.

I'm a lawyer and there are a lot of pressures in this profession. Time is a big pressure. We have a lot of deadlines, and we always have to get a lot of work done in a short time. Another pressure is staying current. Laws and regulations change all the time, and we have to know about the changes, so we have to pay attention. I think those are the two biggest pressures, time and paying attention to changing laws. Then there are the daily pressures of any job, finding new clients, getting along with everyone at the office, things like that.

Wheelchair-Accessibility Issues

WORDS (page 221)

1. B
2. C
3. A
4. D
5. I
6. G
7. H
8. F
9. E
10. M
11. J
12. K
13. L
14. N
15. O
16. P
17. T
18. R
19. S
20. Q

READING (page 225)

1. A
2. B
3. B
4. recreation
5. switches
6. ramps
7. updated

WORD FAMILIES

A (page 227)

1. capable
2. capabilities
3. capably
4. disabled
5. disable
6. disabled
7. disability
8. incapacity
9. incapacitated
10. Incapacitation
11. incapacitate
12. necessitate
13. necessarily
14. necessary
15. necessity
16. slippery
17. slipperiness
18. slip
19. Slips

B (page 229)

1. incapacity
2. necessarily
3. disabled
4. capable
5. slipperiness

PARAPHRASES (page 229)

1. B 2. A

DICTIONARY SKILL (page 230)

1. B 2. A 3. A 4. B

LISTENING (page 231)

1. A 2. C 3. E 4. F

WRITING (page 232)

(sample response)

Ninety percent of the people without disabilities in this country are employed. At 85 percent, the employment rate among non-severely disabled people is not a great deal lower. However, severely disabled people have a very low employment rate. Only 25 percent of severely disabled people are employed. But even when disabled people are employed, they are still not as comfortable as people who don't have disabilities. The average monthly salary of people without disabilities is $2,200, and for the non-severely disabled it is $600 lower. Severely disabled people are in an even less comfortable situation, with an average monthly wage of just $1,100. That means that they earn half the amount that people without disabilities earn. These statistics show that employment for people with disabilities is not a simple issue. It is not only about getting a job, but also about how high a salary a disabled person can earn.

SPEAKING (page 232)

(sample response)

There are laws in my country that require public buildings to be accessible to disabled people—not only people in wheelchairs, but also people with other kinds of disabilities. For example, the floor numbers in elevators have to be in Braille so blind people can read them. I think these laws are a good idea because they give disabled people independence. That's really important. Think about if you were in a wheelchair. It would really change your life if you couldn't enter buildings or take the bus because you were in a wheelchair. But if buildings and buses and subways are accessible, you could go on living almost the same life you do now without a wheelchair. There is a drawback though. Changing buildings to make them accessible costs a lot of money. That's really a problem in places where there's a lot of poverty. Accessibility is really important, but it might not always be possible because of the costs.

I work in an office building, and it is accessible to people in wheelchairs. There are elevators, and they are all wide enough for wheelchairs. The buttons on the elevator are low so people in wheelchairs can reach them. On each floor there is a handicapped restroom that can accommodate wheelchairs. There is no need for ramps because the entrance is at the same level as the sidewalk, so there aren't stairs or steps to enter the building. I think the building is really easy for a person in a wheelchair to use, so I can't think of any improvements that are needed.

UNIT 9: EDUCATION

Learning Styles

WORDS (page 233)

1. A	6. J	11. G	16. R
2. C	7. H	12. N	17. P
3. D	8. K	13. M	18. T
4. E	9. I	14. L	19. S
5. B	10. F	15. O	20. Q

READING (page 236)

1. B	4. A	7. B
2. A	5. C	8. A
3. C	6. B	9. D

WORD FAMILIES

A (page 238)

1. confidently	7. dominate	13. Facial
2. confidence	8. dominant	14. face
3. confident	9. dominance	15. Solitary
4. conventions	10. expose	16. solitarily
5. Conventional	11. exposure	17. solitude
6. conventionally	12. face	

B (page 240)

1. Conventional	3. Exposure	5. confident
2. dominates	4. solitude	6. faces

PARAPHRASES (page 241)

1. B 2. C

DICTIONARY SKILL (page 241)

1. A 2. B

LISTENING (page 242)

1. diagrams	3. manipulate
2. recite	4. encouragement

WRITING (page 242)

(sample response)

Confidence is an important element in the learning process. In order to learn, students need to believe that they can learn. When students are given opportunities for success, encouragement from their teachers, and exposure to a variety of experiences, they can develop a strong feeling of confidence.

When students have opportunities to complete tasks successfully, this shows them that they really can learn. If you give a small child a book with lots of pages crowded with words, naturally she will feel it is impossible to ever learn to read. However, if you give that child one page with a few simple words on it, she can learn to read the page quite easily. The child understands that learning to read is not only possible, but probably not all that difficult, either. The child gains confidence in her abilities.

Encouragement is also important. The teacher can show the child how to break a difficult task into small parts and praise the child's small successes. The teacher can give the child support to keep going until a difficult task is completed. If the teacher believes in the child's abilities to complete learning tasks and lets the child know this, the child will believe in herself, too.

Having a variety of types of learning experiences also contributes to a child's feeling of confidence. If a child has opportunities to work alone as well as in groups, then she knows she can work in different situations. If she learns to write about what she learns as well as talk about it, then she knows there are different ways that she can communicate information. Knowing that she can learn in different ways and in different circumstances helps her feel confident about her abilities to learn.

Confidence is an important part of learning. Building students' confidence should be part of all classroom activities.

SPEAKING (page 242)

(sample response)

I think I would have to say that I'm an auditory learner because I like to talk so much. I was always getting into trouble in school because I couldn't keep my mouth closed, especially when the teacher was talking! But now that I think about it, I think that must have been because I am an auditory learner. I need to talk about what I learn. In school, I always liked it best when we had small-group discussions. I enjoyed listening to what others had to say and talking about my ideas with them. I always preferred classroom discussions to reading. It was hard for me to understand something I had read until we talked about it in class.

I'm definitely a social learner because I need to talk about the things I'm learning. I see some students spend a lot of time in the library, reading and taking notes. That's always been difficult for me. When I was in high school, if I had to go to the library to study, I always asked some friends to go with me. I didn't like studying alone. Even if my friends weren't working on the same assignments, I liked being around them when I studied. That must mean I'm a social learner.

Being alone hinders my learning, definitely. I'd rather have company when I study. When I was in high school, sometimes in class we would have to sit quietly and read the assignment. That was usually a waste of time for me. I just couldn't learn that way, in silence. On the other hand, when I'm with people who talk too much, that also hinders me. If I don't get a chance to talk, too, and have people listen to my ideas, that's not helpful to me.

The Homeschool Option

WORDS (page 243)

1. B	6. H	11. K	16. Q
2. E	7. I	12. J	17. R
3. D	8. G	13. L	18. T
4. A	9. F	14. P	19. S
5. C	10. M	15. O	20. N

READING (page 246)

1. B	3. E	5. True	7. False
2. D	4. False	6. Not Given	8. True

WORD FAMILIES

A (page 247)

1. alternative	7. instruct	13. obligatory
2. alternatively	8. instructionally	14. obligate
3. alternative	9. instruction	15. periodically
4. concerned	10. instructors	16. periodic
5. concerns	11. instructional	17. periods
6. concern	12. obligation	

B (page 249)

1. alternative	3. concern	5. obligation
2. instruct	4. periodically	

PARAPHRASES (page 250)

1. A
2. C

WORD SKILL (page 250)

1. pleased
2. not pleased

LISTENING (page 251)

1. A 2. D 3. F 4. G

WRITING (page 251)

(sample response)

I strongly believe that school should be compulsory for all children, with very few exceptions. Most parents do not have the professional teaching skills and range of knowledge that their children are exposed to at school. Only children who have special circumstances that prevent them from attending school should be taught at home, in my opinion.

Parents teach their children many things. They teach them skills they need in daily life, such as how to keep their rooms clean or how to tie their shoes. They teach them moral values such as honesty and kindness. These are very important lessons, but they are very different from the academic lessons children learn at school. Most parents, unless they are professional teachers themselves, do not have professional teaching skills. They have not been trained to teach academic skills such as reading, writing, and arithmetic. The best place for children to learn these things is at school under the guidance of professional educators.

Children are exposed to a much wider range of knowledge at school than they ever could be at home, no matter how well educated their parents are. At home, children have their parents and possibly also their grandparents. This is a limited number of adults. At school, on the other hand, children study with a variety of teachers. Each of these teachers has specialized knowledge about his or her subject area. This gives schoolchildren the opportunity to learn about many more things than their parents could teach them at home.

Some children cannot attend school for special reasons. Some live too far away from school. Some are professional actors and have to work during the school day. Some have physical disabilities or health problems that make it difficult for them to move around. In cases such as these, learning at home is the only choice. However, these are exceptional cases.

No matter how well educated parents are or how much they love their children, they cannot provide the same level of education that a school can. That is why I believe that school should be compulsory for all children.

SPEAKING (page 251)

(sample response)

I think education should be compulsory for ages six through eighteen, that is, for first through twelfth grades. Some people think that compulsory education should start in kindergarten, but I don't think that's necessary. In kindergarten the kids just play and learn things like colors and numbers and look at storybooks. These are all things they can do at home, and five years old is too young, I think, to be away from home all day. Six is a good age to start school. In some countries you have to do only six or eight years of school, but I think it's really important to finish high school. The modern world gets more and more complicated every day, and I think everyone needs the things they learn in high school, even if they don't plan to go to the university afterward.

In most high schools, students have to learn some math, such as algebra and geometry. They have to take the basic science courses: biology, chemistry, and physics. They have to study the history and literature of their own country. I think all these things are important. Usually high school students have to learn a foreign language, and I think that's very important, too. These are all things that an educated person should know. It's basic knowledge. Maybe the only thing I would add would be international politics. The world is getting smaller every day, isn't it? We all should understand something about how other countries operate.

A problem with the schools in my country, especially in the primary schools, is the size of the classes. It isn't unusual to see a classroom with forty or even fifty children in it. Imagine if that's a first grade classroom with forty or fifty six-year-old children. It's impossible for the teacher to give so many children the attention they need. It's a really difficult situation, and the quality of education for little children really suffers from it. I guess it's a problem with money. To make smaller classes they would have to build more classrooms and hire more teachers. I guess the real concern is that the government is not spending enough money on education.

Educating the Gifted

WORDS (page 252)

1. C	6. F	11. K	16. M
2. E	7. I	12. L	17. T
3. B	8. H	13. N	18. S
4. D	9. G	14. P	19. R
5. A	10. J	15. O	20. Q

READING (page 255)

1. extraordinary	4. recognize	7. curriculum
2. profoundly	5. peers	8. dedicate
3. moderately	6. transferred	9. inquisitiveness

WORD FAMILIES

A (page 256)

1. assess
2. assessment
3. assessor
4. enriching
5. enrich
6. enriched
7. enrichment
8. unrecognizable
9. recognizable
10. recognition
11. recognize
12. simultaneously
13. simultaneous
14. sophistication
15. sophisticated
16. withdraw
17. Withdrawal
18. withdrawn

B (page 258)

1. recognition
2. sophistication
3. assessments
4. enrichment
5. simultaneously
6. withdraw

PARAPHRASES (page 259)

1. C
2. B

WORD SKILL (page 260)

1. turn up
2. turn into
3. turned out

LISTENING (page 260)

1. recognize
2. sophisticated
3. discipline
4. constructive
5. curriculum

WRITING (page 261)

(sample response)

The charts show information about enrollment in remedial education at two different universities. The statistics are percentages of first-year students.

There are significantly more students enrolled in remedial education at University A than at University B. Close to half (45 percent) of the first-year students at University A take remedial education courses. A little more than a third (35 percent) of first-year students at that school are enrolled in remedial math courses, and close to one-quarter are enrolled in other remedial courses: 22 percent in remedial reading courses and 26 percent in remedial writing courses.

At University B, only 15 percent of first-year students are enrolled in remedial education courses. The smallest number, 5 percent, take remedial math courses, and 10 percent are enrolled in remedial writing and 12 percent in remedial reading. Clearly, there are many more students with math difficulties at University A than at University B. University B may have stricter requirements for math when they admit new students.

SPEAKING (page 261)

(sample response)

If I could choose to have any extraordinary talent, I think I would choose to be a painter. I really enjoy looking at art. I enjoy the work of many famous painters. I love going to museums and studying the paintings. I have tried painting a little myself, but I'm not very good at it. If I could paint even half as well as Picasso, I would be very happy. However, I don't think that's very likely to happen. I'm not gifted in the arts.

I don't know too much about gifted education in my country. I think in some schools they have special programs for gifted children where they spend an hour or two in a class with other gifted children, and then spend the rest of the day in a regular classroom. I don't know of any full-time gifted education programs. Maybe some private schools have them—I'm not sure. When children have special artistic or musical talents, usually their parents hire private teachers to teach them after school.

I think education for everyone will be very different in the future. I think all education will be through the Internet, and that way education can be individualized. That means that any child with exceptional abilities will have a specialized program that fits those abilities. At the same time, children who have difficulties in certain areas will have special instruction to help with those difficulties. The Internet will make this possible because then children won't have to study just with the children who live in their neighborhood or just with the teachers in their local school. They'll be able to find the children and the teachers who match their abilities and needs and study with them. This will be good for everybody, whether or not they have exceptional abilities.

UNIT 10: TECHNOLOGY/INVENTIONS

The Development of the Lightbulb

WORDS (page 263)

1. B	6. K	11. G	16. L
2. E	7. J	12. O	17. R
3. D	8. I	13. N	18. Q
4. A	9. F	14. P	19. T
5. C	10. H	15. M	20. S

READING (page 266)

1. inventors	4. device	7. F
2. current	5. refinement	8. B
3. unveiled	6. D	9. A

WORD FAMILIES

A (page 267)

1. invent
2. inventor
3. invention
4. investment
5. invest
6. investor
7. inspired
8. inspiration
9. inspired
10. inspiring
11. refinement
12. refine
13. refined
14. specifications
15. specific
16. specify
17. specifically
18. suitably
19. suits
20. suitable
21. suitability

B (page 269)

1. inspiration
2. invention
3. refine
4. invest
5. Suitable
6. specific

PARAPHRASES (page 270)

1. A
2. B

DICTIONARY SKILL (page 270)

1. A
2. B

LISTENING (page 271)

1. patent search
2. an application
3. pay a fee
4. investors/backers

WRITING (page 271)

(sample response)

There have been many important inventions in the past 100 years, and they have changed our lives in dramatic ways. One of the more important of these inventions, in my opinion, is the cell phone. It is a device that has made both our work and our personal lives more convenient.

Because of cell phones, people are no longer tied to their offices. If someone has a business meeting in another part of town, she does not have to miss important phone calls because she is away from the office. Also, since it is possible to send and receive e-mail with many cell phones, it is very easy to take advantage of travel time to catch up on sending and responding to business e-mails. Cell phones are also very useful for people who travel a lot on business. Specifically, they make communication with the home office extremely convenient, and they make it easy for the traveler to continue attending to normal business responsibilities even when on the road. For reasons like these, cell phones have changed the way most companies do business.

Cell phones have also had a big impact on our personal lives. For one thing, they make it easier for families to stay in touch with each other throughout the day. Parents do not have to worry about their children because they can always reach them by cell phone. Children feel secure because they know that their parents are just a phone call away. Cell phones also make it very convenient for people to make or change plans with their friends and relatives. Cell phones have changed the way we interact with each other and the way we go about our daily lives.

Cell phones are always changing and becoming capable of more and more things. As cell phones continue to evolve, their impact on our daily lives will become even greater.

SPEAKING (page 271)

(sample response)

When I was growing up, my cousin was an inspiration to me. He is a good deal older than I am, maybe ten or twelve years older. When I was a child, he seemed like a grown-up to me. He was always doing interesting things, and I wanted to do what I saw him doing. He was on his school's soccer team, so I wanted to play soccer, too. His favorite subject in high school was biology, so I was interested in biology, too. By following his example, I learned to apply myself in sports and in school. He really was a good role model for me.

The person who is an inspiration to me now is the president of the company where I work, Mr. Gomez. It's a small company, but a very successful one. Mr. Gomez started it from nothing. He had an idea, a dream, and he made it into a reality. He did it with hard work and brains. I'm learning all I can while I work for this company, because one day I want to start a company of my own just like Mr. Gomez did.

I find classical music very inspiring—certain types of it, fast-paced music. When I'm working, I always play classical music because it helps me concentrate, and if the music is fast paced or energetic, it gives me energy to keep working.

The Invention of Variable-Pitch Propellers

WORDS (page 272)

1. A	6. G	11. O	16. R
2. E	7. J	12. M	17. P
3. B	8. H	13. N	18. S
4. D	9. I	14. K	19. Q
5. C	10. F	15. L	20. T

READING (page 275)

1. True	4. True	7. D
2. False	5. Not Given	
3. True	6. B	

WORD FAMILIES

A (page 276)

1. enthusiasts
2. enthusiastically
3. enthusiasm
4. enthusiastic
5. inflexibly
6. inflexible
7. inflexibility
8. isolation
9. isolate
10. isolated
11. reliable
12. reliably
13. rely
14. reliance
15. revolutionary
16. revolutionize
17. revolution
18. variable
19. varies
20. variably
21. variables

B (page 278)

1. enthusiastic
2. inflexible
3. rely
4. isolated
5. vary
6. revolution

PARAPHRASES (page 279)

1. C
2. C

WORD SKILL (page 279)

1. able to change
2. not able to change

LISTENING (page 280)

1. A
2. C
3. F
4. G

WRITING (page 281)

(sample response)

By looking at these charts we can see that very light jets are larger and faster than light sport aircraft. Light sport aircraft can carry at the most one passenger, and one of the models shown does not have the capacity to carry any passengers at all. The very light jets, on the other hand, can carry two to six passengers. Very light jets are much faster than light sport aircraft, with cruise speeds between 300 and 425 miles per hour. The fastest light sport aircraft, on the other hand, has a cruise speed of just 130 miles per hour. With their higher passenger capacity and greater speeds, very light jets are naturally a great deal more expensive than light sport aircraft. Prices range from just under $1 million to well over $3 million. Prices for light sport aircraft are much lower, ranging from $39,000 to $194,000 for the models shown.

SPEAKING (page 281)

(sample response)

I definitely prefer to work in isolation. I think it's much more efficient. When I work alone, I don't have to wait for other people to do their part.

I don't have to change my work habits or methods to fit in with other people. I can work the way I work best and at my own pace. I get a lot more done when I work on my own, and I enjoy it a lot more, too.

It depends on the problem. Sometimes I have to confer with others. Sometimes I know that a certain other person will have the information I need or has had experience with a similar type of problem. In that case, I confer with that person. But most of the time I try to solve problems on my own. It's like a puzzle. If I can come up with a good solution on my own, I feel proud of myself. Mostly, I prefer working alone, and I prefer solving problems on my own, too.

I like my work because it's all about numbers. I'm an accountant, and I chose this field because I love numbers. I could spend all day working with numbers. It may sound strange, but I really am enthusiastic about numbers. I'm happiest when I'm in my office by myself working on accounts.

The Transatlantic Cable

WORDS (page 282)

1. F	6. B	11. L	16. O
2. D	7. J	12. P	17. T
3. E	8. H	13. N	18. Q
4. C	9. G	14. K	19. R
5. A	10. I	15. M	20. S

READING (page 285)

1. F	4. B	7. snapped
2. C	5. insulation	8. transmitted
3. E	6. towed	9. triumph

WORD FAMILIES

A (page 286)

1. catastrophic	7. insulator	13. perseverance
2. catastrophically	8. insulated	14. triumphant
3. catastrophe	9. insulate	15. triumph
4. compensation	10. insulation	16. triumphed
5. compensatory	11. persevering	17. triumphantly
6. compensate	12. persevere	

B (page 288)

1. catastrophes	3. triumphant	5. compensate
2. persevering	4. insulate	

PARAPHRASES (page 289)

1. B
2. A

WORD SKILL (page 289)

1. set out
2. set up
3. set back

LISTENING (page 290)

1. 1975
2. set out
3. 1982
4. 1985
5. cable TV

WRITING (page 290)

(sample response)

Both perseverance and good luck are helpful ingredients for success. People may work hard to reach their goals, but finding some luck along the way is also nice. However, I believe that perseverance is much more likely to help someone reach success than plain old luck. You may sit around waiting fruitlessly for luck to come your way, but perseverance is something you can always control. In addition, you can create your own luck through perseverance.

From one point of view, luck is something we do not have any control over. Your friend may win the lottery, but you do not. That is not something that happens because your friend is somehow more deserving. It just happens. If you believe that reaching your goals similarly depends on luck, then you probably will not get anywhere at all. You might waste your time just sitting around all day waiting for opportunity to fall into your lap. It will not. It would be better to go out and do something yourself every day that will bring you closer to your goals.

From another point of view, luck is not really luck but the result of our own perseverance. Sometimes people say that getting that special opportunity you have been hoping for is just a matter of being in the right place at the right time—a lucky chance. But how did you get to be in that place at that time? It is probably because you have been working hard toward your goals. If you want to get a certain kind of job, for example, you answer job ads, talk to other people in your field, and do other things to find out where the job openings are. Pursuing these activities makes it more likely that you will come across people who are hiring. You may have to persevere, but eventually you will meet the person who has the job for you. The day you meet this person it might look like luck, but it really comes about because of your own effort.

Luck is nice when it comes our way, but I think that perseverance is the thing that will help us reach our goals.

SPEAKING (page 291)

(sample response)

I'm in training to become a nurse. I think this is a really interesting profession because it has so many possibilities. To become a nurse you have to have specialized training, but there are different levels of nursing, so your training depends on what level you're interested in. At a minimum you need a certificate that means you've been trained in basic nursing skills like giving medicines and assisting patients. Some nurses have bachelor's degrees and some have master's or doctoral degrees. To get a nursing degree, you study a variety of subjects such as science, public health, administration, and more. You have to know about all these things. You definitely need a certificate or a diploma to become a nurse, but the exact kind you need depends on your goals and interests.

Nurses have to be good at a lot of things; the skills required for this profession are disparate. To be a good nurse you have to have a range of interests and be good at learning new things. You should be good at science and technology. At the same time, you need good "people skills." This is really important because the job of nursing is to help sick people. You have to be able to work well with them, to be kind and compassionate, to transmit a certain type of message through your interactions with your patients: "I care and I'm here to help you." If you don't have that attitude when you set out to care for your patients, you won't be completely successful. Good medical skills can't compensate for a lack of compassion or kindness.

Audioscripts

Track 1

Unit 1: Natural World—Environmental Impacts of Logging

Narrator: Listen to a lecture about trees.

Lecturer:
When you look at a tree, you may notice only the branches and leaves. A closer look shows that there's actually a great deal more going on. Trees provide homes to a large variety of terrestrial animals, from tiny insects to large birds such as owls. Insects live beneath the bark, providing a source of food for many types of birds. Squirrels and birds nest on the branches or in the trunk. Small animals defend themselves by hiding among the leaves. The benefits of trees also extend to aquatic animals. The shade from trees keeps water cool, protecting aquatic animals from the heat of the summer sun. The roots hold on to the soil, which keeps it from being eroded by the rain. This is a protection for aquatic habitats, as it prevents soil from running into the rivers and polluting them. Clearly trees are very important. If forests vanish because of logging or other activities, the impacts on the environment will be great.

Track 2

Unit 1: Natural World—Bird Migration

Narrator: Listen to a tour guide at a bird sanctuary.

Tour Guide:
Welcome to the National Bird Sanctuary. The bird sanctuary provides us with the opportunity to study many aspects of the lives of the migratory birds that pass through here every year. This is a breeding area for many different species, and we'll likely see a number of them on our walk today. On our right, just past the entrance, you'll see a list of all the species that have been observed here. You'll notice several nocturnal species as well as diurnal. They spend the warm months here but leave in the autumn, as they can't endure our cold winters. Okay, take a look at your maps. We're beginning here at the entrance. As we walk through the sanctuary, it's imperative that you not stray off the trail and that you be particularly careful to stay out of the

restricted area, all along the trail to the left here. The restricted area protects breeding birds from disturbance. All right, then. That trail over to the right leads to the gift shop, but before we head there, let's continue to the end of this trail on the left, to the observation platform. *[pause]* Here we are. We can look out over the wetlands from here and observe the waterbirds. I'll leave you here to observe as long as you like, and I'll meet you afterward at the gift shop. It's at the end of that trail I pointed out to you earlier. Before I leave you, I'd like to remind you that this bird sanctuary was built entirely by volunteer labor and donations. You can imagine what a feat that was and what it takes to maintain it. Please consider giving a donation before you leave. You'll find a box for that purpose along the trail right before you arrive at the gift shop.

Track 3

Unit 1: Natural World—Plant Life in the Taklimakan

Narrator: Listen to a class discussion about plants in the Taklimakan Desert.

Professor: We've looked at plant life in various deserts around the world. Let's talk today about plants in the Taklimakan Desert.

Student 1: What I understood from the reading is that there aren't a lot of plants throughout the Taklimakan Desert but that many plants live in the transitional area on the desert fringe.

Professor: That's exactly correct. Conditions in the desert are extremely harsh, but around the edges, plants have been able to adapt and thrive, and some species are actually quite prolific. Of course, the environment there is still extreme, and the plants have some interesting adaptations.

Student 2: There are still a lot of stressors on the desert fringe. The rain there is sparse, right?

Professor: That's true. The desert fringe is very dry and is subject to extreme temperature swings, and these conditions can cause plants a lot of stress.

Student 1: Another stressor is, because of the dry air, there's rapid evaporation, so it's difficult for the plants to hold on to the water they take in.

Student 2: I read that some plants are actually able to determine when they've lost enough moisture and have the ability to close their pores so they don't lose more.

Professor: Yes, that's one of the interesting desert plant adaptations. Another way plants thrive in the desert is by having large root systems so that they can accumulate water taken from deep in the ground.

Track 4

Unit 2: Leisure Time—Peripheral Vision in Sports

Narrator: Listen to a class discussion about vision and basketball.

Professor: We've been discussing the way the eye works and the importance of vision. Let's apply some of this and talk today about how vision affects an athlete's performance. Okay, so when a basketball player, let's say, is out there on the court, what does he need to pay attention to?

Student 1: The player needs to focus on the ball. He needs to always know where the ball is.

Professor: Correct. That's important. But that's not all. The player also has to be aware of what the other players are doing. He has to anticipate their maneuvers so he can be ready to respond. This is where peripheral vision is important. The player may be looking directly at the ball, but he also has to be aware of what's going on near the boundaries of his visual range. He has to be aware of the actions around him.

Student 2: Players look at the ball, but they also scan the whole court, right?

Professor: That's right. They need to go back and forth between focusing on one point and scanning the entire game, so they can know what the rest of the players are doing. Of course, they don't stop to think about it. There isn't time. Good athletes do this unconsciously.

Student 1: They do it so fast, it's indiscernible to us when we're watching the game.

Professor: But they don't respond indiscernibly. When you see a player move in to shoot a basket, he's there because he was able to coordinate all the information he took in about the action of the game so he could make his move.

Track 5

Unit 2: Leisure Time—History of the Circus

Narrator: Listen to a tour guide at a circus.

Tour Guide:
Good afternoon and welcome to the tour of the Springfield Circus. Today you'll get to see the circus rings up close, visit the places where the performers work and rest, and even meet an animal trainer and some animals. Let's start our tour with a brief history of the Springfield Circus. It was founded a century ago right here in Springfield and has been going ever since. The original owner sold it after twenty-five years, and it's been under ownership of the same company for the past seventy-five years. Although the owners have changed, the place has not. The Springfield Circus has always put on its performances in this venue. Unlike other circuses, it has never traveled around with tents but has always held its performances in this permanent spot. When the Springfield Circus was first founded, it put on large entertainments filled with grandeur for massive audiences. Since then, the show has been reduced in size somewhat with fewer performers and acts. The show always begins with its famous parade of exotic animals. This is followed by dancers on horseback, and then the clowns enter the ring. We may get a chance to meet some of them today. They're always the most popular part of the show. Okay, let's go out to the rings now, so we can see where the performers work. Hold on to your tickets, as you will need them to be admitted to the show after the tour.

Track 6

Unit 2: Leisure Time—Uses of Leisure Time

Narrator: Listen to a talk about leisure time.

Lecturer:
There has been a good deal of research on how we use our leisure time. Study after study has shown the importance of using leisure time well. According to research, people who spend their leisure time engaged in passive pastimes such as watching TV actually end up feeling less rejuvenated than people who choose more active leisure-time activities. People who report feeling the most satisfaction with how they spend their leisure time engage in a range of activities for relaxation, both physical and intellectual. Among the most popular pastimes reported by adults, physical activities include a variety of sports, playing with their children, and gardening. Intellectual activities include reading, playing computer games, doing puzzles, and using the Internet. People who engage in a variety of active pastimes tend to be

healthier, both physically and emotionally. It is obvious that we need to engage in leisure activities that exercise both our minds and bodies to avoid suffering problems such as obesity and depression.

Track 7

Unit 3: Transportation—First Headlamps

Narrator: Listen to a talk about early train travel.

Lecturer:
Train travel became increasingly common in the mid- to late-nineteenth century, despite the difficulties involved with this mode of travel. In many ways, trains were more efficient than other available means of transportation, but there were still drawbacks. Travel at night was tricky, for example, because trains lacked effective methods of illumination. Rides on early trains were often rough because of the way the train tracks were laid, although this improved over time and riding the train became more comfortable. As train travel became more popular, the tracks became more crowded, and this was one reason why trains were frequently vulnerable to delays. Train travel could also be dirty because the smoke from the locomotive could not be kept away from the rest of the train. In the early years of train travel there were few disasters, so passengers generally felt safe. Trains were the major means of long-distance travel for a long time and had major effects on society and the economy. Clearly, the initial cost of building the railroads was well worth it, despite the drawbacks involved.

Track 8

Unit 3: Transportation—Major Subways of Europe

Narrator: Listen to two students discussing subways.

Student 1: We need to organize the information for our report on the history of subways. We agreed that our topic would be the London Underground.

Student 2: Yes, it's such an intrinsic part of London. It's famous worldwide. It really is the centerpiece of the city.

Student 1: And it's been around for a long time. We should mention that it first began operation in 1863. I think it's important to point out that at that time they used steam engines to pull the trains.

Student 2: Yes. That's really important information because steam engines were intrinsic to the way the system was built. The tracks couldn't be very deep because the engines had to release steam.

Student 1: Right. The tunnels had to be close to the surface of the ground, and there were vents to release the steam to the streets.

Student 2: So we should explain all that and then talk about how the system changed when electric trains were introduced.

Student 1: That made a big difference because the tunnels could be deeper since they didn't have to worry about releasing steam.

Student 2: And they had developed methods that made it possible to dig deeper tunnels because they used a sort of shield to support the tunnel while the workers were digging.

Student 1: Right. The Harlow-Greathead Shield.

Student 2: People were happy with the deeper tunnels because it wasn't necessary to destroy streets and buildings to dig them.

Track 9

Unit 3: Transportation—Electric Cars Around the Globe

Narrator: Listen to a tour guide introduce a city tour.

Tour Guide:
Welcome to City Bus Tours. Our tour today will take us not only through the city but also to some of the nearby suburbs as we explore the historical development of the area. Before we begin, let's take a look at this map, which shows the places we'll be visiting today. We'll start here, on the west side of the river, which is all urban area. We'll pass by the commuter rail station here, right by the river and near the bridge. This is a brand new station since the train system was completed just last year. Commuter traffic was becoming a huge problem in our area, and there's been a marked improvement in the traffic situation since the trains started running. After we look at the station, we'll cross this bridge, which spans the Rocky River. The bridge was built 100 years ago. At that time, we had the city on this side, but it was all rural area on the other side of the bridge. The building of the bridge accelerated development on the east side of the river, and now it's a growing suburban area with a lot of sprawl. On that side of the river, we'll take a look at some historic houses that still exist there, and then stop for lunch at Miss Mary's Restaurant.

Track 10

Unit 4: Culture—Origins of Writing

Narrator: Listen to a tour guide at a museum.

Tour Guide:
Welcome to the university's Museum of Ancient Studies. As you may be aware, this museum was created by professors and students as a place to exhibit objects and information about ancient civilizations that they've uncovered in their research. Visiting scholars to the university have also contributed a great deal to the museum, and there's a room created especially for items they've donated. However, that's in Room D, near the end of our tour, so we'll talk more about that later. We'll begin here near the entrance, in Room A. This room is all about agricultural tools. It encompasses tools from several different cultures, and it's interesting to note the similarities and differences among them. You'll also find a few examples of agricultural-related objects in Room C, where we have an exhibit of items found in more recent excavations, but most of them are here in this room. Let's move ahead now to Room B. This is my favorite part of the museum. The exhibit you see in here explains the mythology of several ancient civilizations. Some of the old myths are lovely, fascinating. If you're interested in mythology, our gift shop has a number of books for sale on the subject. Okay, let's move now to our right, to Room C. Here's the Recent Excavations Exhibit I mentioned earlier. There are a variety of things in here that've been recently uncovered by scholars connected with the university: tools, cooking implements, clay tablets and tokens, and more. Just ahead is the Visiting Scholars' Room, and past that's the gift shop, in Room E. There, in addition to the books I mentioned, you can buy copies of many of the items on exhibit in the museum, so don't forget to spend some time there before you exit. Now, I'd be happy to answer any questions you may have.

Track 11

Unit 4: Culture—Hula Dancing in Hawaiian Culture

Narrator: Listen to two students planning a hula demonstration.

Student 1: We have to get ready for our hula demonstration for our class. We need to show what we've learned about Hawaiian culture.

Student 2: Let's start with the decorations. I don't think they should be too elaborate, but we want to evoke a feeling of being in Hawaii.

Student 1: I think floral decorations would work. We can make garlands and leis out of paper flowers. They would be easy to make, and still give the right feeling.

Student 2: That's a good idea. What about our costumes? We need to be careful to avoid stereotypes like grass skirts.

Student 1: Since we're going to demonstrate the ancient style of hula, we don't need elaborate costumes. We can make simple costumes that look like tapa bark.

Student 2: Okay, I guess that wouldn't be hard to do. What about garlands of leaves? Aren't they part of the traditional costume?

Student 1: Yeah, they are, but I think the tapa skirts are enough. Otherwise we'll spend all our time making decorations and costumes.

Student 2: I suppose so. No garlands then. But we do need an altar. That's really important because that's part of what we learned about the place of hula dancing in Hawaiian culture.

Student 1: Of course. We'll have to spend some time on creating an altar. But we can't forget to actually practice the dances that we're going to demonstrate.

Student 2: Did we decide to use the graceful movements with all the swaying?

Student 1: No, we're demonstrating the ancient style. Remember? We're doing the energetic dances.

Student 2: Right, of course. With the traditional music, the drums and chants. Okay, let's start practicing.

Track 12

Unit 4: Culture—The Art of Mime

Narrator: Listen to a talk about mime.

Speaker:
Mime is a type of performance carried out without the use of props or language. The mime's skill is the ability to make the audience believe that objects are present when in reality they're not.

Mimes create illusions of everyday activities. For example, a mime may act out climbing the stairs or opening a window, and do it so skillfully that it almost appears that the stairs or window are really there. Mimes use gestures to show the presence of objects. For example, a mime may use his hands to outline the shape of a box, then climb inside the imaginary box. In addition to interacting with imaginary objects, mimes may act out stories in which they portray different characters. The stories usually show the characters involved in some sort of conflict, but it's all done in a humorous way meant to make the audience laugh.

Track 13

Unit 5: Health—Nurse Migration

Narrator: Listen to a talk about training for nurses.

Speaker:
Qualified nurses must have several years of specialized training following high school. In the United States, for example, the bulk of nursing schools offer four-year programs. A nurse who graduates from such a program and then passes a licensing test is qualified for a variety of professional-level jobs. Many nurses choose to go on to graduate school and get higher-level degrees. In the United Kingdom, about 25 percent of nurses have graduated from degree programs. The rest generally have studied in two-year programs. This situation will change soon, however, and in the future all nurses in the U.K. will be required to have a degree in order to qualify for professional nursing jobs. Despite the need for nurses everywhere, there is still a decline in applicants for nursing programs. Many nursing schools in the United States have reported a decline of applicants of 5 percent or more over the past decade. This situation stems from a variety of causes. An important one is that more women are interested in professions, such as doctor or lawyer, which in the past were considered to be men's professions. It's been estimated that there will be 114,000 vacant nursing jobs in the United States by the year 2015.

Track 14

Unit 5: Health—Aerobic Exercise and Brain Health

Narrator: Listen to a woman talking to a trainer at a fitness center.

Patient: Hello? Is this the hospital fitness center?

Trainer: Yes. I'm Tim Smith, a trainer here. How may I help you?

Patient: I'm interested in taking classes.

Trainer: Just let me take down your information. May I have your name?

Patient: Yes, it's Amanda Clark. That's Clark, C-l-a-r-k.

Trainer: R-k. Right. And what kind of classes were you interested in?

Patient: I need to get some exercise. Do you have aerobics exercise classes?

Trainer: Yes, we do. We have several levels of exercise classes. Are you a beginner?

Patient: Yes, I am, for aerobics classes, but I've taken other classes previously. I took yoga classes last year.

Trainer: So you've taken yoga classes. Very good. And why are you interested in exercise classes with us now? Do you have a referral?

Patient: Yes, I do. My doctor told me to call you. I've been feeling depressed, and she said it would improve my mood.

Trainer: I think we'll be able to help you with that problem. Medical research shows a clear link between exercise and mood.

Patient: Also I've been getting a little heavy, and the doctor thought that regular exercise would help me stave off any big weight gain.

Trainer: It certainly will. Exercise has many benefits. We also work a lot with the elderly here, who may be suffering from dementia or decrease of cognition. But you, of course, are much too young for that! However, we can help you with the issues your doctor wants you to work on.

Track 15

Unit 5: Health—How Drugs Are Studied

Narrator: Listen to two students discussing their research assignment.

Student 1: Our lab assignment is due soon. We need to go over the steps to follow for our experiment.

Student 2: The professor gave us an outline. We're investigating the effects of certain substances on a certain type of bacteria, right? So the first thing we have to do is grow our culture in the lab.

Student 1: Right. Okay. Then we'll have to introduce the different substances to the culture.

Student 2: Yeah, and then carefully monitor it at regular intervals. I think every twelve hours would be about right. We should take turns doing that.

Student 1: Good idea. Let's leave a notebook in the lab so we can each record what we see. We'll have to ascertain whether there are any changes.

Student 2: Yes. It's fairly straightforward, isn't it? At the end we'll get together to write up the report. We'll have to describe the outcome.

Student 1: Okay. I'm ready to get started.

Track 16

Unit 6: Tourism—Hiking the Inca Trail

Narrator: Listen to a tour guide at an archeological site.

Tour Guide:
Good morning and welcome. I'm sure you'll enjoy your visit to this archeological site. One of the greatest mysteries of this site is the question of how it was built. How were the ancient people able to construct such spectacular buildings out of such heavy stones without the help of modern technology? We'll explore this and other mysteries pertaining to their culture during our tour today. Before we begin, let me go over a few restrictions. In order to preserve the site, we ask you to walk only on the network of paths, which is clearly marked. After the tour, you may walk around the site as you please, but remember that you can access the buildings only between ten o'clock and four o'clock. The grounds stay open until six. You can access any building you wish on your own except for the ceremonial area. That building is open only to groups with guides, and we'll be visiting it on our tour today. If you haven't bought your tickets yet, please do so now. They're available over here at the counter, fifteen dollars for adults and ten dollars for children. After the tour is over, you might want to visit out gift shop, where we have an array of native crafts for sale.

Track 17

Unit 6: Tourism—What Is Ecotourism?

Narrator: Listen to a customer talking to a tour company agent.

Agent: Good afternoon. Excellent Eco Tours.

Customer: Hello. Yes. I have a vacation coming up, and I haven't taken a pleasure trip in a long time. I'm interested in ecotourism. Can you tell me about any trips you have coming up soon? My vacation is in January.

Agent: I'd be happy to help you. Let me just take down your information. What's your name, please?

Customer: Bob Henderson.

Agent: What kind of tour are you interested in? Our most popular tours are the Wilderness Adventure Tour and the Local Culture Tour.

Customer: Tell me more about the first one.

Agent: That's a nature tour. We take you to a remote area of the rain forest where you learn all about the local plants and animals.

Customer: It sounds interesting, but I'm a little wary of tours that feature wild animals.

Agent: Don't worry. You'll be in the hands of experts, and everything will be perfectly safe. Also, there will always be a barrier between you and the animals.

Customer: It sounds like an interesting trip.

Agent: It is. Shall I sign you up for the Wilderness Adventure Tour then?

Customer: Yes. What are the dates?

Agent: January twelfth through the twenty-fifth.

Customer: That sounds perfect. I have a question about the accommodations. What are they like?

Agent: There are two types. You have a choice between a fairly basic hotel or camping at the campground.

Customer: Oh, I'd definitely prefer the campground.

Agent: Great. I'll put you down for that. Now do you mind if I ask you something? How did you hear about our company? Did you see our publicity somewhere?

Customer: Yes, I saw it in a travel magazine.

Track 18

Unit 6: Tourism—Learning Vacations

Narrator: Listen to a customer talking to a tour company agent.

Agent: Good afternoon. Learning Vacations Limited. May I help you?

Customer: I'm interested in taking a learning vacation. I understand you organize vacations with painting classes.

Agent: We do. We offer learning trips for a broad range of tastes and interests, and painting trips are among the most popular. Do you have a particular destination in mind?

Customer: Not really. I'd just like to go someplace pretty with colorful scenery for painting and maybe some nice ocean breezes.

Agent: Then you would probably be interested in our painting trip this summer. You spend two weeks at a beach resort in Mexico and attend painting classes under the supervision of university art professors.

Customer: University professors? That's impressive.

Agent: Yes. The trip is sponsored by the art department at Springfield University. It's part of their summer school.

Customer: That sounds great. My other interest is international cuisine. Do you have any cooking trips?

Agent: We certainly do. However, I don't know whether you'd be interested because almost all our cooking trips take place in a city, not by the ocean. Our clients get to enroll in ongoing cooking classes at the National Cooking Institute, which sponsors the trips.

Customer: So I would really learn to cook, not just watch someone else cook?

Agent: Yes. You learn how to choose ingredients, how to prepare them, everything.

Customer: What are the accommodations like? Would I stay at a hotel?

Agent: No. For the cooking trip, participants stay at a residential college that's close to the National Cooking Institute.

Customer: I think either one of those trips would suit my taste.

Agent: You need to decide soon. You'll have to enroll in the class of your choice, and then we make the travel arrangements for you.

Customer: When would I have to decide?

Agent: Enrollment for the painting classes ends on June 15 and for the cooking classes on July 1.

Customer: Thanks. I'll let you know soon.

Track 19

Unit 7: Business—What Makes a Small Business Successful?

Narrator: Listen to two students discussing a small business.

Student 1: Okay, so our assignment for our business class is to explain the reasons for the success of a particular small business. We agreed to use the Sunshine Bakery for our model, right?

Student 2: Yes. It's a good example of several of the characteristics that are typical of successful small businesses. For one thing, it has its own particular niche.

Student 1: Uh huh, because there are no other bakeries in the neighborhood.

Student 2: Right. So even though its product isn't unique—it just sells normal baked goods—there aren't any competitors in the area.

Student 1: Yes, I think that's a vital part of its success. And its product is really good, so it already has a great reputation. Everybody knows about the delicious bread you can get there.

Student 2: So it has lots of customers. I don't remember reading anything about market research that the owners did before opening the business, but I guess it doesn't matter because there are lots of customers now.

Student 1: But the owners did start with a sound business plan. I mean, they projected all their expenses and how long it would take to start earning a profit and all that.

Student 2: Right, and the business became profitable in about two years. I think that's pretty good. And since they had enough financial support to start off with, they were able to keep the business afloat until then.

Student 1: Okay, so let's start writing up these ideas for our report.

Track 20

Unit 7: Business—Brand Loyalty

Narrator: Listen to a lecture in a marketing class.

Lecturer:
We'll talk today about promoting new products. Your main goal in promoting your products is to create brand loyalty, a bond between you and your customers. That way, your customers will keep coming back to you. How do you do this? The main point is to make your customers feel that your brand is somehow special so that they'll feel special when they buy it. They want to feel that using products with your brand gives them status. A common method is to get endorsements from famous people. Customers will think, "If I use the same brand as that movie star or athlete or television actor, then I'll be as special as that person." This also gives the idea that your brand is bought by selective people, which makes customers feel very good about buying it themselves. If you can make customers feel passionate about your brand, then they'll always buy it, whether your products are common household staples or expensive luxury items. This is what you want, a brand loyalty that's hard to reverse.

Track 21

Unit 7: Business—Global Outsourcing

Narrator: Listen to a tour guide at a factory.

Tour Guide:
Welcome to the Apex factory tour. Let's begin with a little history of the factory. The Apex Manufacturing Firm has been in existence since 1900, when the company built the first factory right here on this site. It was quite a boon to the local economy since it was the first factory in this region. In fact, Apex was at the epicenter of manufacturing in this region for many, many years. Business was so good that in 1910, the firm's owners decided to add a night shift in order to keep the factory operating twenty-four hours a day. As you can imagine, the firm's owners became quite wealthy. The first branch factory was built in 1915. In 1940, the original old factory was completely torn down

and replaced with a new larger one on the same site. That's the building we're standing in now. Over the years, there have been a number of changes, of course. Then came 1998, which was perhaps the most decisive year for the company. The decision had to be made about outsourcing some of the labor, as many other companies were doing and are doing. The firm's owners ultimately decided not to do so. That decision means that at the present time, Apex remains a major employer in this region. There's a high level of satisfaction among our staff, as shown by the fact that our employee turnover is quite low.

Track 22

Unit 8: Society—Social Networking

Narrator: Listen to a class discussion about social networking.

Professor: Let's talk today about the online social networking trend. There's been an explosion of interest in this form of communication. What effects do you think this will have on our lives as the trend unfolds?

Student 1: It's clear that the advantages are immense. Think about it. These online social networking sites make it possible to have contact with people all over the world.

Student 2: I agree. You can pursue all kinds of opportunities, both personal and professional, through social networking. You can make friends, you can find jobs, you can exchange all kinds of information with people everywhere. It really expands your world.

Professor: These are important advantages, but do you also see any disadvantages to this phenomenon? What might be some of the negative consequences?

Student 1: I see that in one way it expands your world, but in another way it hurts it. I mean, you might spend so much time with your online friends that you don't pay attention to your local friends and family. It can mean the loss of your local community.

Student 2: There are also dangers with your online community. You can make many acquaintances online, but you don't necessarily know a lot about them. You might not know their true identity.

Track 23

Unit 8: Society—Why Are Women Leaving Science Careers?

Narrator: Listen to a tour guide at a research lab.

Tour Guide:
Welcome to the Robertson Research Lab. On our tour today you'll see where researchers work, and you'll learn what scientific research is all about. Today, the Robertson Research Lab is one of the most important labs devoted to scientific research in the country, but it took a long struggle for the lab to gain the status that it enjoys today in the scientific and academic communities. It required an inordinate effort to get the support necessary to build the lab. In fact, it took approximately ten years to collect enough funding to start construction. That would not have been possible without the invaluable help of a number of individuals whose names are listed here on this wall. Although much of the funding came from government resources, and, of course, some of it also came from the Robertson family, the lab is located here at the university and it's the university that bears the responsibility for maintaining and running the lab. In fact, one purpose of the lab is to give university students experience with research. Professional research scientists at the lab provide guidance to science students as they design and carry out their own research studies.

Track 24

Unit 8: Society—Wheelchair-Accessibility Issues

Narrator: Listen to two students discussing wheelchair accessibility.

Student 1: We have to plan our report on wheelchair accessibility in this building. The professor wanted us to see what accommodations are already in place and what changes need to be made.

Student 2: Right. So the first thing we need to do is walk around the building and see what's here.

Student 1: We've already done some of that. I have, anyway. I measured the corridors, and they're wide enough to accommodate wheelchairs.

Student 2: That's good to know because I measured some doors, both exterior and interior, and none of them has the necessary width.

Student 1: Then that's the first recommendation we'll have to make: wider doors.

Student 2: I think the building's exterior is fine. There's a ramp at the front entrance so wheelchairs can get inside the building easily.

Student 1: That's true, but didn't you notice that there aren't any curb cuts? The curb is too high for a wheelchair to get over. So, there's a parking place for disabled people in front of the building, but they still can't get a wheelchair over the curb and onto the sidewalk.

Student 2: Yeah, I guess that really would be a problem. So we'll have to recommend curb cuts.

Student 1: The building already has an elevator, so wheelchairs can get to all the floors.

Student 2: Right, so elevators aren't a problem. What about the light switches? Are they low enough on the walls?

Student 1: Yes, I tested some of them by sitting in a chair. They're low enough to reach.

Track 25

Unit 9: Education—Learning Styles

Narrator: Listen to a lecture about learning styles.

Lecturer:
As teachers, when you plan your lessons, you'll need to keep in mind the different learning styles of your students. Remember that visual learners need to see things. Allow them to sit where they can easily see your face as you give the lesson. Remove any obstructions that might prevent this. Include visual items such as diagrams and pictures in your lesson to address the needs of these students. Auditory learners need to hear things. When they read, they may want to hear the words as well as see them, so allow them to read aloud and to recite information they're studying. Don't hinder their learning by requiring them to keep quiet during study time. Kinesthetic learners need to do things. To help these students, include activities that give them opportunities to move around and to manipulate items. While students may have different learning styles, they all have one thing in common: the need for frequent encouragement.

Track 26

Unit 9: Education—The Homeschool Option

Narrator: Listen to a parent explain homeschooling requirements in her city.

Speaker:
Welcome to the City Homeschooling Association. Most of you are interested in homeschooling your children, and I know you have many concerns and questions about how to begin. I'll start by explaining to you the legal requirements for homeschoolers in our city, then in the latter part of the program, you'll have a chance to ask questions. There are certain things that are compulsory for homeschoolers in our city. First, to start, you'll need to inform the city that you plan to homeschool your children. Many people think that they'll have to hire professional tutors for their children, but that isn't required. Nor do you need to have prior teaching experience yourself. You do, however, have to follow an educational program mandated by the city, which addresses all the same subjects that are taught in the local schools. The city can provide you with textbooks, but, even though the vast majority of families choose to use these books, they aren't required. You can use any books you want as long as you follow the city's program. Periodic tests, usually twice a year, are required by the city. You can give them to your children in your home and send them to the Board of Education for scoring. It's easy to do and doesn't cost any money. At the end of the school year, you have to submit a report to the city, which is also simple to do. It's a short report, and the city provides you with easy-to-follow guidelines. Homeschooling is no longer considered a novel idea but is becoming more widespread. There are a lot of experienced families around who can help you get started.

Track 27

Unit 9: Education—Educating the Gifted

Narrator: Listen to a class discussion about gifted children.

Professor: I asked you to read an article about recognizing gifted students in the classroom. So, tell me. How can a teacher recognize gifted children?

Student 1: One thing gifted children do is read. They usually read books for older children, or sometimes books for adults.

Professor: Yes, that's an important sign. Profoundly gifted children, especially, may be seen reading adult books at a very early age. What else?

Student 2: When it comes to problem solving, gifted children use sophisticated approaches, unlike their peers.

Student 1: Not all the signs of giftedness are positive. Gifted children might be bored in the classroom and behave badly. They often need help with discipline.

Professor: That's exactly right, and one reason why it's so important to recognize these children and place them in the proper environment and give them the support they need.

Student 2: One way to support them is to give them constructive activities that are interesting to them. If they don't have activities that satisfy their inquisitiveness and creativity, that's when discipline can become a problem.

Student 1: And, of course, we need to provide a special curriculum for these children. They need more than just some interesting activities. They need a whole course of study that matches their abilities.

Track 28

Unit 10: Inventions—The Development of the Lightbulb

Narrator: Listen to a talk about producing and marketing inventions.

Lecturer:
When you have an invention that you think you can sell, you have to protect it. You must get a patent so that there will be no infringement on your rights to produce and sell the device you've invented. The first thing you must do is find out if anyone else has a patent on a similar type of invention. This is called a patent search. Often, people hire specialized lawyers to do this for them. Once you've ascertained that there are no patents on inventions similar to yours, then you can get an application and file it with the Patent Office. Generally you'll have to pay a fee when you send in the application. Next, you can start looking for investors. This is critical. Inventors tend to be solitary people and don't give much thought to finding financial backers to help them. However, if you want to successfully market your invention, you'll need people to provide money to start production and begin marketing. You'll need to think like an entrepreneur. Inspiration is not enough. Hard work and money are important ingredients for success.

Track 29

Unit 10: Inventions—The Invention of Variable-Pitch Propellers

Narrator: Listen to two students discussing a flight demonstration.

Student 1: That was a fascinating flight we saw. Now we have to write up the report for the school newspaper.

Student 2: Okay. Well, we should start with the name of the designer of the plane.

Student 1: Right. I'll just write that down. The designer was Steve Wilson, and the pilot's name was Joe Applewood. What about the names of the passengers? Did you get those?

Student 2: No, but there were two of them, we can just put that. We don't need their names.

Student 1: We should say something about the design of the plane, like the size of the propeller. How big was it?

Student 2: I'm not sure. It was big, but I couldn't say the exact size.

Student 1: Well, we should say something about it. What about the speed of rotation? How fast did that propeller move?

Student 2: I don't know. If we'd had a chance to confer with the pilot, we could've found out. But he left too quickly.

Student 1: Okay, so we can't include that information. We'll have to write more about the flight. It was a really prolonged flight.

Student 2: Yeah, he was cruising up there for at least thirty minutes, a lot longer than I expected. So write that down. And what a flexible machine. It handled the turns really well.

Student 1: Yeah, especially considering the weather conditions. It was so windy and cloudy, there must have been some turbulence.

Student 2: There probably was. We'll put that in the report, too.

Track 30

Unit 10: Inventions—The Transatlantic Cable

Narrator: Listen to a tour guide at a museum.

Tour Guide:
Welcome to the City Museum of Invention. We'll begin our tour with a brief overview of the history of the museum. This museum first opened its doors in 1985, the result of years of effort by the mayor and others in our city. In 1975, the city's mayor first got the idea to start a museum about inventions. After he got several experts interested, he set out to rally the necessary funds. In 1976, several events were held to raise the requisite amount of money to begin construction of a building to house the museum. They had almost raised enough money when there was an unexpected setback. A family that had promised a large percentage of the needed funds inexplicably withdrew their offer. It was toward the end of 1977 that this large gift was lost. Although there was an inquiry, it was never made clear why the funds were withdrawn. Plans for the museum were put aside for five or six years. But a group of interested people renewed the efforts, and by 1982 they had rallied enough monetary support to go ahead with the plans. That year, construction on the building began. In just under three years, the museum was completed, the result of the perseverance of a number of dedicated people. The museum continues to be a popular part of our city's culture. Although everything in the museum follows the theme of inventions, the variety of the exhibits will appeal to visitors of disparate interests. Our most popular exhibit, which is all about cable TV, was first opened in 1998.

MP3 Track Listing

Introduction

Unit 1: Natural World
Track 1 Environmental Impacts of Logging
Track 2 Bird Migration
Track 3 Plant Life in the Taklimakan

Unit 2: Leisure Time
Track 4 Peripheral Vision in Sports
Track 5 History of the Circus
Track 6 Uses of Leisure Time

Unit 3: Transportation
Track 7 First Headlamps
Track 8 Major Subways of Europe
Track 9 Electric Cars Around the Globe

Unit 4: Culture
Track 10 Origins of Writing
Track 11 Hula Dancing in Hawaiian Culture
Track 12 The Art of Mime

Unit 5: Health
Track 13 Nurse Migration
Track 14 Aerobic Exercise and Brain Health
Track 15 How Drugs Are Studied

Unit 6: Tourism
Track 16 Hiking the Inca Trail
Track 17 What Is Ecotourism?
Track 18 Learning Vacations

Unit 7: Business
Track 19 What Makes a Small Business Successful?
Track 20 Brand Loyalty
Track 21 Global Outsourcing

Unit 8: Society
Track 22 Social Networking
Track 23 Why Are Women Leaving Science Careers?
Track 24 Wheelchair-Accessibility Issues

Unit 9: Education
Track 25 Learning Styles
Track 26 The Homeschool Option
Track 27 Educating the Gifted

Unit 10: Inventions
Track 28 The Development of the Lightbulb
Track 29 The Invention of Variable-Pitch Propellers
Track 30 The Transatlantic Cable